570

ACPL ITEM
DISCARDED

SO-BWX-607

SOCIALISM

AND

THE GREAT STATE

SOCIALISM
AND
THE GREAT STATE

ESSAYS IN CONSTRUCTION
BY

H. G. WELLS, FRANCES EVELYN WARWICK
L. G. CHIOZZA MONEY, E. RAY LANKESTER
C. J. BOND, E. S. P. HAYNES, CECIL CHESTERTON
CICELY HAMILTON, ROGER FRY, G. R. S. TAYLOR
CONRAD NOEL, HERBERT TRENCH, HUGH P. VOWLES

335
Sol

Essay Index Reprint Series

BOOKS FOR LIBRARIES PRESS
FREEPORT, NEW YORK

First Published 1912
Reprinted 1972

Library of Congress Cataloging in Publication Data
Main entry under title:

Socialism and the great state.

  (Essay index reprint series)
  1. Socialism--Addresses, essays, lectures. I. Wells
Herbert George, 1866-1946.
HX246.S7 1972   335   75-156719
ISBN 0-8369-2863-6

PRINTED IN THE UNITED STATES OF AMERICA

1713698

CONTENTS

PREFATORY NOTE

THIS book is the outcome of a conversational suggestion that the time was ripe for a fresh review of our general ideas of social organisation from the constructive standpoint. A collection of essays by contemporaries actively concerned with various special aspects of progress was proposed, and then the project was a little enlarged by the inclusion of a general introduction which should serve as a basis of agreement among the several writers. This introduction, which is now the first paper in the volume, was written and copies were made out and sent by Lady Warwick, Mr. Wells, and Mr. Taylor (who are to be regarded jointly as the general editors) to various friends who seemed likely to respond and participate, and this book came into being. A sort of loose unity has been achieved by this method; but each writer remains only responsible for his own contribution, and the reader must not fall into the very easy mistake of confusing essays and suggestions with a programme We were not able in the time at our disposal to secure a sympathetic writer upon the various problems arising out of racial difference, which remain, therefore, outside

PREFATORY NOTE

ʝur scope. We failed, also, to secure a detached and generalised paper upon religion. We believe, however, that, except for these omissions, we are presenting a fairly complete picture of constructive social ideals. It is interesting to note certain juxtapositions; this is not a socialist volume, and the constructive spirit has long since passed beyond the purely socialist range. Neither Sir Ray Lankester, nor Mr. Haynes nor Mr. Fry would dream of calling himself a socialist; the former two would quite readily admit they were individualists. That old and largely fallacious antagonism of socialist and individualist is indeed dissolving out of contemporary thought altogether.

E. W.

G. R. S. T.

H. G. W.

THE PAST AND THE GREAT STATE

BY H. G. WELLS

SOCIALISM
AND
THE GREAT STATE

I

THE PAST AND THE GREAT STATE

I

THIS volume of essays is essentially an exercise in
restatement. It is an attempt on the part of its
various writers to rephrase their attitude to contemporary social changes. *Each writes, it must be
clearly understood, from his or her own standpoint;*
there is little or no effort to achieve a detailed con-
sistency, but throughout there is a general unanimity,
a common conception of a constructive purpose.
What that common conception is, the present writer
will first attempt to elucidate.

In order to do so it is convenient to coin two expressions, and to employ them with a certain defined
intention. They are firstly: The Normal Social
Life, and secondly: The Great State. Throughout
this book these expressions will be used in accordance
with the definitions presently to be given, and the
fact that they are so used will be emphasized by the

employment of capitals. It will be possible for any one to argue that what is here defined as the Normal Social Life is not the normal social life, and that the Great State is indeed no state at all. That will be an argument outside the range delimited by these definitions.

Now what is intended by the Normal Social Life here is a type of human association and employment, of extreme prevalence and antiquity, which appears to have been the lot of the enormous majority of human beings as far back as history or tradition or the vestiges of material that supply our conceptions of the neolithic period can carry us. It has never been the lot of all humanity at any time, to-day it is perhaps less predominant than it has ever been, yet even to-day it is probably the lot of the greater moiety of mankind.

Essentially this type of association presents a localized community, a community of which the greater proportion of the individuals are engaged more or less directly in the cultivation of the land. With this there is also associated the grazing or herding over wider or more restricted areas, belonging either collectively or discretely to the community, of sheep, cattle, goats, or swine, and almost always the domestic fowl is a commensal of man in this life. The cultivated land at least is usually assigned, temporarily or inalienably, as property to specific individuals, and the individuals are grouped in generally monogamic families of which the father

4

is the head. Essentially the social unit is the Family, and even where as in Mahomedan countries there is no legal or customary restriction upon polygamy, monogamy still prevails as the ordinary way of living. Unmarried women are not esteemed, and children are desired. According to the dangers or securities of the region, the nature of the cultivation and the temperament of the people, this community is scattered either widely in separate steadings or drawn together into villages. At one extreme, over large areas of thin pasture this agricultural community may verge on the nomadic; at another, in proximity to consuming markets it may present the concentration of intensive culture. There may be an adjacent Wild supplying wood, and perhaps controlled by a simple forestry. The law that holds this community together is largely traditional and customary, and almost always as its primordial bond there is some sort of temple and some sort of priest. Typically the temple is devoted to a local God or a localized saint, and its position indicates the central point of the locality, its assembly place and its market. Associated with the agriculture there are usually a few imperfectly specialised tradesmen, a smith, a garment-maker perhaps, a basket-maker or potter, who group about the church or temple. The community may maintain itself in a state of complete isolation, but more usually there are tracks or roads to the centres of adjacent communities, and a certain drift of travel, a certain trade in non-essential things. In the fundamentals of life this normal community is independent and self-subsisting, and where it is not beginning to be modified by the novel forces of the new times it produces its own food and drink, its own clothing, and largely intermarries within its limits.

This in general terms is what is here intended by the phrase the Normal Social Life. It is still the substantial part of the rural life of all Europe and most Asia and Africa, and it has been the life of the great majority of human beings for immemorial years. It is the root life. It rests upon the soil, and from that soil below and its reaction to the seasons and the moods of the sky overhead have grown most of the traditions, institutions, sentiments, beliefs, superstitions, and fundamental songs and stories of mankind.

But since the very dawn of history at least this Normal Social Life has never been the whole complete life of mankind. Quite apart from the marginal life of the savage hunter, there have been a number of forces and influences within men and women and without that have produced abnormal and surplus ways of living, supplemental, additional, and even antagonistic to this normal scheme.

And first as to the forces within men and women. Long as it has lasted, almost universal as it has been, the human being has never yet achieved a perfect adaptation to the needs of the Normal

6

Social Life. He has attained nothing of that frictionless fitting to the needs of association one finds in the bee or the ant. Curiosity, deep stirrings to wander, the still more ancient inheritance of the hunter, a recurrent distaste for labor, and resentment against the necessary subjugations of family life have always been a straining force within the agricultural community. The increase of population during periods of prosperity has led at the touch of bad seasons and adversity to the desperate reliefs of war and the invasion of alien localities. And the nomadic and adventurous spirit of man found reliefs and opportunities more particularly along the shores of great rivers and inland seas. Trade and travel began, at first only a trade in adventitious things, in metals and rare objects and luxuries and slaves. With trade came writing and money; the inventions of debt and rent, usury and tribute. History finds already in its beginnings a thin network of trading and slaving flung over the world of the Normal Social Life, a network whose strands are the early roads, whose knots are the first towns and the first courts.

Indeed all recorded history is in a sense the history of these surplus and supplemental activities of mankind. The Normal Social Life flowed on in its immemorial fashion, using no letters, needing no records, leaving no history. Then, a little minority, bulking disproportionately in the record, come the trader and sailor, the slave, the landlord and the tax - compeller, the townsman and the king.

All written history is the story of a minority and their peculiar and abnormal affairs. Save in so far as it notes great natural catastrophes and tells of the spreading or retrocession of human life through changes of climate and physical conditions it resolves itself into an account of a series of attacks and modifications and supplements made by excessive and superfluous forces engendered within the community upon the Normal Social Life. The very invention of writing is a part of those modifying developments. The Normal Social Life is essentially illiterate and traditional. The Normal Social Life is as mute as the standing crops; it is as seasonal and cyclic as nature herself, and reaches towards the future only an intimation of continual repetitions.

Now this human over-life may take either beneficent or maleficent or neutral aspects towards the general life of humanity. It may present itself as law and pacification, as a positive addition and superstructure to the Normal Social Life, as roads and markets and cities, as courts and unifying monarchies, as helpful and directing religious organisations, as literature and art and science and philosophy, reflecting back upon the individual in the Normal Social Life from which it arose, a gilding and refreshment of new and wider interests and added pleasures and resources. One may define

8

certain phases in the history of various countries when this was the state of affairs, when a country-side of prosperous communities with a healthy family life and a wide distribution of property, animated by roads and towns and unified by a generally intelligible religious belief, lived in a transitory but satisfactory harmony under a sympathetic government. I take it that this is the condition to which the minds of such original and vigorous reactionary thinkers as Mr. G. K. Chesterton and Mr. Hilaire Belloc for example turn, as being the most desirable state of mankind.

But the general effect of history is to present these phases as phases of exceptional good luck, and to show the surplus forces of humanity as on the whole antagonistic to any such equilibrium with the Normal Social Life. To open the book of history haphazard is, most commonly, to open it at a page where the surplus forces appear to be in more or less destructive conflict with the Normal Social Life. One opens at the depopulation of Italy by the aggressive great estates of the Roman Empire, at the impoverishment of the French peasantry by a too centralised monarchy before the revolution, or at the huge degenerative growth of the great industrial towns of western Europe in the nineteenth century. Or again one opens at destructive wars. One sees these surplus forces over and above the Normal Social Life working towards unstable concentrations of population, to

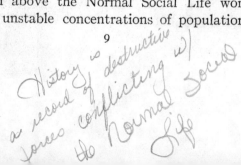

History is destructive w/ a record of conflicting forces conflicting w/ the Normal Social life

centralisation of government, to migrations and conflicts upon a large scale; one discovers the process developing into a phase of social fragmentation and destruction and then, unless the whole country has been wasted down to its very soil, the Normal Social Life returns as the heath and furze and grass return after the burning of a common. But it never returns in precisely its old form. The surplus forces have always produced some traceable change; the rhythm is a little altered. As between the Gallic peasant before the Roman conquest, the peasant of the Gallic province, the Carlovingian peasant, the French peasant of the thirteenth, the seventeenth, and the twentieth centuries, there is, in spite of a general uniformity of life, of a common atmosphere of cows, hens, dung, toil, ploughing, economy, and domestic intimacy, an effect of accumulating generalising influences and of wider relevancies. And the oscillations of empires and kingdoms, religious movements, wars, invasions, settlements leave upon the mind an impression that the surplus life of mankind, the less-localised life of mankind, that life of mankind which is not directly connected with the soil but which has become more or less detached from and independent of it, is becoming proportionately more important in relation to the Normal Social Life. It is as if a different way of living was emerging from the Normal Social Life and freeing itself from its traditions and limitations.

10

Turn to 13

And this is more particularly the effect upon the mind of a review of the history of the past two hundred years. The little speculative activities of the alchemist and natural philosopher, the little economic experiments of the acquisitive and enterprising landed proprietor, favoured by unprecedented periods of security and freedom, have passed into a new phase of extraordinary productivity. They have added preposterously and continue to add on a gigantic scale and without any evident limits to the continuation of their additions, to the resources of humanity. To the strength of horses and men and slaves has been added the power of machines and the possibility of economies that were once incredible. The Normal Social Life has been overshadowed as it has never been overshadowed before by the concentrations and achievements of the surplus life. Vast new possibilities open to the race; the traditional life of mankind, its traditional systems of association, are challenged and threatened; and all the social thought, all the political activity of our time turns in reality upon the conflict of this ancient system whose essentials we have here defined and termed the Normal Social Life with the still vague and formless impulses that seem destined either to involve it and men in a final destruction or to replace it by some new and probably more elaborate method of human association.

Because there is the following difference between

the action of the surplus forces as we see them to-day and as they appeared before the outbreak of physical science and mechanism. Then it seemed clearly necessary that whatever social and political organisation developed, it must needs rest ultimately on the tiller of the soil, the agricultural holding, and the Normal Social Life. But now even in agriculture huge wholesale methods have appeared. They are declared to be destructive; but it is quite conceivable that they may be made ultimately as recuperative as that small agriculture which has hitherto been the inevitable social basis. If that is so, then the new ways of living may not simply impose themselves in a growing proportion upon the Normal Social Life, but they may even oust it and replace it altogether. Or they may oust it and fail to replace it. In the newer countries the Normal Social Life does not appear to establish itself at all rapidly. No real peasantry appears in either America or Australia; and in the older countries, unless there is the most elaborate legislative and fiscal protection, the peasant population wanes before the large farm, the estate, and overseas production.

Now most of the political and social discussion of the last hundred years may be regarded and re-phrased as an attempt to apprehend this defensive struggle of the Normal Social Life against waxing novelty and innovation, and to give a direction and guidance to all of us who participate. And it is very largely a matter of temperament and free choice still, just where we shall decide to place ourselves. Let us consider some of the key words of contemporary thought, such as Liberalism, Individualism, Socialism, in the light of this broad generalisation we have made; and then we shall find it easier to explain our intention in employing as a second technicality the phrase of The Great State as an opposite to the Normal Social Life, which we have already defined.

II

THE Normal Social Life has been defined as one based on agriculture, traditional and essentially unchanging. It has needed no toleration and displayed no toleration for novelty and strangeness. Its beliefs have been of such a nature as to justify and sustain itself, and it has had an intrinsic hostility to any other beliefs. The god of its community has been a jealous god even when he was only a tribal and local god. Only very occasionally in history until the coming of the modern period do we find any human community relaxing from this ancient and more normal state of entire intolerance towards ideas or practices other than its own. When toleration and a receptive attitude towards alien ideas was manifested in the Old World, it was at some trading centre or political centre; new ideas and new religions came by water along

2   13

the trade routes. And such toleration as there was rarely extended to active teaching and propaganda. Even in liberal Athens the hemlock was in the last resort at the service of the ancient gods and the ancient morals against the sceptical critic.

But with the steady development of innovating forces in human affairs, there has actually grown up a cult of receptivity, a readiness for new ideas, a faith in the probable truth of novelties. Liberalism —I do not of course refer in any way to the political party which makes this profession—is essentially anti-traditionalism; its tendency is to commit for trial any institution or belief that is brought before it. It is the accuser and antagonist of all the fixed and ancient values and imperatives and prohibitions of the Normal Social Life. And growing up in relation to Liberalism and sustained by it is the great body of scientific knowledge, which professes at least to be absolutely undogmatic and perpetually on its trial and under assay and re-examination.

Now a very large part of the advanced thought of the past century is no more than the confused negation of the broad beliefs and institutions which have been the heritage and social basis of humanity for immemorial years. This is as true of the extremest Individualism as of the extremest Socialism. The former denies that element of legal and customary control which has always subdued the individual to the needs of the Normal Social Life, and the latter that qualified independence of dis-

14

tributed property which is the basis of family autonomy. Both are movements against the ancient life, and nothing is more absurd than the misrepresentation which presents either as a conservative force. They are two divergent schools with a common disposition to reject the old and turn towards the new. The Individualist professes a faith for which he has no rational evidence, that the mere abandonment of traditions and controls must ultimately produce a new and beautiful social order; while the Socialist, with an equal liberalism, regards the outlook with a kind of hopeful dread and insists upon an elaborate legal readjustment, a new and untried scheme of social organisation to replace the shattered and weakening Normal Social Life.

Both these movements, and indeed all movements that are not movements for the subjugation of innovation and the restoration of tradition, are vague in the prospect they contemplate. They produce no definite forecasts of the quality of the future towards which they so confidently indicate the way. But this is less true of modern socialism than of its antithesis, and it becomes less and less true as socialism, under an enormous torrent of criticism, slowly washes itself clean from the mass of partial statement, hasty misstatement, sheer error and presumption, that obscured its first emergence.

But it is well to be very clear upon one point at this stage, and that is, that this present time is not

a battle-ground between individualism and socialism; it is a battle-ground between the Normal
Social Life on the one hand and a complex of forces
on the other which seek a form of replacement and
seem partially to find it in these and other doctrines.

Nearly all contemporary thinkers who are not
too muddled to be assignable fall into one of three
classes, of which the third we shall distinguish is
the largest and most various and divergent. It
will be convenient to say a little of each of these
classes before proceeding to a more particular account of the third. Our analysis will cut across
many accepted classifications, but there will be
ample justification for this rearrangement. All of
them may be dealt with quite justly as accepting
the general account of the historical process which
is here given.

Then first we must distinguish a series of writers
and thinkers which one may call—the word conservative being already politically assigned—the
Conservators.

These are people who really do consider the
Normal Social Life as the only proper and desirable
life for the great mass of humanity, and they are
fully prepared to subordinate all exceptional and
surplus lives to the moral standards and limitations
that arise naturally out of the Normal Social Life.
They desire a state in which property is widely
distributed, a community of independent families
protected by law and an intelligent democratic

statecraft from the economic aggressions of large accumulations, and linked by a common religion. Their attitude to the forces of change is necessarily a hostile attitude. They are disposed to regard innovations in transit and machinery as undesirable, and even mischievous disturbances of a wholesome equilibrium. They are at least unfriendly to any organisation of scientific research, and scornful of the pretensions of science. Criticisms of the methods of logic, scepticism of the more widely diffused human beliefs, they would classify as insanity. Two able English writers, Mr. G. K. Chesterton and Mr. Belloc, have given the clearest expression to this system of ideals, and stated an admirable case for it. They present a conception of vinous, loudly singing, earthy, toiling, customruled, wholesome, and insanitary men; they are pagan in the sense that their hearts are with the villagers and not with the townsmen, Christian in the spirit of the parish priest. There are no other Conservators so clear-headed and consistent. But their teaching is merely the logical expression of an enormous amount of conservative feeling. Vast multitudes of less lucid minds share their hostility to novelty and research; hate, dread, and are eager to despise science, and glow responsive to the warm, familiar expressions of primordial feelings and immemorial prejudices. The rural conservative, the liberal of the allotments and small-holdings type, Mr. Roosevelt—in his Western-farmer, philopro-

17

genitive phase as distinguished from the phase of his more imperialist moments—all present themselves as essentially Conservators, as seekers after and preservers of the Normal Social Life.

So, too, do Socialists of the William Morris type. The mind of William Morris was profoundly reactionary. He hated the whole trend of later nineteenth-century *modernism* with the hatred natural to a man of considerable scholarship and intense æsthetic sensibilities. His mind turned, exactly as Mr. Belloc's turns, to the finished and enriched Normal Social Life of western Europe in the middle ages, but unlike Mr. Belloc he believed that, given private ownership of land and the ordinary materials of life, there must necessarily be an aggregatory process, usury, expropriation, the development of an exploiting wealthy class. He believed profit was the devil. His *News from Nowhere* pictures a communism that amounted in fact to little more than a system of private ownership of farms and trades without money or any buying and selling, in an atmosphere of geniality, generosity, and mutual helpfulness. Mr. Belloc, with a harder grip upon the realities of life, would have the widest distribution of proprietorship, with an alert democratic government continually legislating against the protean reappearances of usury and accumulation, and attacking, breaking up, and redistributing any large unanticipated bodies of wealth that appeared. But both men are equally set towards the Normal

Social Life, and equally enemies of the New. The so-called "socialist" land legislation of New Zealand again is a tentative towards the realisation of the same school of ideas: great estates are to be automatically broken up, property is to be kept disseminated; a vast amount of political speaking and writing in America and throughout the world enforces one's impression of the wide-spread influence of Conservator ideals.

Of course it is inevitable that phases of prosperity for the Normal Social Life will lead to phases of overpopulation and scarcity, there will be occasional famines and occasional pestilences and plethoras of vitality leading to the blood-letting of war. I suppose Mr. Chesterton and Mr. Belloc at least have the courage of their opinions, and are prepared to say that such things always have been and always must be; they are part of the jolly rhythms of the human lot under the sun, and are to be taken with the harvest home and love-making and the peaceful ending of honoured lives as an integral part of the unending drama of mankind.

III

Now opposed to the Conservators are all those who do not regard contemporary humanity as a final thing nor the Normal Social Life as the inevitable basis of human continuity. They believe in secular change, in Progress, in a future for our species differing continually more from its past. On the whole, they are prepared for the gradual disentanglement of men from the Normal Social Life altogether, and they look for new ways of living and new methods of human association with a certain adventurous hopefulness.

Now this second large class does not so much admit of subdivision into two as present a great variety of intermediaries between two extremes. I propose to give distinctive names to these extremes, with the very clear proviso that they are not antagonised, and that the great multitude of this second, anti-conservator class, this liberal, more novel class modern conditions have produced, falls between them, and is neither the one nor the other, but partaking in various degrees of both. On the one hand, then, we have that type of mind which is irritated by and distrustful of all collective proceedings, which is profoundly distrustful of churches and states, which is expressed essentially by Individualism. The Individualist appears to regard the extensive disintegrations of the Normal Social Life that are going on to-day with an extreme hopefulness. Whatever is ugly or harsh in modern industrialism or in the novel social development of our time he seems to consider as a necessary aspect of a process of selection and survival, whose tendencies are on the whole inevitably satisfactory. The future welfare of man he believes in effect may be trusted to the spontaneous and planless activities of people of good-will, and nothing but state intervention can effectively impede its attainment. And curiously close to this extreme optimistic school in its moral quality and logical consequences, though contrasting widely in the sinister gloom of its spirit, is the socialism of Karl Marx. He declared the contemporary world to be a great process of financial aggrandisement and general expropriation, of increasing power for the few and of increasing hardship and misery for the many, a process that would go on until at last a crisis of unendurable tension would be reached and the social revolution ensue. The world had in fact to be worse before it could hope to be better. He contemplated a continually exacerbated Class War, with a millennium of extraordinary vagueness beyond as the reward of the victorious workers. His common quality with the Individualist lies in his repudiation of and antagonism to plans and arrangements, in his belief in the overriding power of Law. Their common influence is the discouragement of collective understandings upon the basis of the existing state. Both converge in practice upon *laissez faire*. I would therefore lump them together under the term of Planless Progressives, and I would contrast with them those types which believe supremely in systematised purpose.

The purposeful and systematic types, in common with the Individualist and Marxist, regard the Normal Social Life, for all the many thousands of years behind it, as a phase, and as a phase which is now passing, in human experience; and they are prepared for a future society that may be ultimately different right down to its essential relationships from the human past. But they also believe that the forces that have been assailing and disintegrating the Normal Social Life, which have been, on the one hand, producing great accumulations of wealth, private freedom, and ill-defined, irresponsible and socially dangerous power, and, on the other, labour hordes, for the most part urban, without any property or outlook except continuous toil and anxiety, which in England have substituted a dischargeable agricultural labourer for the independent peasant almost completely, and in America seem to be arresting any general development of the Normal Social Life at all, are forces of wide and indefinite possibility that need to be controlled by a collective effort implying a collective design, deflected from merely injurious consequences and organised for a new human welfare upon new lines. They agree with that class of thinking I have distinguished as the Conservators in their recognition of vast contemporary disorders and their denial of the essential beneficence of change. But while the former seem to regard all novelty and innovation as a mere inundation to be met, banked back, defeated and survived, these more hopeful and adventurous minds would rather regard contemporary change as amounting on the whole to the tumultuous and almost catastrophic opening-up of possible new channels, the violent opportunity of vast deep new ways to great unprecedented human ends, ends that are neither feared nor evaded.

Now, while the Conservators are continually talking of the "eternal facts" of human life and human nature and falling back upon a conception of permanence that is continually less true as our perspectives extend, these others are full of the conception of adaptation, of deliberate change in relationship and institution to meet changing needs. I would suggest for them, therefore, as opposed to the Conservators and contrasted with the Planless Progressives, the name of Constructors. They are the extreme right, as it were, while the Planless Progressives are the extreme left of Anti-Conservator thought.

I believe that these distinctions I have made cover practically every clear form of contemporary thinking and are a better and more helpful classification than any now current. But of course nearly every individual nowadays is at least a little confused, and will be found to wobble in the course even of a brief discussion between one attitude and the other. This is a separation of opinions rather than of persons. And particularly that word Socialism has become so vague and incoherent that for a man to call himself a socialist nowadays is to give no indication whatever whether he is a Conservator like William Morris, a non-Constructor like

23

Karl Marx, or a Constructor of any of half a dozen different schools. On the whole, however, modern socialism tends to fall towards the Conservative wing. So, too, do those various movements in England and Germany and France called variously nationalist and imperialist, and so do the American civic and social reformers. All these movements are agreed that the world is progressive towards a novel and unprecedented social order, not necessarily and fatally better, and that it needs organised and even institutional guidance thither, however much they differ as to the form that order should assume.

For the greater portion of a century socialism has been before the world, and it is not perhaps premature to attempt a word or so of analysis of that great movement in the new terms we are here employing. The origins of the socialist idea were complex and multifarious, never at any time has it succeeded in separating out a statement of itself that was at once simple, complete, and acceptable to any large proportion of those who call themselves socialists. But always it has pointed to two or three definite things. The first of these is that unlimited freedoms of private property, with increasing facilities of exchange, combination, and aggrandisement, become more and more dangerous to human liberty by the expropriation and reduction to private wages slavery of larger and larger proportions of the population. Every school of socialism states this in some more or less complete form, however divergent the remedial methods suggested by the different schools. And next every school of socialism accepts the concentration of management and property as necessary, and declines to contemplate what is the typical Conservator remedy, its re-fragmentation. Accordingly it sets up not only against the large private owner, but against owners generally, the idea of a public proprietor, the State, which shall hold in the collective interest. But where the earlier socialisms stopped short and where to this day socialism is vague, divided, and unprepared, is upon the psychological problems involved in that new and largely unprecedented form of proprietorship, and upon the still more subtle problems of its attainment. These are vast, and profoundly, widely, and multitudinously difficult problems, and it was natural and inevitable that the earlier socialists in the first enthusiasm of their idea should minimise these difficulties, pretend in the fulness of their faith that partial answers to objections were complete answers, and display the common weaknesses of honest propaganda the whole world over. Socialism is now old enough to know better. Few modern socialists present their faith as a complete panacea, and most are now setting to work in earnest upon these long-shirked preliminary problems of human interaction through which the vital problem of a collective head and brain can alone be approached. This present volume is almost entirely the work of writers, still for the most part calling themselves socialists, who have come to this stage of admission.

A considerable proportion of the socialist movement remains, as it has been from the first, vaguely democratic. It points to collective ownership with no indication of the administrative scheme it contemplates to realise that intention. Necessarily it remains a formless claim without hands to take hold of the thing it desires. Indeed, in a large number of cases it is scarcely more than a resentful consciousness in the expropriated masses of social disintegration. It spends its force very largely in mere revenges upon property as such, attacks simply destructive by reason of the absence of any definite ulterior scheme. It is an ill-equipped and planless belligerent who must destroy whatever he captures because he can neither use nor take away. A council of democratic socialists in possession of London would be as capable of an orderly and sustained administration as the Anabaptists in Munster. But the discomforts and disorders of our present planless system do tend steadily to the development of this crude socialistic spirit in the mass of the proletariat; merely vindictive attacks upon property, sabotage, and the general strike are the logical and inevitable consequences of an uncontrolled concentration of property in a few hands, and such things must and will go on, the deep undertone in the deliquescence of the Normal Social

Life, until a new justice, a new scheme of compensations and satisfactions is attained, or the Normal Social Life re-emerges.

Fabian socialism was the first systematic attempt to meet the fatal absence of administrative schemes in the earlier socialisms. It can scarcely be regarded now as anything but an interesting failure, but a failure that has all the educational value of a first reconnaissance into unexplored territory. Starting from that attack on aggregating property, which is the common starting-point of all socialist projects, the Fabians, appalled at the obvious difficulties of honest confiscation and an open transfer from private to public hands, conceived the extraordinary idea of *filching* property for the state. A small body of people of extreme astuteness were to bring about the municipalisation and nationalisation first of this great system of property and then of that, in a manner so artful that the millionaires were to wake up one morning at last, and behold, they would find themselves poor men! For a decade or more Mr. Pease, Mr. Bernard Shaw, Mr. and Mrs. Sidney Webb, Mrs. Besant, Dr. Lawson Dodd, and their associates of the London Fabian Society did pit their wits and ability, or at any rate the wits and ability of their leisure moments, against the embattled capitalists of England and the world, in this complicated and delicate enterprise, without any apparent diminution of the larger accumulations of wealth. But in addition they developed

27

another side of Fabianism, still more subtle, which professed to be a kind of restoration in kind of property to the proletariat, and in this direction they were more successful. A dexterous use, they decided, was to be made of the Poor Law, the public health authority, the education authority, and building regulations and so forth, to create, so to speak, a communism of the lower levels. The mass of people whom the forces of change had expropriated were to be given a certain minimum of food, shelter, education, and sanitation, and this, the socialists were assured, could be used as the thin end of the wedge towards a complete communism. The minimum, once established, could obviously be raised continually until either everybody had what they needed or the resources of society gave out and set a limit to the process.

This second method of attack brought the Fabian movement into co-operation with a large amount of benevolent and constructive influence outside the socialist ranks altogether. Few wealthy people really grudge the poor a share of the necessities of life, and most are quite willing to assist in projects for such a distribution. But while these schemes naturally involved a very great amount of regulation and regimentation of the affairs of the poor, the Fabian Society fell away more and more from its associated proposals for the socialisation of the rich. The Fabian project changed steadily in character until at last it ceased to be in any sense antagonistic to wealth as such. If the lion did not exactly lie down with the lamb, at any rate the man with the gun and the alleged social mad dog returned very peaceably together. The Fabian hunt was up.

Great financiers contributed generously to a School of Economics that had been founded with moneys left to the Fabian Society by earlier enthusiasts for socialist propaganda and education. It remained for Mr. Belloc to point the moral of the whole development with a phrase, to note that Fabianism no longer aimed at the socialisation of the whole community, but only at the socialisation of the poor. The first really complete project for a new social order to replace the Normal Social Life was before the world, and this project was the compulsory regimentation of the workers and the complete state control of labour under a new plutocracy. Our present chaos was to be organised into a Servile State.

IV

Now to many of us who found the general spirit of the socialist movement at least hopeful and attractive and sympathetic, this would be an almost tragic conclusion, did we believe that Fabianism was anything more than the first experiment in planning—and one almost inevitably shallow and presumptuous—of the long series that may be necessary before a clear light breaks upon the road humanity must follow. But we decline to be forced by this one intellectual fiasco towards the *laissez faire* of the Individualist and the Marxist, or to accept the Normal Social Life with its atmosphere of hens and cows and dung, its incessant toil, its servitude of women, and its endless repetitions as the only tolerable life conceivable for the bulk of mankind—as the ultimate life, that is, of mankind. With less arrogance and confidence, but it may be with a firmer faith than our predecessors of the Fabian essays, we declare that we believe a more spacious social order than any that exists or ever has existed, a Peace of the World in which there is an almost universal freedom, health, happiness, and well-being, and which contains the seeds of a still greater future, is possible to mankind. We propose to begin again with the recognition of those same difficulties the Fabians first realised. But we do not propose to organise a society, form a group for the control of the two chief political parties, bring about "socialism" in twenty-five years, or do anything beyond contributing in our place and measure to that constructive discussion whose real magnitude we now begin to realise.

We have faith in a possible future, but it is a faith that makes the quality of that future entirely dependent upon the strength and clearness of purpose that this present time can produce. We do not believe the greater social state is inevitable.

Yet there is, we hold, a certain qualified inevitability about this greater social state because we believe any social state not affording a general contentment, a general freedom, and a general and increasing fulness of life, must sooner or later collapse and disintegrate again, and revert more or less completely to the Normal Social Life, and because we believe the Normal Social Life is itself thick-sown with the seeds of fresh beginnings. The Normal Social Life has never at any time been absolutely permanent, always it has carried within itself the germs of enterprise and adventure and exchanges that finally attack its stability. The superimposed social order of to-day, such as it is, with its huge development of expropriated labour, and the schemes of the later Fabians to fix this state of affairs in an organised form and render it plausibly tolerable, seem also doomed to accumulate catastrophic tensions. Bureaucratic schemes for establishing the regular lifelong subordination of a labouring class, enlivened though they may be by frequent inspection, disciplinary treatment during seasons of unemployment, compulsory temperance, free medical attendance, and a cheap and shallow elementary education, fail to satisfy the restless cravings in the heart of man. They are cravings that even the baffling methods of the most ingeniously worked Conciliation Boards cannot permanently restrain. The drift of any Servile State must be towards a class revolt, paralysing sabotage, and a general strike. The more rigid and complete the Servile State becomes, the more thorough will be its ultimate failure. Its fate is decay or explosion. From its débris we shall either revert to the Normal Social Life and begin again the long struggle towards that ampler, happier, juster arrangement of human affairs which we of this book, at any rate, believe to be possible, or we shall pass into the twilight of mankind.

This greater social life we put, then, as the only real alternative to the Normal Social Life from which man is continually escaping. For it we do not propose to use the expressions the "socialist state" or "socialism," because we believe those terms have now by constant confused use become so battered and bent and discoloured by irrelevant associations as to be rather misleading than expressive. We propose to use the term The Great State to express this ideal of a social system no longer localised, no longer immediately tied to and conditioned by the cultivation of the land, world-wide in its interests and outlook and catholic in its tolerance and sympathy, a system of great individual freedom with a universal understanding among its citizens of a collective thought and purpose.

Now the difficulties that lie in the way of humanity in its complex and toilsome journey through the coming centuries towards this Great State are fundamentally difficulties of adaptation and adjustment. To no conceivable social state is man inherently fitted: he is a creature of jealousy and suspicion, unstable, restless, acquisitive, aggressive, intractible, and of a most subtle and nimble dishonesty. Moreover, he is imaginative, adventurous, and inventive. His nature and instincts are as much in conflict with the necessary restrictions and subjugation of the Normal Social Life as they are likely to be with any other social net that necessity may weave about him. But the Normal Social Life had this advantage, that it has a vast accumulated moral tradition and a minutely worked-out material method. All the fundamental institutions have arisen in relation to it and are adapted to its conditions. To revert to it after any phase of social chaos and distress is and will continue for many years to be the path of least resistance for perplexed humanity.

Our conception of the Great State, on the other hand, is still altogether unsubstantial. It is a project as dreamlike to-day as electric lighting, electric traction, or aviation would have been in the year 1850. In 1850 a man reasonably conversant with the physical science of his time could have declared with a very considerable confidence that, given a certain measure of persistence and social security, these things were more likely to be attained than not in the course of the next century. But such a prophecy was conditional on the preliminary accumulation of a considerable amount of knowledge, on many experiments and failures. Had the world of 1850, by some wave of impulse, placed all its resources in the hands of the ablest scientific man alive, and asked him to produce a practicable paying electric vehicle before 1852, he would have at best produced some clumsy, curious toy, or more probably failed altogether; and, similarly, if the whole population of the world came to the present writers and promised meekly to do whatever it was told, we should find ourselves still very largely at a loss in our projects for a millennium. Yet just as nearly every man at work upon Voltaic electricity in 1850 knew that he was preparing for electric traction, so do we know that we are, with a whole row of unsolved problems before us, working towards the Great State.

Let us briefly recapitulate the main problems which have to be attacked in the attempt to realise the outline of the Great State. At the base of the whole order there must be some method of agricultural production, and if the agricultural labourer and cottager and the ancient life of the small householder on the holding, a life laborious, prolific, illiterate, limited, and in immediate contact with the land used, is to recede and disappear, it must recede and disappear before methods upon a much larger scale, employing wholesale machinery and involving great economies. It is alleged by modern writers that the permanent residence of the cultivator in close relation to his ground is a legacy from the days of cumbrous and expensive transit, that the great proportion of farm work is seasonal, and that a migration to and fro between rural and urban conditions would be entirely practicable in a largely planned community. The agricultural population could move out of town into an open-air life as the spring approached, and return for spending, pleasure, and education as the days shortened. Already something of this sort occurs under extremely unfavourable conditions in the movement of the fruit and hop pickers from the east end of London into Kent, but that is a mere hint of the extended picnic which a broadly planned cultivation might afford. A fully developed civilisation employing machines in the hands of highly skilled men will minimise toil to the very utmost, no man will shove where a machine can shove, or carry where a machine can carry; but there will remain, more particularly in the summer, a vast amount of hand operations, invigorating and even attractive to the urban population. Given short hours, good pay, and all the jolly amusement in the evening camp that a free, happy, and intelligent people will develop for themselves, and there will be little difficulty about this particular class of work to differentiate it from any other sort of necessary labour.

One passes, therefore, with no definite transition from the root problem of agricultural production in the Great State to the wider problem of labour in general.

A glance at the country-side conjures up a picture of extensive tracts being cultivated on a wholesale

1713698

scale, of skilled men directing great ploughing, sowing, and reaping plants, steering cattle and sheep about carefully designed enclosures, constructing channels and guiding sewage towards its proper destination on the fields, and then of added crowds of genial people coming out to spray trees and plants, pick and sort and pack fruits. But who are these people? Why are they in particular doing this for the community? Is our Great State still to have a majority of people glad to do commonplace work for mediocre wages, and will there be other individuals who will ride by on the roads, sympathetically no doubt, but with a secret sense of superiority? So one opens the general problem of the organisation for labour.

I am careful here to write "for labour" and not "of Labour," because it is entirely against the spirit of the Great State that any section of the people should be set aside as a class to do most of the monotonous, laborious, and uneventful things for the community. That is practically the present arrangement, and that, with a quickened sense of the need of breaking people in to such a life, is the ideal of the bureaucratic Servile State to which in common with the Conservators we are bitterly opposed. And here I know we are at our most difficult, most speculative, and most revolutionary point. We who look to the Great State as the present aim of human progress believe a state may solve its economic problem without any section whatever of the community being condemned to lifelong labour. And contemporary events, the phenomena of recent strikes, the phenomena of sabotage carry out the suggestion that in a community where nearly every one reads extensively, travels about, sees the charm and variety in the lives of prosperous and leisurely people, no class is going to submit permanently to modern labour conditions without extreme resistance, even after the most elaborate Labour Conciliation schemes and social minima are established. Things are altogether too stimulating to the imagination nowadays. Of all impossible social dreams that belief in tranquillised and submissive and virtuous Labour is the wildest of all. No sort of modern men will stand it. They will as a class do any vivid and disastrous thing rather than stand it. Even the illiterate peasant will only endure lifelong toil under the stimulus of private ownership and with the consolations of religion; and the typical modern worker has neither the one nor the other. For a time, indeed, for a generation or so even, a labour mass may be fooled or coerced, but in the end it will break out against its subjection even if it breaks out to a general social catastrophe.

We have, in fact, to invent for the Great State, if we are to suppose any Great State at all, an economic method without any specific labour class. If we cannot do so, we had better throw ourselves in with the conservators forthwith, for they are right and we are absurd. Adhesion to the conception of the Great State involves adhesion to the belief that the amount of regular labour, skilled and unskilled, required to produce everything necessary for every one living in its highly elaborate civilisation may, under modern conditions, with the help of scientific economy and power-producing machinery, be reduced to so small a number of working hours per head in proportion to the average life of the citizen, as to be met as regards the greater moiety of it by the payment of wages over and above the gratuitous share of each individual in the general output; and as regards the residue, a residue of rough, disagreeable, and monotonous operations, by some form of conscription, which will devote a year, let us say, of each person's life to the public service. If we reflect that in the contemporary state there is already food, shelter, and clothing of a sort for every one, in spite of the fact that enormous numbers of people do no productive work at all because they are too well off, that great numbers are out of work, great numbers by bad nutrition and training incapable of work, and that an enormous amount of the work actually done is the overlapping production of competitive trade and work, upon such politically necessary but socially useless things as Dreadnoughts, it becomes clear that the absolutely unavoidable labour in a modern community and its ratio to the available vitality must be of very small account indeed. But all this has still to be worked out even in the most general terms. An intelligent science of Economics should afford standards and

38

technicalities and systematised facts upon which
to base an estimate. The point was raised a quarter
of a century ago by Morris in his *News from Nowhere*,
and indeed it was already discussed by More in his
Utopia. Our contemporary economics is, however,
still a foolish, pretentious pseudo-science, a fester-
ing mass of assumptions about buying and selling and
wages-paying, and one would as soon consult Bradshaw
or the works of Dumas as our orthodox professors of
Economics for any light upon this fundamental matter.

Moreover, we believe that there is a real disposition to work in human beings, and that in a well-
equipped community, in which no one was under an
unavoidable urgency to work, the greater proportion
of productive operations could be made sufficiently
attractive to make them desirable occupations. As
for the irreducible residue of undesirable toil, I owe
to my friend the late Professor William James this
suggestion of a general conscription and a period of
public service for every one, a suggestion which
greatly occupied his thoughts during the last years
of his life. He was profoundly convinced of the
high educational and disciplinary value of universal
compulsory military service, and of the need of
something more than a sentimental ideal of duty in
public life. He would have had the whole population taught in the schools and prepared for this
year (or whatever period it had to be) of patient
and heroic labour, the men for the mines, the fish-
eries, the sanitary services, railway routine, the

women for hospital, and perhaps educational work, and so forth. He believed such a service would permeate the whole state with a sense of civic obligation. . . .

But behind all these conceivable triumphs of scientific adjustment and direction lies the infinitely greater difficulty on our way to the Great State, the difficulty of direction. What sort of people are going to distribute the work of the community, decide what is or is not to be done, determine wages, initiate enterprises; and under what sort of criticism, checks, and controls are they going to do this delicate and extensive work? With this we open the whole problem of government, administration, and officialdom.

The Marxist and the democratic socialist generally shirk this riddle altogether; the Fabian conception of a bureaucracy, official to the extent of being a distinct class and cult, exists only as a starting-point for healthy repudiations. Whatever else may be worked out in the subtler answers our later time prepares, nothing can be clearer than that the necessary machinery of government must be elaborately organised to prevent the development of a managing caste, in permanent conspiracy, tacit or expressed, against the normal man. Quite apart from the danger of unsympathetic and fatally irritating government, there can be little or no doubt that the method of making men officials for life is quite the worst way of getting official duties done. Officialdom is a species of incompetence. The rather priggish, timid, teachable and well-

behaved sort of boy who is attracted by the prospect of assured income and a pension to win his
way into the civil service, and who then by varied
assiduities rises to a sort of timidly vindictive importance, is the last person to whom we would
willingly intrust the vital interests of a nation. We
want people who know about life at large, who will
come to the public service seasoned by experience,
not people who have specialised and acquired that
sort of knowledge which is called, in much the same
spirit of qualification as one speaks of German Silver, Expert Knowledge. It is clear our public servants and officials must be so only for their periods
of service. They must be taught by life, and not
"trained" by pedagogues. In every continuing job
there is a time when one is crude and blundering,
a time, the best time, when one is full of the freshness and happiness of doing well, and a time when
routine has largely replaced the stimulus of novelty.
The Great State will, I feel convinced, regard
changes in occupation as a proper circumstance in
the life of every citizen; it will value a certain ama-
teurishness in its service, and prefer it to the trite
omniscience of the stale official.

And since the Fabian socialists have created a
wide-spread belief that in their projected state every
man will be necessarily a public servant or a public
pupil because the state will be the only employer
and the only educator, it is necessary to point out
that the Great State presupposes neither the one

nor the other. It is a form of liberty and not a form of enslavement. We agree with the bolder forms of socialism in supposing an initial proprietary independence in every citizen. The citizen is a shareholder in the state. Above that and after that, he works if he chooses. But if he likes to live on his minimum and do nothing—though such a type of character is scarcely conceivable—he can. His earning is his own surplus. Above the basal economics of the Great State we assume with confidence there will be a huge surplus of free spending upon extra-collective ends. Public organisations, for example, may distribute impartially and possibly even print and make ink and paper for the newspapers in the Great State, but they will certainly not own them. Only doctrine-driven men have ever ventured to think they would. Nor will the state control writers and artists, for example, nor the stage —though it may build and own theatres—the tailor, the dressmaker, the restaurant cook, an enormous multitude of other busy workers-for-preferences. In the Great State of the future, as in the life of the more prosperous classes of to-day, the greater proportion of occupations and activities will be private and free.

I would like to underline in the most emphatic way that it is possible to have this Great State, essentially socialistic, owning and running the land and all the great public services, sustaining everybody in absolute freedom at a certain minimum of comfort and well-being, and still leaving most of the interests, amusements, and adornments of the individual life, and all sorts of collective concerns, social and political discussion, religious worship, philosophy, and the like to the free personal initiatives of entirely unofficial people.

This still leaves the problem of systematic knowledge and research, and all the associated problems of æsthetic, moral, and intellectual initiative to be worked out in detail; but at least it dispels the nightmare of a collective mind organised as a branch of the civil service, with authors, critics, artists, scientific investigators appointed in a phrensy of wire-pulling—as nowadays the British state appoints its bishops for the care of its collective soul.

I will not venture here to invade the province of my colleagues in the treatment of the Great State in its relation to individual education, in the discussion of the methods by means of which the accumulating results of the free activities of the free collective mind will be brought to bear upon the development of the young citizen, nor will I do more than point out our present extreme ignorance and indecision upon those two closely correlated problems, the problem of family organisation and the problem of women's freedom. In the Normal Social Life the position of women is easily defined. They are subordinated but important. The citizenship rests with the man, and the woman's relation to the community as a whole is through a man. But within that limitation her functions as mother, wife, and

43

home-maker are cardinal. It is one of the entirely unforeseen consequences that have arisen from the decay of the Normal Social Life and its autonomous home that great numbers of women while still subordinate have become profoundly unimportant. They have ceased to a very large extent to bear children, they have dropped most of their home-making arts, they no longer nurse nor educate such children as they have, and they have taken on no new functions that compensate for these dwindling activities of the domestic interior. That subjugation which is a vital condition to the Normal Social Life does not seem to be necessary to the Great State. It may or it may not be necessary. And here we enter upon the most difficult of all our problems. The whole spirit of the Great State is against any avoidable subjugation; but the whole spirit of that science which will animate the Great State forbids us to ignore woman's functional and temperamental differences. A new status has still to be invented for women, a Feminine Citizenship differing in certain respects from the normal masculine citizenship. Its conditions remain to be worked out. We have indeed to work out an entire new system of relations between men and women, that will be free from servitude, aggression, provocation, or parasitism. The public Endowment of Motherhood as such may perhaps be the first broad suggestion of the quality of this new status. A new type of family, a mutual alliance in the place of a

44

subjugation, is perhaps the most startling of all the conceptions which confront us directly we turn ourselves definitely towards the Great State.

And as our conception of the Great State grows, so we shall begin to realise the nature of the problem of transition, the problem of what we may best do in the confusion of the present time to elucidate and render practicable this new phase of human organisation. Of one thing there can be no doubt, that whatever increases thought and knowledge moves towards our goal; and equally certain is it that nothing leads thither that tampers with the freedom of spirit, the independence of soul in common men and women. In many directions, therefore, the believer in the Great State will display a jealous watchfulness of contemporary developments rather than a premature constructiveness. We must watch wealth; but quite as necessary it is to watch the legislator, who mistakes propaganda for progress and class exasperation to satisfy class vindictiveness for construction. Supremely important is it to keep discussion open, to tolerate no limitation on the freedom of speech, writing, art and book distribution, and to sustain the utmost liberty of criticism upon all contemporary institutions and processes.

This briefly is the programme of problems and effort to which this idea of the Great State, as the goal of contemporary progress, directs our minds. My colleagues deal more particularly with various aspects of this general proposal.

4   45

SOCIALISM AND THE GREAT STATE

I append a diagram which shows compactly the gist of the preceding chapter.

THE NORMAL SOCIAL LIFE

produces an increasing surplus of energy and opportunity, more particularly under modern conditions of scientific organisation and power production; and this through the operation of rent and of usury generally tends to

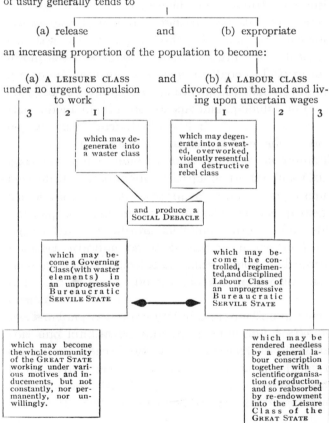

(a) release   and   (b) expropriate

an increasing proportion of the population to become:

(a) A LEISURE CLASS under no urgent compulsion to work   and   (b) A LABOUR CLASS divorced from the land and living upon uncertain wages

3   2   I   I   2   3

which may degenerate into a waster class

which may degenerate into a sweated, overworked, violently resentful and destructive rebel class

and produce a SOCIAL DEBACLE

which may become a Governing Class (with waster elements) in an unprogressive Bureaucratic SERVILE STATE

which may become the controlled, regimented, and disciplined Labour Class of an unprogressive Bureaucratic SERVILE STATE

which may become the whole community of the GREAT STATE working under various motives and inducements, but not constantly, nor permanently, nor unwillingly.

which may be rendered needless by a general labour conscription together with a scientific organisation of production, and so reabsorbed by re-endowment into the Leisure Class of the GREAT STATE

THE GREAT STATE AND THE COUNTRY-SIDE

BY THE COUNTESS OF WARWICK

II

THE GREAT STATE AND THE
COUNTRY-SIDE

THE dividing line which separates the Country
from the Town, the countryman from the townsman, is a comparatively recent phenomenon in
human affairs. Almost to the end of the eighteenth
century—except in a very few great cities, such as
London, Rome, Constantinople, and Paris, for example—there were not many members of a civilised
State who were entirely divorced from a share in
the work and the pleasures of the fields and woods.
The great towns of the Middle Ages and the earlier
Modern Period were of a size that would now be
entitled to the name of little market towns, except
for the few of the rank exampled above. As for
their inhabitants, take the case of the woollen-
spinners when they began to build up England's
industrial supremacy: they were at first merely an
agricultural peasantry who occupied their spare
time and the time of the unemployed members of
their families in spinning in the rooms and sheds
around their cottages. They were much more entitled to the name of agriculturists than the descrip-

tion of industrial artisans. But this is not the place for a study of the history of the Country-side, suffice it to sum up the matter by a specific illustration; the town of Warwick, as it stands to-day, is a fairly typical example of the normal towns of the earlier period; while Manchester or Birmingham is a typical city of modern life. The radical distinctions between the two classes are fairly obvious; and a clear conception of this fundamental fact of the modern city will be a convenient starting-point for our examination of the possibilities of country life under the ideal conditions of the Great State.

It will be for others to discuss the phenomena of the intervening period of transition from the present to the future: it is the business of this essay to describe the Country as it visualises itself to the mind of one who accepts and hopes for the Great State as the most probable and most desirable condition of human society, as it will one day be organised. It will be a frankly ideal presentation of the Country-side of the Great State. But although it will be a statement of an ideal place, it does not necessarily follow that it is based on phantoms of the imagination. On the contrary, we idealists of the Great State claim that our visions are founded on a substantial ground-work of hard, material facts; we reach our ideal by rational conclusions from things which already exist. We argue from the known to the unknown.

At the beginning of this statement it seems very

clear that no rational ideal can admit the possibility of the continued existence of such an unsightly social sore as Manchester or Liverpool or Newcastle or the suburbs of London or its East End. There will, of course, be no room in the Great State for towns of factories belching forth yellow fog; there will be no place for congested areas of slums. But our rebellion will go further than this: for the fresh air of the country, with its quiet sunshine and open fields, with its flowers and birds, is all such a vital part of a rational human life that no civilised beings will be content to be buried in the middle of great cities, however healthy they may be made. Perhaps the most fundamental change in the ideal Great State will be the abolition of the overswollen town and the revival of the saner towns of earlier days. There will be fewer enormous cities like New York and Chicago, there will be more boroughs of the size of Ipswich, Chester, Reading, and York. The radical distinction between the Country and the Town will have disappeared.

This change will be rendered possible because the means of transit—railways, trams, light-railways, and motor traction, perhaps aeroplanes or something better—will be so vastly improved that there will be no need for people to herd together in closely packed groups. When it is a simple matter for the citizens to move themselves and their belongings and the produce of their labour from one point to another, almost the whole advantage of town segregation will vanish. The railways and trams and cars will then be communal and free services, just as the roads are communal and free to-day. The waste of innumerable ticket-collectors and booking-clerks will be saved: the citizens of the Great State will regard transit as a commonplace, which they will provide without stint and encourage every one to use without a moment's hesitation.

But there may be some readers who are asking what all this concerning towns has to do in an essay on the Country. It has everything to do with the subject, for we cannot know what will be Country until we have decided what will belong to the Town. If the population is to be distributed in a larger number of smaller-sized towns, instead of in the huge towns as at present, then it is clear that our conception of the Country is materially altered by the fact that there will not be many parts of the State which are very distant from a town. Here we reach an all-important factor in the problem. There will be no need in the Great State for any rural dwellers to be utterly divorced from those unlimited advantages of civilised life which can only be obtained by intercourse with a centralised collection of human activities at one spot.

Town life has brought many evils in its train; but there are certain invaluable advantages which only the town segregation can procure. For example, a well-equipped opera-house, a theatre, a concert-hall; art galleries and museums; libraries, swimming-baths; specialised medical advice and special instruction; facilities for higher education; large shops, with a full variety of choice for their customers; the invigorating interchange of the social intercourse of large gatherings; all these things demand a town of a fairly extensive size for their accomplishment. The torpor of the rural dwellers of to-day is largely the consequence of having to do without these advantages of the city: and they will remain torpid until some method is discovered of placing them within the reach of the countryman and woman. The countryman of the Great State will always be within easy reach of the town. Indeed, when we consider the organisation of the agricultural work of this Great State it will seem probable that comparatively few people will live outside the town. This agricultural business we will now consider in some detail; after which we shall be the better able to view the picture as a whole.

After all, the main purpose of the country, in the material sense at least, is to pasture beasts and grow corn and fruits and vegetables and trees. It is the manufacturing place of our food: and the people who live there are the producers of animal and vegetable wealth. The country must be organised and worked with that end in view. No one who knows anything of the technicalities of farming will deny that this work of producing agricultural wealth is done exceedingly inefficiently to-

day, in England at least. In spite of all the teaching of science, in spite of all the actual practice of
many foreign nations, we are still farming our land
after the manner of rule-of-thumb rustics. Our
large farmers are content with a mere minimum of
produce which will pay a minimum interest on the
capital expended; our small holders are trying to
extract a larger yield by methods which are little
better than the working of a village allotment in
a man's evening hours. There are many farmers
who are doing sufficiently well to pay their landlords' rent, with enough over to give themselves a
comfortable living, but entirely ignoring the fact
that the nation is losing all the surplus wealth which
might be grown if they had the knowledge and the
energy. Our small holders are struggling along—
often going under—as isolated units, when every
Continental country is an object-lesson of the truth
that small holdings are only really successful when
there is close co-operation between the farmers.

But the Great State will have got beyond anything so unscientific as small holdings or so transitory as larger farmers bound down by the will of
rent-exacting landlords. Both large and small
farmers are as uneconomical and mediæval as is
the village craftsman when compared with the
great modern industrial companies and trusts.
There is, indeed, a better case for the small craftsman in industry than there is for the small farmer
in agricultural organisation. The small holding

which is part of a complicated system of co-operation—and that is its only chance of real success—
is, in fact, not strictly speaking a small holding at
all in any more reality than one field of a large
farm is a small holding. Everything about co-
operative farming goes to show that there is no
good reason why the organisation should stop short
at the marketing of the produce or the buying of
the seeds and implements. If it is well to co-operate
in these ways, it is also well to co-operate in the
production of the goods. And when small holders
co-operate in the management of their farms, then,
to all intents and purposes, they are a large, united
farm.

Under the rule of the Great State, the landlord
and the small and large private farmers will no
longer exist. The State will own the land, and it
will not make itself ridiculous by letting it out in
petty patches, to be farmed on the scale that one
would run a village general-shop. It will, on the
contrary, be divided up into convenient tracts, of
a size determined by the nature of the soil and the
kind of produce to be grown; and these will be
worked as State farms under the control of a director and assistants, who are highly trained in the
latest science and art of their department of knowledge. Farming will be a profession of the same
rank as medicine, public administration, and education. The ideal of these agriculturalists will be
to produce as much wealth per acre as the soil is

capable of yielding. The farm-workers, likewise, will be specially trained in their duties by a course of apprenticeship on the land. The idea of getting good farming out of untrained farmers and unskilled labourers will be thought of as a comical tradition of the past.

The vast difference between the present amateur farmers and the professionals we contemplate for the future, will require some consideration before it is grasped by the reader who does not know the ridiculous inefficiency of present agricultural methods. It is not by any means the fault of the farmers and landlords: they are in the grip of a thoroughly bad system. They have to compete against well-organised co-operating Danes, or against United States farmers who have great tracts of land at their disposal without urgent need for careful economy of every rood. The farmers of to-day are content if they can get a living for themselves; it is not part of their desires to produce as much agricultural wealth as their land is capable of growing. Again, if some foreign competitors can grow corn or potatoes more cheaply than they can be grown in England, then the private farmer is compelled to allow his land to remain proportionately uncultivated. Whereas, under the system of State farms, the land would be cultivated to its utmost capacity, until some other use was found for the men and land. It is always wasteful to allow men and land to stand idle.

The Great State will very probably not grow corn in England at all, for it will have under its control more suitable land as it is now found in Canada or India. Here we come across a practical advantage of the Great State system—namely, it has, or will have, a large variety of choice within its own domain; it will not be compelled to grow potatoes on a few feet of rock as do the west-coast peasants of Ireland. It is this ridiculous economic waste which is the dire penalty of the highly localised small-farm system. The State Farm Board will not waste its time cultivating bare rocks or inferior soil until it has brought its richest soil to its fullest fruition; it will allot each crop to the locality most suitable in the area. It will grow its corn in the vast plains of the great continents, for corn can be easily shipped from the other end of the world to its consumers. On the other hand, every large town may have its milk farm and its vegetable gardens just outside its boundaries; for milk and vegetables are not easily carried without loss of freshness. But even in these latter departments it is probable that improved facilities of transit will make the highly specialised milk farm or potato farm—on the most suitable soil—supplying a large number of towns and large tracts of country, a reasonable possibility.

Certainly, this present niggling system of little holdings, or even bigger farms, all starved for want of capital and compelled to use the wasteful methods that come from small production, all this will be swept away contemptuously by a State Farm Board which sets out to do its work under the rules of science and common sense. The most carefully organised co-operative farm becomes a mediæval method when compared with the larger schemes of the Great State. Agricultural organisation will not be squeezed within the limits of small local necessities and the stinted capital of needy men. It will be managed with all the scope and all the national resources at the disposal of a great state department. The Great State agriculture will be to the agriculture of to-day what the Oil Trust is to the oil-shop in the back streets of a slum district: only the profits will go to the whole community instead of into the pockets of a Mr. Rockefeller.

Needless to say, the farm-labourer will be altogether a different person from the man of to-day. His wages will not be based on a standard of what is just possible for the minimum of a rigidly simple country life. He will take an equal share with his fellow-citizens of the towns in the standard of living which the community has reached. It is not tolerable to us to suppose that there should be members of the community doomed year after year to sacrifice their leisure, the larger interests, and all the variety of life in order that their fellows can be free. Yet that is the position of the agricultural workers to-day; they are cut off from the full advantages of civilised life, pushed into a corner, and underpaid; they are the serfs of society. The essence of modern culture is the possibility of contact with a large amount of varied human fellowship. It is absurd to say that the solitary countryman— shut off from the main currents of social develop- ments—is as good a man as the best product of the more complex life of the towns. The rustic may be as good a man or far better than the slum dweller: but then the slum dweller is not the product of the advantages of the town; he is, rather, the result of all its unnecessary failure. There is a great deal of absurd sentiment talked of the charming "simpli- city" of the peasant. We are not out to cultivate "charming simplicity"—"charming" chiefly to the patronising observer; we want able and adaptable men.

And to make a civilised man of himself, the agri- culturalist must have full leisure to get away from the working monotony of his own trade. The most satisfactory of trades must become narrowing if they absorb the whole of life. A portrait-painter or a poet who gave his whole time to painting or poesy would be a poor stunted creature, and his art a poor stunted art. And so likewise with the farmer. A rural life, with all its freshness, is not a complete life: it lacks the variety of a fully developed exist- ence. A man must no more spend his whole time with bent back, hoeing or digging from dawn to dusk, than a cotton-spinner should spend all his waking hours at his loom. When his reasonable hours of labour are ended, the farm-worker must be able to

59

reach all the culture and stimulus which are within the reach of the dweller in the complex town.

We have said that the normal town of the Great State will probably be of between fifty and sixty thousand inhabitants. That will be large enough to make social organisation in the way of theatres and libraries, and so on, quite possible, while there will be no interminable circle of suburbs to cut off the citizens from the fresh country. But the point which concerns us here is that the rural dweller will be, by an efficient transit system, in easy reach of these towns. As we have also suggested, the agricultural workers may easily live in the towns; a very slight care in the organisation of light railways and motors may enable them to reach their fields and return to the towns for the night. However, the village may also remain under the Great State system; many people may still prefer to live in little groups of a few hundreds rather than in a town, however fresh and clean. Still fewer may prefer the isolated houses; and these will have the opportunity to act as guardians of the outlying crops and herds. But all, villages or solitary cottagers, will possess the leisure and the facilities for reaching the complex town when they please to go thither. The general rule will probably be that most of the agricultural population will live in the "big" towns; the rest will be scattered in fairly large villages within easy reach of those towns. Here and there, for those who have a passion for retirement, will be lonely houses.

One factor which is worth noting in passing is the fact that, under the big-scale agriculture of the Great State, work will not be done as it is to-day when it is customary to see solitary workers in the fields; for under the centralised system, with plenty of workers for the job and systematic organisation taking the place of the present haphazard methods, it will be much more possible for the labour to be done by groups of workers which will give fellow-ship, instead of the dreary solitude which is so dead-ening to many minds; also there will be better facilities for controlling the work by expert overseers.

But there is another aspect from which we must view the Country-side of the Great State. So far we have seen that the rural dwellers will tend to collect in the towns as their permanent dwelling-place or as the habitual haunt of their leisure. There will be a corresponding approach from the other side: the town artisans will tend to come out into the country towns and villages as the mon-strous city of the present breaks up from sheer discomfort and uselessness. The public industrial department of the Great State will not—like the callous companies and employers of to-day—plant its factories and workshops in the midst of over-grown cities, when the work can be as efficiently done within reach of fresh air and pleasant recrea-tion. To-day it may pay the employing classes to huddle all their factories together and build all their workers' dwellings in long strings of endless streets.

But when an educated democracy demands something better, its State transit department will find the organisation of the carrying trade a matter of comparative simplicity. When the community works to live and does not live to work, the first consideration will be to select a spot where men and women can dwell with the greatest satisfaction to themselves; and few people are likely to find solace in paved streets which lead to other paved streets and so on for miles—the fate of the Londoner and the dwellers in Manchester. So the factory and workshop and mill will be placed in the reasonably sized towns. They may even migrate to the village. In this matter we must remember that the increased use of electricity as a motive power will render it possible to have power supplied "on tap" at great distances from the generating stations, just as gas and water are now supplied. Electricity in the days of the Great State will not be the monopoly of the towns. There will be no need to have a smoking stack of factory chimneys in every village which possesses a factory.

There is another probable development to consider. The industrial artisan and the agricultural worker will not necessarily be two distinct persons. The bulk of the work on the fields is seasonal; and the winter, on the whole, is a slack time for farmers. A well-organised agricultural system will get much of its work done at limited periods, leaving its workers free to remain in the towns or villages during the darker months of the year. The man who makes hay and digs potatoes will probably have a town craft—for example, boot-making or wood-work or house-decorating—for a winter occupation, just as the town artisans will supply the extra hands to allow the countrymen to keep their reasonable hours during the stress of harvesting.

Indeed, in the Great State the Town and the Country will be much more closely allied than they are now. They will interchange their work and their pleasures. It is only the private employer who cannot manage to admit a fluid exchange in his system. The public officials of the Great State will have the names of the whole of the workers on their lists; and one can take the place of another; whereas the private employer has his limited staff; and it is no advantage for him to go to the trouble of re-arrangement to suit the convenience of his workmen.

Such, then, is the general aspect of the Country as it will be in the Great State. There are innumer-able details which it is scarcely in place to expand here. There will be, for example, vast tracts of State forests, which few private owners seem ready or able to grow and manage under the present sys-tem. There will be great expanses of open moun-tains and moorlands which will be left wild and untouched—not to breed stags and grouse for mil-lionaires, but for the sheer pleasure of the culti-vated mind in beholding nature at its most solitary moments. Those who imagine that a well-developed country-side and a larger number of country dwellers will necessarily mean the passing-away of the rural solitude and peace of the woodland glade and heathered hills, are needlessly in dread. Indeed, under the Great State there will be less danger to the sanctuary of the country-side than under the present haphazard individualism which is producing Garden Cities and Garden Suburbs of to-day. The levelling-up of education will tend to a stronger desire to live near one's fellows rather than to escape from them. Also, the manifold advantages of co-operative housekeeping, with common kitchens and dining-rooms and libraries and recreation-rooms, will make most people hesitate before they throw away these advantages for the sake of an exclusive villa of the present suburban type. So it may well come to pass that houses will be grouped together, or built on the block system, even in the country. When towns are built on healthier lines, there will not be the same race to escape into a rather unsightly chaos of straggling suburbs. So the towns, on the whole, will tend to be more compact. That means that the country will be more preserved than even now. The Garden Suburb will not be built when there is no urgent need for either a suburb or a garden; and that will be the case when the town is a fit place of habitation, and every one will have a share in the communal gardens and be within easy reach of open country.

But on these points it is not necessary to dogmatise. There is nothing in the structure of the Great State which will restrict a free choice of dwelling-places—certainly more free than is possible to-day. We can only try to foresee general tendencies: and the impulse of human beings to group together certainly seems a more permanent and normal development than the present tendency to scatter. We all feel that there is something rather vulgar about a suburb: it is an almost instinctive judgment: it is neither a solitude nor a society.

To sum up, the Country-side of the Great State, as we have tried to visualise it, will be a very different thing from the poor and mean extent of small holdings and scattered cottages which seem to have such an attraction for the Liberal and Tory political speakers. We do not believe that there is any perverse twist in the human mind which will lead it to waste its energy in cultivating little isolated scraps of soil when the results would be so manifold better under the larger and more scientifically organised system which will be possible under the experts of a State Agricultural Board.

The desire to possess a few acres of land, and so many private cows and pigs and hens, is, we are told, one of the elemental passions of men. We shall be more certain of that "eternal" truth when mankind can choose between his little Whig or Tory patch and a share in the richer produce of the Great State farm.

65

SOCIALISM AND THE GREAT STATE

There are some who say that the small-holding system is picturesque. We think of it, rather, as but a slightly better version of that most hideous sight on earth—the collection of mean wooden huts and cramped heaps of vegetables which the locally minded and narrow-sighted politician hails with pride as the "allotments" and which he regards as one of the glories of his town. In the light of modern advantages and modern possibilities we see the Normal Social Life as the disjointed scraping for a pittance it has always been. Man has been the serf of the country-side long enough, and now he becomes its master: not only to cultivate it for his profit, but to use it for his pleasure. What conceivable glory to humanity is a servitude to cabbages, a prolification of potatoes in the narrow margins of men's leisure?

＼

WORK IN THE GREAT STATE

BY L. G. CHIOZZA MONEY, M.P.

III

WORK IN THE GREAT STATE

I

THE DIVORCING OF WEALTH AND WORK

It was a wise old woman who sat her down in Cheapside and waited for the crowd to go by. To the average London citizen she is a perfect picture of the ill-informed rural intelligence. To the man who understands she had good cause to contemplate the stream of passers-by with amazement, and to expect it to cease. What, indeed, are all the people doing who may be seen thronging the streets of the city of London?

It is not difficult to answer this question in the negative sense. Observation shows us that, almost in its entirety, the ceaselessly moving City crowd is composed of non-producers. The centre of London is fed from about 8 A. M., the hour at which workmen's trains cease to arrive at the termini, until eleven o'clock, with tens of thousands of men and women, and boys and girls, who are not merely non-producers, but persons who could not give you an intelligent idea as to how any useful material thing is made. Whether our point of observation be the Mansion House, or the top of Ludgate Hill, or westwards at the Marble Arch, it is rarely that there passes before the vision the dirty clothes which, in England, we are unhappily accustomed to regard as the proper costume of a working-man. We are in a land of "officials," where an enormous number of people are traffickers in material commodities, who eat without sowing or reaping, who dress without spinning or weaving, who house themselves without building or planning. From merchant to clerk, from shopkeeper to girl typist, from stock-broker to commission-agent, from banker to office-boy, from lawyer to doorkeeper, it is a land in which an army of people consumes without producing.

Traced homewards, the individuals who form the City stream may be found living in places widely remote, from rows of little houses in Tooting or Walthamstow to expensive and hardly less ugly red-brick villas in Hendon or Woking, in Hampstead or Surbiton. There spending the big and little incomes which they gain by non-productive work, they support by their expenditure, to build and repair their homes, to sustain and beautify their persons, a very large proportion of the inhabitants of London, and of Greater London, and of the places immediately beyond.

Not all these attendants on the city crowd are non-producers. Apart from the shopkeepers and their assistants and the menials, there are brought into the economic chain a considerable number of nominally useful producers who spend their work at the bidding of the non-producers who traffic at the centre.

The result, in large, is to bring into the Metropolis and its surroundings, imports of material commodities which have been either created in those parts of the country where men work usefully or which have been gained by commerce from abroad. It is not forgotten that London is itself a manufacturing centre—are not even food factories to be found in the filthy abysses of the East?—but the matter may be put in true perspective by pointing out that the London County Council area contains only 387,-000 factory workers in a population of 4,500,000.

It is a far cry from the place of central traffic and private officialdom to the springs of British wealth. British prosperity is built upon the possession of one of the greatest and richest coal areas in the world, and the British coal-mines are not situated near London. They are to be found in the West, and in the Midlands, and in the North. Curiously, there are not so many red-brick villas near the springs of work as there are near the centres of mere traffic. You shall seek in vain in Cardiff or in Newcastle for endless streams of real and imitation swells. Mean and sordid, even as measured by the standard of a sordid Metropolis, are the highways and byways of the places from which flow the mineral streams which have done so much for Britain.

What was it that Jevons so truly wrote nearly fifty years ago? I quote from page 234 of *The Coal Question*:

"The history of British industry and trade may be divided into two periods, the first reaching backward from about the middle of the eighteenth century to the earliest times, and the latter reaching forward to the present and the future. These two periods are contrary in character. In the earlier period Britain was a rude, half-cultivated country, abounding in corn and wool and meat and timber, and exporting the rough but valuable materials of manufacture. Our people, though with no small share of poetic and philosophic genius, were unskilful and unhandy; better in the arts of war than those of peace; on the whole, learners rather than teachers.

"But as the second period grew upon us many things changed. Instead of learners we became teachers; instead of exporters of raw materials we became importers; instead of importers of manufactured articles we became exporters. What we had exported we began by degrees to import; and what we had imported we began to export."

A wise man having thus pointed out for all time to the British people that the use of coal changed the entire character of British trade, and made the United Kingdom great, and in the ordinary sense prosperous, it might be imagined that the lesson would be so surely learned, especially seeing that coal-getting is arduous and exceedingly dangerous, that mining would rank amongst the most honoured of callings, and that mining districts would flow with the milk and honey bestowed by a grateful people upon the indispensable creators of wealth. In reality, the mining districts of the United Kingdom are devoid of every trace of beauty and of nearly every rational means of happiness. Take, for example, the unique South Wales coal-field and its unhappy valleys. Perched on the hillsides, in close contiguity to the pit-head, gloomy rows of uncomfortable boxes shelter those who work and die to produce a little for themselves and a great deal for the soft-handed ones who dwell afar off. Once smiling valleys have been shorn of every natural attribute and changed into pandemoniums of work and pain. Even a mining manager in one of these little Welsh villages—and how few can hope to rise to become mining managers!—lives in a small and obscure house where the delight of a garden is unknown. So melancholy is the impression created by these places that one discovers almost with surprise that the people have not lost their gift of song.

Wherever the coal is found, whether it be in Scotland, or in the Black Country, or in Yorkshire, or in Northumberland, or in Lancashire, there also the greater part of useful British industrial work is necessarily done (for work naturally gravitates to Nature's power areas), and there also, strangely, are to be found the chief evidences of an all-pervading poverty. The nearer the source of wealth, the nearer the abodes of squalor. The nearer to honourable, useful, and necessary labour, the nearer to desolation. Who that has seen the purlieus of our industrial towns, and who understands that these are the places where the greater part of the material wealth of the country is created, can fail to wonder why so few commodities remain with those whose lives are spent in productive labour?

It would astonish me to learn that the majority of the readers of these words reached this point without feeling an ardent desire to remind the author of the fact that a man or woman who does not work with his hands in the direct production of material commodities is not necessarily a non-producer. I therefore hasten to add that I am very familiar with the fact, and with all that has been said about it by the long and dreary line of economists, and that I shall discuss it hereafter.

II

THE FEW WHO PRODUCE

BECAUSE so many of us are wasting our time, the material production of the United Kingdom is not large enough, even if equally distributed, to redeem us from poverty. In the Mean State that is, the waste of work is so grievous that it is but the minority of the working population which is engaged in material production, and even as to that minority it is most unhappily true that it is largely engaged in making material things which ought not to be produced at all—things which the Great State of our dreams would ban as economic indecencies.

It is quite simple to demonstrate the truth of these propositions.

In 1906 I took a good deal of interest in the passage into law of the Census of Production Act of the United Kingdom. It was a belated piece of legislation, and its clauses are marked with that timidity which has been the curse of so many British legislative endeavours, and which is largely responsible for the accusing arrears of legislation which are beginning to tell seriously in Britain. I tried to get an inquiry into wages and capital added to its provisions, but the House of Commons, although, as subsequent events have shown, then within measurable distance of a general strike against low wages (I correct this article for press on March 15, 1912, when a general strike of miners is bringing trade to a standstill), was not sufficiently interested to order a compulsory examination of wages and capital. Nevertheless, the Act has given us most valuable if incomplete information. For the first time we have a measurement of the value of the material

75

production of British industries, accompanied by a record of the number of wage-earners and salaried persons, men, women, boys, and girls, who did the work which yielded the commodities. The harvest of British productive work is measured and spread out before us.

The first thing to observe is a thing amazing to the man who has not acquainted himself with the rougher measurement of productive workers exhibited by the ordinary Census of the United Kingdom.

There were, in 1907, the year in which the Board of Trade conducted the Census of Production, about 20,000,000 men, women, boys, and girls engaged in occupations for gain. As the population in 1907 was about 44,000,000, it follows that *nearly one-half of the entire population was working for gain*. When allowance is made for infants, school children, and the aged, we get a decided impression that the British people are a busy people. And indeed they are.

But what are they busy with?

Let us see what the Census of Production tells us as to the number of people occupied in material output in 1907.

The Census dealt with every sort and kind of material production for gain, save and except agricultural production. It covered, that is, not only the manufacturing accomplished in factories, mills, and workshops, but the preparation of food for gain in bakeries, the brewing of beer, the distilling of spirits, and the public works of construction carried out by State departments and local authorities, and it included the value of repairs. It also covered all mining and quarrying. The only exception appears to be the manufacturing of food by restaurants.

Each employer returned the number of salaried persons and wage-earners employed by him, with details as to the proportions of men, women, boys, and girls composing each group. To be precise, those aged eighteen years and over were distinguished from those under eighteen, for each sex.

The inquiry showed that about 6,900,000 persons were engaged in producing in 1907, and that of these 6,400,000 were wage-earners, officered by some 500,000 salaried persons. This is sufficiently remarkable, but the more closely the figures are examined the more remarkable they appear. Further analysis shows that the 6,400,000 wage-earners were thus made up:

UNITED KINGDOM INDUSTRIAL EMPLOYMENT
IN 1907

Males aged 18 years and over.. 4,250,000
Females " 18 " " " .. 1,200,000
Males and Females under 18.... 950,000
—————————
Total.................. 6,400,000

Thus, in the year 1907—and the facts in 1912 can exhibit little variation—*there were only 4,250,000 men occupied in industry in the United Kingdom, terming a man a male person over eighteen years of age.*

And how many men, counting as men the males over eighteen years of age, did the United Kingdom boast of in 1907? The answer is 13,000,000. So that, in what is a great manufacturing country—a country reputed to be industrialised more than any other country—*less than one-third of the males over eighteen are actually engaged in industry.* And not all these are manufacturing. Nearly 1,000,000 of them are engaged in mining and quarrying, so that not more than about one in four of our male population over eighteen is a "manufacturer."

Let us see what addition has to be made to our 4,200,000 miners and manufacturers on account of agricultural production. To judge by the last Census of 1901, and the subsequent drain through emigration, we had in 1907 about 2,000,000 persons engaged in agriculture, including farmers, farmers' relatives working on their farms, agricultural labourers, market gardeners, nurserymen, dairymen, etc., and of these about 1,600,000 were males over eighteen.

Therefore, reviewing material production of every sort and kind, save only the trifling and negligible exceptions which have been mentioned, the number of males over eighteen engaged in material output in 1907 was only about 5,800,000. This total does not include the captains of industry, but their inclusion would, of course, scarcely affect the total. There are only some 250,000 registered factories and workshops in the United Kingdom.

It is true that we supplement the labour of these 5,800,000 "men" by employing in industry 1,200,000 females aged eighteen and over, and some 950,000 boys and girls, and that in agriculture there are perhaps a further 400,000 women, boys, and girls employed. These additions, however, merely serve to raise the total of productive workers to 8,400,000, or, if we throw in the 500,000 salaried persons connected with the industrial operations, 8,900,000. We thus arrive at the extraordinary conclusion that, in a nation containing in 1907 about 44,000,000 of people, about 20,000,000 of whom figure in the Census as "engaged in occupations," only about 9,000,000, or *less than one-half of those working for gain, are engaged in either agricultural or industrial production.*

But let us in particular consider the case of the males. In 1907 there were about 14,000,000 male persons "engaged in occupations." Of these 14,-000,000 males, as we have already seen, there were about 13,000,000 aged eighteen and upwards. Including both industry and agriculture, the number of such males at work was only about 5,850,000.

So that only 45 per cent. of our males over eighteen are direct producers of material commodities.

79

Is it reasonable, or is it not rather incredible, that the labours of the remainder of the working population should be needed to transport and to distribute the material production of so small a proportion of our men, aided by a couple of million women and children?

Make every conceivable allowance for the very real productive powers of such workers as railway servants and carmen, seamen and dockers, warehousemen and storekeepers, postmen and telegraphists, with a due proportion of wholesale and retail distributors, architects, designers, doctors, nurses, and teachers, and it still remains a thing most significant and most unsatisfactory that, amid a multitude of workers, so small a proportion should be employed in making those material things a lack of which constitutes poverty in the physical sense.

Take the case of retail distribution. It is the extraordinary fact that there are 1,500,000 shopkeepers and shop assistants in the United Kingdom, in a community which numbers only some 9,000,000 families. That is to say, there is one retail distributor to each six families in the country, an absurdly high proportion. And this figure takes no account of the carmen, horsemen, stablemen, and other agents also concerned in the process of retailing. It excludes, also, the retailing of coal, which is accomplished, not by shopkeepers, but by "coal-merchants" with another army of clerks, vans, carmen, horsemen, labourers, etc. And the number of retail agents is equally striking when compared with the number of producers. As we have seen, there are only 8,400,000 men, women, boys, and girls engaged in industrial and agricultural production. The shopkeepers and their assistants number 1 for every 5.6 persons engaged in production.

And as for the mass of clerks, agents, travellers, brokers, merchants, canvassers, and other between-agents, their number is altogether disproportionate, either to the number of producers or to the aggregate of those producers' outputs.

III

THE WASTE OF PRODUCERS' WORK

WE must not readily conclude that we have even as many as 4,250,000 men, 1,200,000 women, and 950,000 boys and girls engaged in useful industrial production.

For one thing, the Census of Production was taken in an exceedingly good year of trade, when employment was good. If it had been taken in the following year, the number of producers would have been shown as about 4 per cent. less than the above figures. We have also to take account of short time and of the operation of industrial disease and accident, which cut deeply into the available working time of industrial workers.

81

But these considerations, important as they are, pale before the waste of work which is involved in industrial processes that are but the servants of unnecessary competition.

Analysis of the work of the few millions of industrial producers shows us that no small part of them are engaged, not in the manufacture of things of economic value or personal utility, but in the manufacture of articles or commodities which merely serve the purpose of competitive selling.

Take the printing trade, for example. An unmeasurable but certainly large proportion of the men, women, boys, and girls who rank in the Census of Production as working in the printing trades are engaged in printing, not books or newspapers or magazines, but advertising matter, competitive price-lists, wrappers, trade labels, bill-heads, account books, posters, etc., which are merely called into existence in the struggle of various competitive sellers to reach the consumer. The consumer has to pay the bill for all this printing in the price of the competitive articles which he buys; but what does he gain by the mass of printing which is daily thrust upon him? He is bewildered by the printed appeals which are made to him, which are nearly always misleading in some degree, and which in many cases are deliberately intended to deceive. The newspaper reader pays for his newspaper, he fondly believes, only a halfpenny or a penny. As a matter of fact, he pays for his newspaper in two ways; there is the direct payment of a copper to the news-agent, and there is the indirect payment which he contributes in the prices of things which he buys from tradesmen, prices which are calculated to cover the cost of the advertisements which he fondly imagines are presented to him by the newspaper proprietors. One feels sorry for the uninstructed man who, desiring to buy, say, a pianoforte, consults advertisements as the best means of discovering where to buy.

And not printing alone, but many other trades give a considerable part of their output to the uses of advertisement. Iron, copper, zinc, enamel, colour, ink, paper, string, gum, wood—the list of articles which are built up into advertisements to deface towns, despoil scenery, and confuse the traveller is a lengthy one. The workers upon these things are amongst our few "producers," but their production is in vain.

In recent years, the absurdity of competition by advertisement, which is sufficiently obvious in regard to what are commonly called manufactures, has been imported even into the domain of food supply. Enormous sums are spent by competitive firms to persuade the public that there are a number of different individual teas, butters, or bacons. Tea bought in the ordinary process in the London market is put up into special packets and labelled with fancy names and advertised in terms which suggest that it possesses individual quality like a

Beethoven symphony. The consumer does not dream that, in 1911, 348,000,000 pounds of tea were imported into the United Kingdom for the small sum of £13,000,000, or only 9d. per pound, and that when he buys tea he pays a tax of 5d. to the government and a tax of from 4d. to 8d. and upwards per pound to the host of wholesale and retail middlemen, railway shareholders, advertising agents, brokers, etc., who stand between tea at the port and tea on the breakfast-table. To furnish forth the newspaper advertisements, the posters, the lead wrappers, the paper wrappers, the boxes, and the other paraphernalia connected with the tea-selling means a good deal of "manufacturing," but it is manufacturing which from the point of view of economic production is for the most part a good deal worse than useless. I hope no one will suppose from this that retail grocers make big net profits on tea, for they do not. Their *gross* profit is about 20 per cent. on the wholesale price at which they buy, but much of that goes in rent, etc. The great waste of work brings small *net* gain out of large *gross* profit to ordinary shopkeepers.

And if the manufacturing of competitive materials is bad, the manufacturing of rubbish in nearly every department of industry is worse. I repeat here what I have said before, that rubbish-making is our largest industry. It is one of the saddest things in our industrial system to see an ingenious machine, worked by an intelligent man, and driven by an engine which is a triumph of human skill, exercised upon shoddy material. The average workman is so used to working upon rubbish that he fails to perceive the irony of it. The bricklayer takes the bricks and mortar as they come along; it is all the same to him whether the bricks be soft or hard, or whether the mortar be good cement or pure mud. The carpenter uses the timber supplied to him by the jerry-builder, however green, however shaky. The weaver will as readily weave you a shoddy weft on a cotton warp as produce a piece of good, honest woollen cloth. *Twenty per cent. of the material used by the British woollen and worsted industries consists of shoddy.* This shoddy is worked up with pure wool in various proportions. It is safe to say that no poor man ever wears a garment wholly made of honest woollen material. If our workmen began questioning their materials, I really shudder to think what would happen to their next wages bill, or to what sort of dimensions our industrial production would be reduced. We are surrounded by rubbish on every side. All but a tiny proportion of the houses of the country are furnished with rubbish and curtained with rubbish and fastened up with rubbish. The greater part of household coal, which costs its getters so much in life and its purchasers so much in money, is wasted in rubbish grates and rubbish ranges. It is impossible to exaggerate in this connection; the reality is an exaggeration beyond all imagining.

I cannot pretend to express these things of which I have written in statistical terms. I cannot pretend to decide how many of the 4,250,000 producing males over eighteen make honest stuff and how many, on the other hand, are amongst the rubbish producers. It is only too clear, however, that the rubbish producers are an exceedingly large part of the whole, and that the number of people in the country who make articles worth buying is ridiculously small.

IV

A STARVED PRODUCTION

FROM what has been said, no one will be surprised to learn that the output of our mines, mills, factories, and workshops, while actually great, is small relatively to the labour power of the nation.

Passing from the workers to the results of their work, the Census of Production shows us for each producing industry (1) the factory value of the output, (2) the cost of the materials used in the work, and (3), by subtraction, the value added by each trade to the materials which it uses. By this method the duplication of values is avoided, and we get a true aggregate of the total net value of British production.

86

It is shown that the net output of all British industries thus arrived at in 1907 was £712,000,000, or about £100 for each man, woman, boy, and girl employed.

This total is exclusive of the value of materials either imported from abroad or bought from British agriculture.

Now let us see what was the total value of material commodities gained by the United Kingdom in 1907: (1) through productive industry, (2) through agriculture, (3) through the exchange of part of British material production for foreign produce, and (4) through any material imports gained from abroad through services rendered to people abroad. It is quite simple to do this.

First, as to agriculture. We are still waiting the result of the voluntary Census of agricultural production which the Board of Agriculture conducted in 1907. It is probable, however, that the agricultural produce of the United Kingdom, considered as one farm, is not very different in value from the careful estimate which was made some years ago by Mr. R. H. Rew—*viz.*, £200,000,000. Adding this to the net industrial output, we get £912,000,000. We have to add to this sum the imports we received in 1907, and to deduct from it the exports which we sent out of the country in that year. The whole operation may be shown clearly thus:

UNITED KINGDOM INCREMENT OF MATERIAL
WEALTH IN 1907

INDUSTRIAL PRODUCTION:
  Net value of output shown
    by Census of Production £712,000,000

AGRICULTURAL PRODUCTION:
  Estimated at..........   200,000,000
                          ——————————
    TOTAL MATERIAL PRO-
      DUCTION........... £912,000,000

Add: Imports into United
  Kingdom.............. £646,000,000
                          ——————————
                        £1,558,000,000

Subtract: (1) Exports of Bri-
            tish productions,
            £426,000,000
          (2) Exports of im-
            ported goods,
            £92,000,000
          —————————— £518,000,000
RESULT: Net gain of Material ——————————
    Wealth in 1907....£1,040,000,000

Apart from any question as to the quality of the
stuff, here is a faithful picture of the wholesale value
of the gain in material commodities which the United
Kingdom made in the year 1907, whether by home

production or by foreign trade and foreign shipping and investment. The total, it will be seen, amounts in round figures to a little more than one thousand millions. When we remember that in 1907 the British population numbered 44,000,000, we are struck, not with the greatness, but with the paucity of the figure. It amounts to just over £23 per head of the population.

Thus, British poverty is not alone a matter of ill-distribution. If this yearly increment of material things was equally divided amongst the population, it would not be sufficient to give good food and good clothing and good housing, to say nothing of the *matériel* of government, of civic life, of sport, of amusement, and of mental culture, to a population of such magnitude. *It would abolish poverty in its worse sense, but it could confer but an exceedingly poor standard of civilisation.*

It will be perceived that the facts we have examined go much closer to the causes of poverty than even an investigation of income. The income of the United Kingdom, defined as the aggregate of all the wages, salaries, and profits of the individuals who compose the nation, is about twice as great as the one thousand million pounds arrived at above. The national income measures not material increment alone, but all the services, good, bad, and indifferent, useful and useless, beneficent and malefi-cent, which are built up upon the basis of the mate-rial income. The national income measures not merely the wage of a useful boiler-maker, but the salary of a useless clerk, or the fee paid to a lawyer for making a woman, much more moral than himself, confess her failings in the witness-box.

There is, of course, close connection between ill-distribution and poverty of production, and attention was specially directed to this in my *Riches and Poverty*, Chapter XVIII, p. 251. Here I will only point out in passing that the ill-distribution of the national income must connote restriction of material production, since the rich man, by reason of the nature of his expenditure, calls out of production into the region of hand-service and luxury-providing a considerable number of his fellow-creatures. A better distribution of income would thus largely increase material production by changing the character of expenditure; but much more than that is needed to abolish material poverty.

V

SCIENCE HAS SOLVED THE PROBLEM OF PLENTY

No one who is acquainted with modern machine production can fail to have been struck with the extreme facility with which we can now fashion material commodities. The scientist and the engineer have put plenty at our disposal, if we care to have it. It is not the fault of the inventor or the

discoverer that only about 4,000,000 men are irregu-
larly employed upon their wonderful machines and
processes. That is obviously true, for a large proportion of the originators of modern industrial processes are dead, and their inheritance is the common
property of mankind. Even as to the living inventor, we are careful to put a very short time-limit
to his powers of monopoly. The inventor of the
incandescent gas mantle is happily still alive; but
any man can now employ cheap labour to turn out
more or less imperfect examples of his great invention without paying him a cent. There is no secret
about modern machine industry. The great body
of invention is at our disposal with which to produce
plentifulness, and every year the patents of living
inventors are expiring.

To visit a modern cloth factory or cycle factory or
boot factory or furniture factory is to witness
operations which win from a wonderful complication
of devices, and from a division of labour between
machines made for sectional purposes, an extreme
simplicity and rapidity of output. Each part of a
boot or a cycle, however small and seemingly insignificant, is turned out by a specialised machine at
very small cost. The accurately and beautifully
made parts are put together, and the total labour
exerted to make one boot or one cycle is marvellously
small. Looking at boot machines, we understand
that a very limited number of them, worked by a
small fraction of the working population, could

easily make more boots in a year than our entire population could wear out in several years. Looking at a cycle factory, we understand that it would be the simplest possible thing for a very limited number of people to turn out more cycles than there are people in the country to ride them.

It is not manufacturing which is the trouble to the manufacturer. It is not the work of his factory which worries a manufacturer. *The manufacturers' trouble is this, that it is so easy to make things and so difficult to sell things.* It is to selling and not to making that the manufacturer has chiefly to address his mind. From the point of view of economic production, the man who makes boots is a valuable worker, while the man who takes orders for boots and perhaps by his skill in representation takes an order away from a man who sells better boots, counts for nothing, or worse than nothing, as an economic agent. To the manufacturer, however, the boot worker is a commonplace object who can easily be replaced, while the successful salesman is all in all. It is an inversion of proper economic conceptions which goes to the very root of the problem of poverty.

The efficient machinery which has been contrived to meet the needs of large-scale production of every sort and kind is, as we have seen, worked by a small proportion of our population. Yet, even when thus indifferently and partially worked, the machines have but to keep going for a brief period and demand is overtaken. Almost as soon as the wheels begin to run freely, the brake must perforce be put to them, for lack of buyers to command the products which can so easily be made. The machines are run, not with the object of producing goods in plenty, but with the object of reducing costs in connection with a known or an estimated demand. In effect, every machine is run to make one thing and one thing only, and that is individual profit. That profit can only be secured out of the trade which offers. The trade which offers arises from the limited consumption of a community, the mass of which are wage-labourers paid little more than the bare cost of renting a poor home and buying fuel and food for its inmates. To run the machines freely under such conditions is to attempt the impossible. Each manufacturer, in effect, denies customers to every other manufacturer. Each is successful in putting a brake upon the machinery of every other. The hat-worker cannot afford to buy the boots he requires, which can so easily be made by the boot-worker. The boot-worker cannot afford to buy the hats he requires, which can so easily be made by the hat-worker. Neither of them can command the cycles so easily turned out at Coventry, and at Coventry every factory pours out men and women poorly shod and with indifferent head-gear.

As for the product which is actually turned out, and supplemented, as we have seen, by exchanges with foreign parts, it is scrambled for by a host of uneconomic agents who attenuate the poor stream of commodities as it flows through the country.

The case of tea, to which I have referred in these pages, is typical rather than exceptional. To take retailing alone, the average shopkeeper cannot live on a gross profit less than from 30 to 50 per cent. His retail profit may be insignificant, and often is so. The failures amongst shopkeepers are appalling in their number. But whether they succeed or fail, upon every article they sell they must load on a big *gross* profit. When, therefore, the wage-earner takes his poor wage to market, he has first of all to provide a living for middlemen whose living may be as hard to get as his own, while both suffer from the waste of their labour.

There is one certain way of getting very little out of the scramble, and that is to be one of the producers. So long as a man is content to remain a useful economic producer he cannot become even moderately comfortable. If he is worldly wise, he will reason to himself: "There is only one way in which I can get a chance to make an ample subsistence, and that is by ceasing to make goods, and by entering upon one of the paths by which I can make, not goods, but profits." "Getting on" is rarely or never possible for the man who continues honestly to make hats or furniture or boots or carpets or upholstery, as a unit in large-scale economic production. Can we wonder, then, if an increasingly large proportion of the population has realised this

94

and has made what is, under the circumstances, the wise decision to desert production for one of the paths of profit? *When there is neither comfort nor honour to be got out of honest work, need we wonder if so many of us prefer to live without working?* The latter course is at least not less likely to fail than the former and offers so many sublime opportunities.

So it is that the inventors, the scientists, and the engineers have completely failed to make tolerable the lot of the common man. It was in 1828 that George Stephenson ran "The Rocket"; to-day, eighty years after, the great mass of the British people are unable to travel any considerable distance in their own country by railway, for they cannot afford the fares. The steamship is nearly as old as the railway locomotive; yet to-day the masses are only acquainted with steamships when they are driven into emigration. We possess in electric traction the means of spreading our town populations over considerable and healthy areas; the people remain, huddled in their grimy towns, a prey to disease. We are one of the few great coal nations; yet few of our people can afford to warm their houses properly. The mass of the British people warm their beds with their own bodies, and that in a great coal country which enjoys seven months of winter. We have not yet the wit to keep us warm. Vain have been the strivings of the most gifted of men. The machines they have constructed have but created a new race of machine-slaves, and made it

95

possible for an increasing proportion of civilised men to live by useless work, while liberating entirely from work, useful or useless, a limited leisure class which alone enjoys the fruits of the earth as multiplied and harvested by machinery.

Is it necessary for so much work to produce so much pain? After taking so much trouble to facilitate production, does it pass the wit of man to organise our labour to better advantage than is shown in the wretched material increment we have examined, made to be enjoyed chiefly by those who do not produce it? Is it really more difficult to persuade a people to use machinery properly than it is to invent the machinery itself? Must it be said of civilised man that he can analyse the light of Sirius but cannot shelter all his children?—that he can achieve scientific miracles but is baffled by the commonplace?

VI

THE STATE ORGANISED FOR WORK

THE answer to the questions just propounded is that, while scientific accomplishment has in the last few generations been regarded as a proper study of mankind, we have not yet deemed it our duty to provide our people with comfort. As long as science was a forbidden domain, science made little progress. As long as men continue to regard such a thing as an ample supply of clothing a matter to be resigned to haphazard effort, conducted by unorganised and incompletely informed individuals working in opposition to each other for private gain, the masses of people will remain ill-clad. That is as true as what Machiavelli long ago wrote as to the impossibility of conducting successful national military operations by purchasing the services of *condottieri*. No nation will ever be well housed, well clothed, well fed, and well cultured while it is content to cherish industrial *condottieri*. Not until the soldier of fortune is as much an anachronism in the industrial as in the military world will there be an output of commodities of such dimensions as to abolish material poverty, and of such rapidity and ease of production as to abolish the distinction between classes by creating a universal leisure won through the ordered scientific use of economic appliances.

Is this to envisage as a worthy ideal a Great State running as a Great Machine, the well-oiled wheels of which are the lives and labours of drilled and enslaved citizens? Does the reign of Order necessarily mean the loss of liberty, of individuality, of personal choice, of captaincy of one's own soul?

The answer to these questions will appear to those who consider carefully the considerations which have been advanced in these pages. Production has become so simple that, if a people will but consent to organise for the production necessary to yield a high minimum standard of subsistence for the entire community, the necessary labour will occupy so small a proportion of the day of the community's adults of working age, as to produce for every one such a measure of liberty as can now be enjoyed in dishonourable ease by but a few. I have led up to this proposition by showing (1) that present production is the work of a few, (2) that the work of even that few is largely wasted, and (3) that the means of production are now so efficient as to make it possible to produce easily much more than we can possibly consume.

In our community of some forty-five millions of people, there are approaching twenty-eight millions over eighteen years of age. It is clear, then, that if training merged into economic work at eighteen, the number of workers would be so great as to make it possible to organise, in a very brief working day for all, the efficient production and distribution of the materials necessary for a high minimum standard of living. If a few millions of men, aided by a million or two of women, boys, and girls, can create and sustain the material fabric we now know of, in spite of the interruption of unemployment, preventable sickness, and avoidable accident, what could not be done by the entire nation, engaged in economic labour, and working with the aid of the most efficient appliances in each department of production? One cannot pretend to make estimates in such a matter, but I submit with confidence that an ample output in all the departments of civic, home, road, and transport maintenance, construction and repair, of lighting and heating, of cloths and apparel, of foods and beverages, of indoor and outdoor furnishings, of afforestation and land development, of certain public amusements and exhibitions, could be secured in a short working day, leaving the greater part of the life of an adult absolutely free, within the limits of common rule, for the pursuit of individual occupations, researches, travels, and amusements, the leisure dignified and justified by the ordered maximum of labour, and the necessary labours of the Commonwealth deprived of monotony and hardship by the gain of honourable leisure.

But let us endeavour to get definite conceptions of the possibilities of necessary order and admired disorder, of organised work and unorganised work, of law and of liberty, of professionalism and of amateurism, in this Great State that we dare to dream of.

At the age of, say, eighteen years the youth will pass into apprenticeship to some definite branch of the organised work of the Great State. It is not my province here to deal with the education which will fit him for serious professional service. Basing myself upon the known fact that an average child, given proper training, is the inheritor of the normal capacity of his race, and can be developed into a man useful to himself and to his fellows, I postulate an education worthy the name. I see the average boy of eighteen, not only healthy, but understanding why he is healthy, and what branches of the professional work of the State are necessary for the maintenance of that public health in which he shares. I see him thus respecting his own body and the bodies of others. His eye is clear, and his touch is deft and firm. He moves with grace and precision, and his hands are skilful. In the region of acquired knowledge, as distinguished from the education of his inherited powers, he is acquainted with the elements of science. He knows the quality of the Nature from which he has emerged, so far as it has been revealed by the sciences of geology, biology, chemistry, and physics. He has taken up the magnificent inheritance of knowledge which as yet not one in ten thousand of our people enjoys. By virtue of this inheritance, he understands the physical world in which he has his being. For him there are sermons in stones, and good and evil in everything. He rejoices in his knowledge as he rejoices in his strength. His acquaintance with first principles enables him to scan a machine with an eye of intelligence. There is no common object of that conquest of Nature which we call Civilisation which has mystery for him. He, therefore, understands why work is necessary, and why Nature has not merely to be conquered in one final decisive battle, but in the every day of a never-ending struggle. What imagination he has and what native powers he possesses are widened and deepened and multiplied by the knowledge which makes him one of the chain of Nature's conquerors. Withal, he has read in the history of the races of man and in the literature and philosophy which has been the expression of the best of men; and the structure of society and the manner of the governance of society are known to him in their forms and in their conceptions.

Thus I see the normal educated youth of the Great State, and I cannot see a Great State based on anything less. Without general culture of a kind which is not now possessed even by our ruling classes, I can see nothing more than the possibility of a Socialist bureaucracy, a Servile State, a later Peruvian Socialism, with its general order of docile units and its upper order of a ruling and informed caste. I do not deny that a socialistic bureaucratic State might be infinitely superior to our existing admixture of bureaucracy, feudalism, and private individual governance for purposes of individual gain; but let us build as greatly as scientific attainment gives us leave to envisage the future, trusting that we may be really building even greater still.

I picture the educated youth of eighteen choosing his professional lot.

It is necessary here to interpolate the supposition that the Great State will express the results of the professional work done within its borders— the results, that is, of that maximum of individual labour which its citizens will owe it—in money, and that the income, or share of the results of professional work, which all will enjoy, will be spent in the form of money by citizens free to command with that money whatsoever the Great State produces.

A call for commodities being a call for labour, the Great State will be able to measure unerringly for what kind of labour the people call. It will also know what quantity of human work, aided by the most economic appliances known, is needed in each department of production called upon by the people's aggregate expenditure. Thus, in any particular year, as the youth of the nation reaches the age of entry into professional labour, a certain number of apprenticeships or openings will be available for the new workers of the year. It is not difficult to conceive arrangements, combining elements of choice with elements of examination as to qualifications, which shall draft the youth of the year into the professional work of the nation. The average element of choice will be a thousandfold wider than now, and liberty in this respect thus a thousandfold wider. For all but an insignificant fraction of the youth of our State that is, there is in practice no choice, and, even where choice exists, it is but as a choice of evils. Narrow indeed is the gate, and strait exceedingly is the way, for the son of a Glamorganshire miner or of a London bricklayer or of a Leicester boot-hand who reaches the thirteen years of age at which he is ejected from the sham schools wherein we mock the name of Education.

And this enlarged liberty in choosing the way of professional life, it must be remembered, although necessarily finding bounds to its freedom in the necessities of society and the limitations of the individual, is, it is necessary to insist, but the committal of the individual *to that part of his life which is to be professional.* True it is that this side of life must have its limitations to freedom, its elements of compulsion, its inexorable call to duty, and its door shut against escape from honourable toil. But this side of man's life will not necessarily be the larger side. Every professional of the Great State will be also an amateur of what arts, what occupations he chooses.

Again let us remember that in our forty-five millions of people there are twenty-eight millions of over eighteen years of age. What might not twenty-six million persons — to deduct the two million over sixty-five years of age—do even to-day, with science and invention no more developed than they are, if their labour was organised without competitive waste and exerted, not for individual profit, but in the output and economic distribution of useful products and services?

The conception of the Great State is that the whole of the adult population will be *organised to produce a minimum standard of life, expressed by the output and distribution of the material products and services necessary to its maintenance.* This work is what I term the professional life of the individual. It is the performance of his social duty. It is a thing of written law and compulsion. And because it is universal and compulsory, and because the waste of effort will be reduced to an insignificance, the professional or compulsory work of the individual will occupy but a few hours of his day. Even now, were the thing possible, as most unhappily it is not possible, the adult units of our people, officered by the small proportion of informed people we possess, could probably do all that is now usefully done in not more than a five hours' day. With a universal scientific education, less than a five hours' day of labour for adults will produce a bulk of commodities and services many times greater than now obtains.

The economic contraction of professional life means the widening of freedom. Beyond his professional work, the citizen will owe no duty to the State, and he will be free to do anything which is not to the injury of his fellows. For the greater part of his working hours, that is, he may be poet or painter, writer or philosopher, singer or musician, actor or dramatist, carver or sculptor, even sportsman or idler.

I cannot conceive a professional actor in the Great State; I can only see amateur actors, robbed of those unfortunate attributes that come with eternal pose, by healthy work done in a healthy world.

WORK IN THE GREAT STATE

I cannot imagine a poet selling his epics in the Great State; I can only see amateur poets, whose Muses shall visit them the more frequently because they are engaged in the useful work of the world. I cannot conceive in the Great State would-be professional painters ruined by drink and the devil while waiting for rich *parvenus* to appreciate their Venuses; I can only see healthy creatures painting because they needs must, and painting what they want to paint. As for the great army of writers, journalists, ministers of religion of all denominations, dancers, philosophers, lecturers, and others who now escape from legitimate labour, and from their honest share of what needs to be done that we all may live, sometimes escaping because they are clever, sometimes because they are merely artful, and sometimes, Heaven knows how, when they are neither clever nor artful, there will be no room for them as professionals in the Great State. They may write for such as will read; they may mime for such as will look; they may lecture for such as will hear; they may preach to such congregations as their gifts may command; but they will do so as amateurs, and their labour of love will find its reward in that self-respect and public honour which are amongst the chief rewards possible for man.

Thus I picture an amateur life of individual work and recreation embroidered upon the main social fabric formed by exertion in professional work.

The amateur side of life in the Great State will

need its materials. Those materials will be partly purchased with money out of State production through the individual's ordinary income which expresses his minimum wage, and partly supplied by amateur effort and exchanges between amateurs as amateurs. This side of the subject presents no difficulty. We can see the amateur carver working upon wood the produce of State professional production. We can see the amateur company of actors hiring one of the Great State's theatres, and performing with dresses and effects partly purchased out of income from State stores and partly furnished by amateur effort or by amateur elaboration or decoration of State materials. The poet's pen and ink, the artist's tools and colours, the amateur publishers' paper and machinery, will all alike be commanded out of State production by professional income and elaborated or worked with in amateurs' time.

The newspaper of the Great State will be a plain record of home and foreign happenings. It will record the result of elections at home and abroad, the progress of industries, the growth or decline of peoples, the judgments in cases of dispute or arbitration, the births and marriages and deaths, the departures of travellers, the arrival of visitors, the accidents or misfortunes in its homes and factories. It will not record opinions, or be concerned with policies. Organs of opinion will be purely amateur in ownership and direction. An organ of opinion will not be published for gain, but to express the thoughts and desires of those who publish it. Obviously, they will not desire to publish unless they think earnestly and strongly, and for a man or society of men who think thus it will be easy to publish. (As I need hardly point out, there is already growing up a very great output of purely amateur and non-commercial literature of opinion, in the shape of books, pamphlets, reports, journals, etc.) The professional income of twenty men, or even ten, will command paper and machinery, and by their own amateur labour men will speak their minds. If such speaking gains hearers, it will gain supporters, and a large circulation will be possible—not a circulation contracted for with advertisers, or a circulation which needs must be to give so many people a living whether they want to write or not, or whether they have anything to say or not. Thus the organs of opinoin of the Great State will live honestly or not at all, afid even the least of poetasters will find it less difficult than now to produce his little volume of verses for the edification of his friends.

I see that in some ways the professional and amateur worker of the Great State will join hands. "It is my pleasure," said the German municipal architect to me, as he waved his hand towards the municipal dwellings. I see amateur painters competing for the pleasure of decorating with frescoes the panels of a new Town Hall, amateur painters who professionally may be carpenters or clerks or masons or engineers, and who, assured of an ample income by their professional labour, will aim at the honour of making their own monument in amateur work done for their own joy and for the public good. I see no reason to suppose that the professional workers of the Great State will not be as ready to sacrifice their lives, if need be, as some amongst out leisure classes are ready to-day. *The amateurs of the Great State will be the labour class, and the professionals of the Great State will be the leisure class, and all these will be one.* I have faith that there is that in man which will build greatly on this conception, and I see no reason to set limits to the strivings of man under such conditions.

It is possible that for long, if not for ever, there will remain many tasks necessary to civilisation which will call for unusual physical exertion, or the suffering of unpleasant physical conditions, or even the risk of danger. For example, we do not know for how long the world will be dependent upon coal for its supplies of energy. Let us suppose that the Great State will be so dependent. Does the supply of labour for such work present difficulties? The answer is that labour of this kind will be done in the Great State by sharing it amongst the able-bodied. The Great State will regard it as a thing impossible to condemn a man to be a coal-miner for life. For my own part, I always regard the devotion of a definite section of our people to mining as a sentence of penal servitude upon them. It goes without saying that the Great State, if it uses coal, will conserve it, so that coal-mining will be reduced to a minimum. That minimum will be performed, not by a definite few for life, but by all able-bodied men for a year or two. Mining is much more dangerous than soldiering, and calls for the application of the principle of conscription. The mining conscript will go to his term of service as a matter of duty and with pride. In after years he will look back upon his Mining Year, and because of it he will the better understand the society in which he lives and the relation of labour to life.

Such a plan will avoid the cruelty and the waste of setting a definite million, or a definite half-million —for that is what we now do in effect — to do a particularly hard and dangerous form of work. We cannot afford to bury in a coal-mine without chance of redemption lives of we know not what possibilities. We cannot give every man adequate opportunity unless we give every man more than the prospect of unending toil in a single groove, and unless we provide every man with leisure.

Individual saving will be both unnecessary and unknown in the Great State, and the form of saving known as insurance, necessary as it is to-day, will be read of in history with considerable amusement. What capital saving is necessary will, of course, be done out of the product of the State's professional work, and the only waste in connection with this capital saving will be the devotion of a certain amount of labour to experiment in every branch of production, although amateur experiment will be plentiful, because of the fulness of opportunity for the prosecution of individual tastes and inclinations in the arts and sciences. The devotion of the professional work of the State to the best materials and in the best way will, of course, reduce the need for labour upon capital work, since replacements and repairs will be less needed on account of wear and tear. No vested interests will impede the substitution of one process for another, or of a better for a worse invention.

As need hardly be added, there will be a tremendous increase of really personal property in the Great State, and nothing will prevent the bequeathing or the inheritance of such personal property. Obviously, however, a man will not burden himself with more personal property than he can care for, and he will be quite unable to command menials to take charge of an excess. Thus personal property will naturally limit itself to those really personal implements, ornaments, furnishings, garments, books, musical instruments, etc., which pertain to the needs, habits, and tastes of the individual. The means of producing *professional* income will belong to the Great State, and no private individual will, therefore, be able to control the work of his fellows. He will be able to get amateur service from a friend; *he will have no economic lien upon any man.* The citizens of the Great State will be amused when they recall days when men possessed bits of paper representing a fraction of a municipal sewer, or of a railway line, or of a colliery plant, or of a calico shed, or even of a druggist's shop, and when, by virtue of such ownership, a man could live without continuing to labour. No; interest will not exist in the Great State, but every man will realise before he passes into the work of the world that he is one of the nation's common inheritor's, and that it will be his personal interest, as it is not now, to swell the value of the common undertaking—to increase what will be really and not nominally a National Dividend.

The mutation of industrial processes in the Great State will be an exceedingly simple matter. To-day, the man who invented a method of building houses with one-half the present amount of labour would condemn to ruin, and in many cases to utter destitution and degradation, hundreds of thousands of families in every industrial nation, and the economic effects would not pass until tens of thousands of heads had been plunged under water. Indeed, under present conditions it is a mercy when dulness of perception or lack of enterprise of capitalists keeps a new process hanging fire for some years. In the Great State the invention of a process to halve the labour in a great branch of national industry will mean simply the reduction of the working day of the citizen as professional without the reduction of his income, and the *pro tanto* increase of his leisure as amateur. Thus, every new invention will be hailed joyfully *as meaning either the decrease of work with the same income, or a larger income for the same amount of work*. Let that be understood in a community of educated people, and the spur to invention will take us to means of accomplishment as yet undreamed of.

For the woman the Great State spells Economic Independence and the end of marriage as a profession. The marriages of the Great State will be between economic equals, and only maternity will release a woman from her professional duty. Motherhood, of course, will be the peculiar care of the Great State, and for a certain number of years the mother will draw her professional income as mother, in addition to an endowment for each child, and the child will be in no sense dependent upon the work of its father. I see the budding girl's education in the Great State regardful of her supreme function, and the training and nurture of the child regarded as the professional duty of a woman both before and for some time after the beginning of the age when it will begin systematic training in the school. Thus, some ten or fifteen years of the life of most adult women will be divorced from the professional material work of the State, but before the beginning and after the end of that period the adult woman will work at the profession into which she has been inducted in the manner we have already indicated.

It is not necessary, at the end of the first decade of the twentieth century, to say very much by way of argument that it is possible for the major industries of a nation to be unified and placed under State controls. Some forty years ago John Stuart Mill wrote that "The very idea of conducting the whole industry of a country by direction from a single centre is so obviously chimerical that nobody ventures to propose any mode in which it should be done." Since those words were written it has been proved abundantly that large-scale operations conducted under the general direction of a central control are not merely possible, but possess such advantages in practice that business men have been led to consolidate trade after trade in all the great industrial nations, and especially in the country America, which, by reason of the magnitude of her population and natural resources, presents the largest factors to deal with. Thus the United States Steel Corporation, which is a private "State within the State," is a far larger industrial undertaking than would be formed if all the iron and steel works, including the iron-mines, of the United Kingdom were unified under a single public direction.

The truth is that the economic consolidation of all the factors of an industry in the State eliminates difficulties instead of creating them, as was supposed by the older economists. Thus, if we take the very familiar case of the Post Office, the ease with which its operations are conducted is often attributed to the inherent simplicity of the trade. As a matter of fact, the business of collecting, transmitting, and delivering letters is one which, if it were not organised as a single unit, would be one of infinite difficulty and complexity. Imagine it organised under the direction of some hundreds of partly competitive, partly monopolistic, local or district letter-delivery firms, each necessarily having accounts with each other, and the jurisdiction of each running no farther than a certain limit, more or less wide, and sometimes overlapping with the area of operations of a competitor. Imagine, then, the postal communications of an unfortunate people collected by some one firm, transmitted through several others, and finally delivered (or not delivered) by a company in the district of the addressee. Imagine the charges piled up to pay the host of unnecessary between-agents, the vexatious delays that would arise, the consequent restriction of postal facilities and slow growth of communication. With such an economic absurdity in being, we can imagine a second John Stuart Mill gravely pointing out in an economic treatise that such a complicated, such an inherently difficult, such a vexatious trade could never be sucessfully carried on by a State department. But this picture of a disintegrated postal service does not tell one-fiftieth part of the everyday absurdities of our organisation for the distribution of groceries or meat or dairy produce or vegetables. In these, we tolerate the waste of hundreds of millions a year in setting millions of men and women to waste their time as unnecessary, and often unhappy and overworked between-agents, who earn mean and paltry livings while simply serving to attenuate the streams of commodities which under happier conditions they might swell. In the distribution of coal, for example, we have in practice a case much more wasteful than we have imagined if private were substituted for public letter-carrying. It is a case not merely of separate controls in each area, but of insane competition in each area between middle-men whose expenses are necessarily great, and whose expenses, from invoice forms to advertisements, have each and all to be paid for by the consumer in the final price of coal. So it falls out that often the consumer of coal pays a high price for the fuel even while the hewer of coal is obtaining a mere trifle for getting it. The mining of coal by the State and its distribution through local authorities as agents would, on the other hand, with an organisation much simpler than that of the Post Office, put coal at a nation's disposal cheaply and conveniently and with complete guarantee as to grade and suitability for specific use.

And so it is with each of the industries which contribute to what ought to be the comforts of civilisation but in practice are the comforts of a few bought by the largely wasted labour of the comfortless many. To write a plain and unvarnished account of what happens to the milk produced in the

United Kingdom, or to the tea landed in the United Kingdom, or to the wool imported into the United Kingdom, is to describe a series of absurdly complicated and wasteful operations which in great part are as economically useless as to set men to dig holes and to fill them up again. For example, Colonial wool imported into Britain is chiefly used in Yorkshire, but the greater part of it is childishly landed, not at Hull or Goole, but in London, where it is played pranks with by hosts of railway companies, carriers, warehousemen, brokers, auctioneers, etc. After having been played with, and *pro tanto* raised in price, it is gravely conveyed, again by competitive railway companies and carriers, to the worsted and woollen industries in Yorkshire. But this is to imagine no waste prior to the ridiculous landing at a port hundreds of miles from the place where the material is wanted. When we remember that in Australasia similar absurdities occur and similar uneconomic "livelihoods" are made out of the product by the wasted work of thousands, we have a picture of waste from start to finish which gravely reflects upon the competence of mankind. There is, of course, no need for such complications. The Great State of Australia could transmit its wool simply and surely to a wool-consuming land like the United Kingdom; here the wool department of the British Great State would obviously see that the wool was landed at the nearest port to its place of use. Not a broker, not an agent, not an auc-

tioneer would be needed; the number of necessary
carriers and distributors would be few through the
simplicity of direction; the worsted and woollen
industries would get their raw material cheaply and
at last honestly, and thousands of men would be set
free from work upon waste to do the economic work
for lack of which we remain poor.

It is impossible to multiply details in so broad a
sketch as this, but something may usefully be said
with regard to the simplification of exportation and
importation. A hint of the possible improvement of
facilities which would arise between nations properly
organised for work is also to be found in existing
postal arrangements. The ease and certainty with
which postal communications are exchanged between nations have become a commonplace; but,
regarded in relation to the great majority of international dealings, they are miraculous. The economic reasons for interchanges between geographical
areas would remain in a world of federated Great
States; all that would be removed would be the
main difficulties which now impede exchange. No
longer should we witness such sad spectacles as the
holding-up of raw cotton by one set of agents in
America to retard the progress of the very cotton-
manufacturing industry upon the success of which
the real gain of a cotton-planter naturally depends,
or of the Brazilian government arranging for the
solemn burning or holding-up of a fine harvest of
coffee even while millions in the world have not

coffee enough. Nor is it difficult to realise how, in a world organised for economic labour under the captaincy of Great States, all the factors of the great industries throughout the world could be co-ordinated, from the production of the primary materials to the distribution of the finished articles, effecting a proper relation between the producer-consumer and the consumer-producer, making every man a citizen of the world and giving all the world to each man's use.

Such are the hopes which man can legitimately cherish for the control of the Nature from which he has emerged in this one of the least of Nature's worlds. It is a control which cannot be exercised effectively without co-operative effort and proper organisation for work. The struggle with Nature differentiates man from the other animals, and is his hope of redemption from a natural poverty. The struggle is too stern for us to be able to afford to turn from it to spend most of our time in putting forth useless competitive work. The little world to which we are confined is too poor to yield more than poverty for the many while the many are stupidly scraping together a little for the few to enjoy. It is not a world of plenty, such as is often pictured by sentimentalists, in which Nature is bountiful and men naturally wealthy. It is a world of pain, in which a grim Nature stalks relentless, red of tooth and claw; a world so limited in resources that, until modern science had given us some degree of mastery, the majority of men were necessarily poor. To-day, with the endowment of Science at our disposal, we know how to win plenty from an unwilling world. We know how; but, even while we know, we neglect to put our hands to the necessary labour. To organise for work thus becomes the primary duty of our modern civilisations, and organisation for work is Socialism. A State of ill-informed but drilled servile units, under the guidance of a specialised bureaucracy, could doubtless do effective work and abolish poverty as we know it to-day, but it would not be the Great State of our desire. The Great State can only be a nation of free men, educated to the full development and accentuation of their inherent inequalities, equal in point of economic independence and opportunity, understanding the necessity of continuous and unremitting labour, and, therefore, organised for work as the only means of escape from unnecessary toil.

THE MAKING OF NEW KNOWLEDGE

BY SIR RAY LANKESTER, K.C.B., F.R.S.

THE MAKING OF NEW KNOWLEDGE

It is perhaps necessary before considering how this ideal Great State, which is the common basis of all these essays, may best provide for the making of new knowledge, to discuss the question as to how the present or the future rulers of the State are to be brought to such an appreciation of the meaning of new knowledge—new science, whether of extra-human nature or of man's own nature, history, and capacities—as to understand that it is the one factor upon which the happiness and healthy development of mankind depend. I leave this preliminary discussion the more willingly to other writers, since I confess that after spending the best part of my energies during nearly fifty years in endeavouring to increase the number of my fellow-citizens who have arrived at a just estimate of the value of new knowledge and of the consequent need for the organisation of its pursuit by the expenditure of public funds, I am disappointed with the result.

There has been a little, but a very little progress. The mass of the public, both those who should know

better and those who cannot be expected to, have
persistently confused the teaching of the elements of
existing science with what is a very different thing—
namely, the search for new science, the actual creation of knowledge which is not merely new to the
ignorant, but new to the most advanced and capable
investigators. It has been the rule that all effort
and apparent success in securing and organising
means for the creation of new knowledge are sooner
or later misappropriated by those who are bent upon
teaching what is already known. Throughout the
country the holders of both old and new professor-
ships, in both ancient and modern universities, have
been remorselessly compelled to perform the work
of schoolmasters and examination-grinders, and as a
rule for less pay than is received by the latter. The
attempt to make the university professor an investigator and creator of new knowledge (in accordance
with the dictum of Fichte [1]) has failed in consequence
of the overwhelming number of those who are able
to exercise control in the details of these matters and
have either no conception of what creation of new
knowledge means or else have deliberately determined that it shall not go on and that all the resources of our universities and all the strength of

[1] Fichte, in his essay on "The University to be Founded in Berlin,"
says that a university is not a place where instruction is given, but
an institution for the training of experts in the art of making knowledge, and that this end is attained by the association of the pupil
with his professor in the inquiries which the latter initiates and
pursues.

their promising young men shall be used in the task of preparing indifferent youths to pass examinations.

It is perhaps natural that the unqualified persons who, as committees and councils and congregations, are allowed to control the expenditure of university endowments should so frequently destroy the opportunity which those endowments naturally afford and were intended to afford—to the men who are capable of creating new knowledge. These managers and controllers honestly confuse the teaching of the elements of science with the making of new knowledge.[1] They do not know either that this making of new knowledge is of prime importance to the well-being of the State, nor that, when looked at from the point of view of higher education, there is no influence, no training, no development so important and so entirely without possible substitute, as that arising from the association of younger men in research and investigation with an older gifted and authoritative investigator who makes them co-workers with him in some great line of inquiry.

Not only do we suffer in this country from the fact that the control of higher educational institutions is

[1] I read to-day in the *Times* the self-congratulation of the Oxford tutors and lecturers, who have given up a large part of their long (very long) vacation to teaching working-class men and women whom they have induced to come to Oxford and take lessons from them. It is declared that "the respect for knowledge" (whose?) and the eagerness to acquire it shown by the working-class people was most gratifying. Leaving aside the question as to the value of these studies, it is regrettable that the money and resources of a university should be thus dissipated.

9   125

in incapable hands, but it is the fact that no leader in the State ever shows any sympathy with discovery or takes any step to promote its increase. In Germany, where already every university is mainly organised as a series of institutes of scientific research and discovery, the Emperor, at the centenary of the University of Berlin, declared that he desired to see there more institutions for pure research, whose directors should be untrammelled by the demands of ordinary teaching. After a truly admirable account of the splendid work done by the University of Berlin in the regeneration of the fatherland, he himself did something the like of which no prince or statesman has done in Great Britain since the time of Henry VIII.: he handed over to the university (which already has an income of £140,000 a year) a vast sum of money—half a million pounds sterling—for the creation there of institutes of scientific research; and he pledged himself that this was only a provision for initial expenditure and that the Imperial government would find further money for the support and development of these institutions so set on foot.

What I feel is that, in spite of all that has been said and done in the last fifty years, no one in Great Britain would dream of expecting such a provision to be made for scientific research in London as that recently made by the German Emperor in Berlin. It seems to me that the present British governing class, whether they label themselves with one political

name or another, cannot be imagined as acting in
the spirit of the Emperor William. If they were
told of what he has done in this matter, they would
not believe it. They have not arrived at the first
step in conceiving of the possibility of such expenditure—expenditure not to teach and train professional engineers, chemists, or doctors (that is a
thing our politicians might understand, though not
approve), but expenditure for the sole purpose of
creating new knowledge, knowledge pure and simple,
not as the so-called "handmaid" of commerce,
industry, and the arts of war, but knowledge as the
greatest and best thing that man can create—
knowledge as the Master who must be obeyed.

And whilst I feel something like despair in regard
to the appreciation of knowledge by our present
form ᵒf government and state organisation which is
        ᵥanced along the line of the progressive
"Culte de l'Incompetence" so firmly traced by M.
Faguet,[1] of the Académie Française, I find no reason
to hope that, when the democracy has, in this country, gained more complete power, there will be any
change for the better. At present the "masses" are,
if possible, more ignorant of the meaning of science
and the need for making new science, new knowledge,
than are the "classes." As I have said, I must leave
it to others amongst my fellow-essayists to suggest
how or when the toiling millions of the British Empire or of all civilised Europe, Asia, and America

[1] See his book with that title.

together, are going to arrive at, first of all, an under-standing of what the "progress of science" really means and what it does not mean, as distinguished from mere pedagogic instruction, and, secondly, at such a desire for that progress as will lead them to sanction the annual expenditure, out of public resources, on the making of new knowledge, of as large a sum as we now spend annually on the army and navy.

Supposing that very large sums were available in the new Great State for devotion to the business of making new knowledge, what would be probably the best way or the most promising way in which such money could be spent? What sort of an organisation would be required? I will venture to indulge in a speculative consideration of this remote but at the same time interesting problem.

It seems to me that what we who believe in the vital importance of the making of new knowledge must aim at is, in the first place, the selection by the State of really great and specially gifted investigators or makers of new knowledge, in such number as lavish provision of stipend and means of research can secure, as "servants of the State." Secondly, we must aim at the selection of a regular succession of young men who have the gift or talent of discovery of new knowledge, to be associated with the older men in their work and in the course of time to succeed to the positions held by the older men.

THE MAKING OF NEW KNOWLEDGE

Let me at once say that it seems to be quite certain that the special mental quality which enables its possessor to discover new things, to make new knowledge of nature and of man, is not a common one. Probably many youths have it in a greater or less degree, and may be trained or encouraged so as to develop it. But the possession of it in a marked degree so as to make it worth while to secure the services of the possessor for a career of investigation is extremely rare. That is a reason why every care should be taken to discover those who possess it and to enable them to exercise their capacity. There is no reason to suppose that the quality of mind we look for is not as abundantly distributed among the poorer classes as among the well-to-do. The State must cast its net widely so as to include the whole population without distinction of class or sex. But the essence of success lies in wise and honest selection directed to this one quality or gift. How can such a selection be effected?

It seems to me that the necessary first step must be the creation of a limited number of institutes of research in specific subjects such as are recognised to-day (and may be further divided and rearranged hereafter) under the names, Astronomy, Mathematics, Physics (several), Chemistry (several), Geology, Zoology, Botany, Physiology, Pathology, Anthropology, Psychology, Archæology (several), Oceanography, and so on. Necessarily the provision for each branch of these subjects would at first be incomplete, but the number would have to be increased rapidly after the first institutes were created, and from the first it would be laid down that no institute was expected to carry on work in more than a limited portion of the subjects indicated by its title.

For each of these institutes--which would at first be situated in London, but would be multiplied in number and established in every large centre of population in the course of time—a director or chief investigator would have to be chosen by the officials of the State. This would be the most critical step in the whole scheme, since the entire future success not only of each institute, but of the whole body of institutes, must be affected by this first selection. The avowed and unalterable purpose of the officials who make this selection must be to obtain the one man in each case, from the whole civilised world, who is proved and known to be the most capable and active discoverer or maker of new knowledge in his subject. Steps must be taken to ensure the purity and wisdom of the selection. The effect of a correct selection in such a case has been seen in one or two instances in the past. In this country, through the personal influence of the Prince Consort, the husband of Queen Victoria, a really great investigator was appointed as head of the Royal College of Chemistry, founded some sixty years ago and now incorporated with the Imperial College of Science. This was Hoffman, a German, who came from Bonn (he was born and trained at Giessen) to London and made at the college not only invaluable discoveries himself, but trained chemists like himself. His intellectual tradition or heritage remains still with us, although he himself was allowed to leave us and to accept a more honoured and honourable post in Bonn and later in Berlin. Similarly such men as Johannes Müller, of Berlin, the biologist, and the Cambridge successive leaders in physics—Stokes, Kelvin, Clark Maxwell, Raleigh, and J. J. Thomson—exhibit (as many other instances do) the generative activity of a really great investigator on those who work with him. Therefore in the first instance the State must offer whatever salary is necessary (say, in each case £5,000 a year—the salary of those numerous and admirable officials, H. M. judges) and whatever laboratory, apparatus, and assistants (say to the equivalent in each case of £10,000 a year) in order to secure the greatest discoverer in each line, as head of the corresponding "institute." In such a matter the State officials responsible must obtain the advice of the leading makers of new knowledge of all parts of the world and form a judgment.

Once we have got our great heads or directors of institutes, the scheme will work successfully. It will be the duty of the director of each institute to receive a certain number of selected "workers" into his laboratory (or museum, library, or workshop) and to associate them with himself in investigation. These workers must be selected from among those who volunteer for the career. I assume that in the new Great

State there would be efficient general instruction in schools and colleges of a qualifying character, and that it would be possible for the teachers to nominate likely young men of not less than twenty-one years of age to proceed to the State Research Institutions. Every State college should have the right of nominating a number in proportion to the number in each subject of its graduating or final class. I would have the State pay these youths (at present prices) £150 a year for two years. I will suppose that every director of an institute is obliged to receive six such students a year as probationers. At the end of two years the director would decide either to accept one or more of his "probationers" as junior assistants or cut short their career. Every director should have ten junior assistants, paid £300 a year each and holding office for no more than three years; four senior assistants, paid £600 a year each, appointed for life; and two assistant directors, paid £1,200 a year each, also for life. The directors—those appointed after the original nominations—should receive £2,000, rising to £5,000 a year, according to standing and the approval by other researchers of their work, and be appointed for life.

A young man, once admitted as a junior assistant, would have an attractive and well-paid professional career before him, his success in which would be largely determined by the capacity he displayed. Such a career should attract the ablest men. The promotion of junior to senior assistant should be in the hands of the director, it being open to him to appoint either one of his own juniors or one from another laboratory. The same method would be followed in appointing to assistant directorships. But the post of director of any institute should be made on the recommendation of the whole body of existing directors of institutes and submitted to an independent State official who should have power to confirm or to request a reconsideration of the claims of possible candidates. The post of director of an institute should always be regarded as open to any investigator of high distinction in the subject to which the institute is assigned, whatever his nationality or official antecedents. The council or senate of "directors" would accept as one of their most solemn duties the selection of the ablest man as director to fill any vacancy.

As no fees would be received by any of the directors in connection with their work, it is difficult to make sure of a standard of efficiency being maintained in such institutions as I suggest; nor is it obvious, at once, by what precautious jobbery and nepotism in the appointments may be rendered unlikely to occur. In the German universities, the professors who practically elect or invite a new professor to fill a vacancy are pecuniarily interested in the fees of students, and, therefore, in the success and reputation of the university. Some stimulus of this kind might be applied to the State "Institutes of Research" here suggested, by the award of honours and of extension of premises, increase of staff and money-grant for expenses, to those institutes which in a given period, say seven years, had made the most important discoveries. The publication of results would be at State expense, and every institute would produce its own series of memoirs. Expeditions, explorations, and special enterprises of the kind would be undertaken by each institute independently, and the budget of each would comprise funds assigned to such purposes.

Such a scheme seems clumsy and mechanical when sketched in a few words, but with slight modifications to be added as to time of tenure, pension, retirement, etc., as to government and source and amount of funds the most successful centres of research at the present day in Europe, such as the Institut Parseur in Paris, the British Museum, the national libraries of great States, and the laboratories of German universities, are practically conducted in the spirit of the regulations here suggested, if not directed by any written laws embodying such regulations.

A view about "original research" and "opportunities for investigation" exists with which I disagree and should wish to criticise. There is a notion that a large proportion of young men, such as university students, are capable of doing valuable research and making new knowledge if they only are given place and material upon which to work and a competence.

THE MAKING OF NEW KNOWLEDGE

Let us make at once a broad distinction between the educational value to the individual of a brief contact with and participation in actual serious scientific investigation, on the one hand, and the importance to the State of the provision of a permanent body of selected, specially competent investigators appointed for life to high professional office in the public service. The realisation of the second of these two desiderata will secure that of the first named. Youths will be attracted to qualify as "probationers" in large numbers, with the view of having their capacity tested, and thus possibly entering on a great profession. On the other hand, whilst all will benefit by the initial training in research, only a few—namely, those who are found to be really capable of valuable work—will be definitely received as permanent members of the profession. At the present moment, even in our great universities, we do not often get beyond the stage of producing probationers. There is a tendency in our universities, and colleges of like rank, for professors, who should be themselves great and active makers of new knowledge, to spend their energies in inducing students to do "odds and ends" of original investigation with a view to advertising the fact that the professors' laboratories or workrooms are full and their ministrations appreciated. Such fictitious activity in research can be produced by a quite inferior "professor" who devotes himself to the task of rendering "research" amusing, agreeable, and ap-

parently easy to the unfledged and really incapable
student. This undesirable form of activity arises
from the desire to satisfy a demand for research as
the condition of pecuniary support and approval by
the governing bodies of colleges and universities,
whilst really adequate organisation and provision for
the pursuit of scientific research as a serious profession is withheld. In a system of research institutes (such as exists in Germany), properly financed
and organised, the "professor" or "director" does
not make himself the merely complacent host and
finisher of his pupils' little efforts in research (like a
drawing-master who suggests, superintends, and com-
pletes a young lady's "works of art"), but is himself
pursuing a definite and serious investigation. He
receives into his laboratory younger men whom he
regards as really competent, and joins their work to
his in the definite problems which he has set himself
to solve. At the same time the young man who
comes to such a head of a laboratory (or museum or
other workshop) with a suggestion of his own as to a
subject for investigation may be received and given
every facility and assistance if it should appear to
the professor that the subject is one which comes
within his outlook and that the would-be investigator is competent. This system I saw at work when
I studied in the "seventies" with Carl Ludwig at
Leipzig, with Gegenbaur at Gena, and earlier with
Stricker at Vienna. It is well known as the system
by which the professors in German universities attain

their results—and I did my best thirty years ago to introduce it at University College in London and later at Oxford.

What I would deprecate is the notion that the making of new knowledge of any great value or amount is an easy thing and one which any young man who fancies that he has the talent can really achieve. No doubt in such work every kind and degree of talent can be utilised for what it is worth, and there must be hewers of wood and drawers of water in this as in other kinds of enterprise and organisation. But it is true that selection of real quality and the organisation of leadership is essential in the attempt to insure, by State funds, an increase in discovery and the creation of new knowledge. The notion that the needs of the State in this matter can be satisfied by a few groups of temporary workers in pleasant universities, or by, according to every ambitious and untested youth, an independent position enabling him to follow out his possibly valuable but probably ill-founded programme of inquiry, must lead to sterility and ultimate discredit of all provision by the State for such purposes.

Another mistake which I should wish to warn my readers to avoid is that of giving "scholarships" of from £100 to £200 a year tenable for two or three or five years by young men who are supposed to pursue "original investigations" whilst thus supported. This giving of scholarships is mere waste of money unless two other definite provisions are

137

made—*viz.*, (1) that of professional posts tenable for life and capable of attracting men of the highest ability to adopt the profession, and, (2) laboratories or institutions of research directed by first-rate investigators where the "scholars" may be trained by association in the work of these specially gifted investigators. The present government has provided a modest sum to such public departments as the Board of Agriculture which is being, in my opinion, wasted by those departments in a sort of charitable doles to "scholars" all over the country— since no attempt is made to face the essential and far more difficult and costly problem of setting up adequate institutions directed by men of exceptional ability under whom the "scholars" may work and develop. The scheme is a shirking of responsibility and a mere piece of popular bribery in place of real constructive effort.

What we require—and what such a scheme as I have sketched would provide—is a fair and free chance to every young man to enter upon the career of "a maker of new knowledge" whilst at the same time insuring that the definite admission to the profession shall only be open to those who prove their fitness for it during probation. It further provides that the professional career shall be so well paid and furnished with the means of research that the ablest men who have the necessary talent shall prefer it to other professions and means of livelihood.

The scheme admits of large modification and

adaptation. Perhaps it would be as well to provide *ab initio* that any one of any age may be nominated as a probationer by a duly recognised authority, subject to the condition that two-thirds of the nominations shall be reserved to candidates under the age of twenty-one years; and it might also be desirable under special restrictions to extend a candidate's period of probation to four years.

HEALTH AND HEALING IN THE GREAT STATE

BY C. J. BOND, F.R.C.S.

V

HEALTH AND HEALING IN THE GREAT STATE

HEALTH

THE twofold object of the following essay is to put forward a worthy conception of Health in its widest and fullest sense, and to sketch in brief outline some of the possibilities which will exist in the coming time for the attainment of a healthier Life by the citizens of the Great State.

What then must be our conception of Health?

Knowledge concerning disease has increased so much in recent years, and the focussing of individual and public attention on disease organisms and insanitary surroundings has been so keen, that there exists to-day a real danger of our losing sight of the true proportions of the Health Problem. We are apt to forget that, while the Healthy Life includes recovery from the attacks of disease organisms, it should also for the citizens of the modern State embrace resistance to every one of the injurious influences in the environment which tend to depress vital activity or to direct it into wrong channels. And it includes even more than this. Health is more than mere existence: it means in its widest sense "*Joy in Life*"; it presupposes a capacity of response to the beautiful, the health-giving, the soul-elevating stimuli of the surrounding world, as well as the power of overcoming the depressing factors which make for disease.

This is no merely modern view. Let us glance for a moment at the attitude of the old Greeks to this same problem. The citizens of Athens in her best days conceived of the true, the healthy Life as a harmonious development of mental and bodily powers, and as a true adjustment of the man to his environment. Self-realisation meant to the Greek the union of a virtuous soul in a beautiful body, and this was the outcome of the ordered use of natural faculties under the control of a well-balanced mind. It is difficult for us to realise the conditions of life which prevailed among the slave population in the poorer quarters of ancient Athens and imperial Rome. We have reason to think that the less fortunate inhabitants of even these noble cities were familiar with squalor, with poverty and disease; but in spite of this there can be little doubt that if the free Greek or Roman citizen were to catch a glimpse of life in our crowded cities to-day, though he would be lost in wonder at the industrial activity, at the care for the sick and the suffering, and at the complexity of our modern life, he would no less certainly marvel at the dim eye, the inelastic step, the listless demeanour of many of our toiling workers—and he would read in these tokens the signs of a reduced vitality, of a lost joyous activity, and of an absence of that Harmony to which he was so deeply attached. Highly trained in physical culture, familiar with fountains and baths, he would wonder also at the lack of personal cleanliness, the dirt, the ugliness of our surroundings, the evidences of monotonous toil, and he would search in vain in our crowded courts and sunless streets for the grace of movement and the dignity of bearing which come from life in the air and the sun. And he would marvel yet more when he learned that those whom he met were not slaves, but free citizens, and that they might, if they wished, be rulers in their own city and masters in their own homes.

But, after all, this Life of Health and Harmony and full development was only realised by a small portion of the Greek community. In spite of its democratic form of government, the "Many," even in Athens, never lived the fuller Life, and this was indeed one of the causes of her fall. We now realise that the possibility of a healthy and happy Life must be within the reach of every citizen, rich and poor, in every community if that community is to escape the stagnation and decay which eventually overtook these ancient civilisations. The Greek knew but little of the evolution of Human societies; he was ignorant of the forces which control organic development and of the real causes of disease and decay. Although we may fail to apply our knowledge, we, on the other hand, do at any rate know to-day that Health depends on successful adaptation, on adjustment to a very complex social as well as natural environment, and we are beginning to realise that Perfect Health means living in harmony with all that is best in our physical, intellectual, social, and moral atmosphere.

If, then, modern life is the outcome of ages of evolution and struggle, if healthy Life is a matter of adjustment to both good and bad stimuli, then the pursuit of Health must be carried out in accordance with the laws which control Hereditary capacity and Adaptive Response in other fields of human activity.

Neither are we left in entire ignorance as to what these life-controlling forces are. We know that all adaptation, all individual and social development, depends on the mutual interaction of certain factors. These are:

(1). Hereditarily transmitted capacity to respond in different ways and in different degrees to different environmental stimuli.
(2). The Conditions under which this Capacity is exercised.
(3). The Acquirements which are made by the individual or the Community as the result of the exercise of this capacity of Response.

And

(4). The various Environmental Stimuli which have to be responded to, the factors towards which adjustment has to be made.

These are the biological foundations on which the truly Healthy Life must be built. These are the factors with which all who attempt to reconstruct Human Society must reckon, and it is on these lines that the interests of the citizen must be promoted and secured in the Great State. We must safeguard the supply of innate individual Capacity. We must stimulate the exercise of this Capacity in all healthy directions. We must improve the conditions under which the Response of Life is carried on. We must utilise to the utmost the Acquirements already made. But this means that we must deal with both the individual and his environment, we must invoke the aid of Individualism as well as Socialism in the Great State. Now if it be true, as it undoubtedly is, that the conditions of modern industrial life tend to depress rather than call forth the highest activities of our citizens; and if it be also true, as we know it to be, that, while the individual does to a certain extent control his environment, the environment also helps to determine the type of individual, then we must recognise the disquieting fact that present-day conditions of Life in our large cities, although they may be consistent with a low death-rate, do not make for national health in its widest and best sense. Before we can set up a standard of Life worthy of the citizens of the Great State, two things must happen. Individual capacity to live the fuller life must be further developed, and the conditions under which this capacity for wider existence is exercised must be vastly improved at both ends of the social scale. If then, bearing in mind our biological limitations, we define Perfect Health as that state of body and mind which is most resistent to injurious and most responsive to beneficial stimuli, we see at once that it is not enough to banish disease organisms or to bring about immunity against infection. We must not rest content with the removal and purification of sewage, with the regulation of food and water supply, the ventilation of factories, and the control of unhealthy occupations and of licensed houses, we must do these things, but we must also insure that the atmosphere of the Home and the Workroom is flooded with moral sunshine; we must strive by intellectual effort and by artistic surroundings to prevent atrophy of mind as well as stunting of bodily stature.

It is here that we come in contact with all that is meant by Education, with Ethical training, with Intellectual culture, with progressive Legislation—in fact, with all the factors which make for human progress. Judged by this standard, the parent, the schoolmaster, the artist, the man of science, the religious instructor, the municipa councillor, the legislator, all are or should be physicians of the mind or of the body.

For there are only two ways of bringing about harmonious adjustment in matters of life and conduct as well as in matters of health. We must either adapt ourselves to our surroundings, or we must adapt our surroundings to ourselves. The first is the method of primitive organic evolution. Whereas it is by the second method that social man has been enabled to surround himself with the complex environment of civilisation and with the possibilities of physical and psychical development that civilisation brings.

There is no more striking object-lesson in the different application of these two evolutionary methods than that which is afforded by the attitude of civilised and uncivilised societies respectively to harmful environmental agencies like alcohol and disease. In the primitive community, mutual protection and co-operation (the conditions which favour recovery from disease) hardly exist. If primitive man, like the animal, contracts disease, he perishes, hence he must be preadapted, and through the stern process of natural selection in weeding out susceptible individuals he has evolved an innate resistance to those diseases of which he has had sufficient racial experience. But with social man it is different; improved medical treatment, mutual protection, and care during sickness all favour recovery from disease. It follows that the necessity for being Immune by nature grows less as the possibility of becoming Immune by Art grows greater. Hence it comes about that civilised man has evolved a capacity of acquiring Immunity by individual experience in such diseases as allow of recovery, while he still retains some of the natural Immunity against lethal diseases possessed by his earlier ancestors.

One long chapter in the history of civilisation contains the record of the gradually increasing power of control by Social man over that part of his environment which has to do with disease, and the success which has attended his efforts to banish disease must provide the sanction for further effort along these same lines of environmental control. But such methods take us further and further away from crude natural selection. Constant vigilance on the part of Society is urgently needed if we are to escape the dangers of decadence of capacity and relaxation of individual effort which modern social conditions render possible. Moreover, such methods depend on mutual co-operation and they involve some curtailment of individual liberty. For this reason in the coming age it will be wrong to be ill if the illness be avoidable. Under the old régime of natural selection the penalty for non-adaptation was extinction, and, though under the new régime of mutual co-operation and environmental control destruction may be avoided, yet some sort of penalty must still remain; either the individual or society or both must suffer in the long run for the lack of efficiency and the want of adaptation which ill health implies. As under the old régime so under the new, the price of harmonious adaptation to a widening environment—in other words, the price of health in a progressive community—is constant vigilance. Unless the citizen is immune by nature, or unless he becomes immune by Art, or until the organisms of disease are permanently banished from the environment of the Great State, the struggle must still continue, though the methods of warfare may become far less cruel. And when the victory is secured, one result, and that perhaps the greatest, will be the setting free of a larger volume of vital energy in new departments of Life and Labour, new springs of Being, new responses to higher calls in religion, science, and art, and then will gush forth again the eternal fountain of hope and of joy in Life, which has now for a season sunk so low.

Our very familiarity with suffering and disharmony has clouded our vision: we accept the presence of disease as necessary, and we forget the enormous waste of human life which these ages of wandering in the wilderness of disease have caused. We can with difficulty gauge the gain in capacity for productive labour that the saving of even a few infant lives implies. Ignorance and Vice, Vice-caused disease and disease-produced Vice—these have also contributed towards the bankruptcy in Health of our city toilers and city dwellers. Disease and Poverty, leanness of body and leanness of soul, these work hand in hand, and these also must disappear in the Great State in the new era of Free Trade in human capacity as well as in material possessions.

But besides these failures in adjustment to diseases which come from without, there are also disharmonies which come from within. There are deficient capacities as well as injurious surroundings, there are errors in individual development of an hereditary kind.

These inborn deficiencies represent isolated flaws in that mosaic pattern of mental and bodily constitution which recent biological research tells us is the hereditary equipment of each individual; they may even represent a total failure in hereditary design, such as we find in the innately criminal and the congenitally feeble-minded. For such as these there will be neither use nor room in the Great State. Even now the problem of how to eliminate this residuum of human Unimprovability urgently presses for solution. The drain of unproductive existence on productive activity is already far too great, far greater than is necessary, as we believe, to favour the growth or to call forth the exercise of benevolence. The altruistic feelings of mankind can be more efficiently promoted by exercise in other fields and on worthier objects.

Man has no more power to overtake the results of anti-social conduct in the field of race production than in any other field of human activity. Here, as elsewhere, the only way of escape is to set about the elimination of capacity for anti-social conduct, or, if this be as yet impossible, to prevent as far as may be its exercise by those unfortunate individuals who inherit it. Our hope of success lies, not in a return to the old régime of natural selection, but in an extension of the newer method of environmental control. We must learn, and that quickly, to apply to the problem of Race Culture those methods which we have already employed successfully in our struggle with disease. If, owing to lack of knowledge, further advance along Positive Eugenic lines should be at present too difficult, we can at any rate make a beginning by preventing the perpetuation of those characters which lead to race destruction.

It is impossible to consider this vital problem of Race Culture in its relation to National Health without recognising that a movement of world-wide importance has set in in nearly all civilised and progressive communities, in the direction of a voluntary reduction of the human birth-rate. This movement is unconnected with questions of food-supply, standards of life, or human fertility. It has originated in the Upper and Middle Social Classes among the more educated portion of the population as the outcome of recently acquired knowledge concerning the transmission of human life from parents to offspring and the application of this knowledge to a definite end, the voluntary control of the family. From our present point of view it is of especial interest because it affords another instance of the gradual emergence of modern society from the control of crude natural selection. It is another example of the extension of the method of environmental control by Social man into regions of human life formerly almost entirely free from such interference, and, like all other movements which interfere with the free play of natural selection and which aim at rendering the conditions of life less exacting, it is fraught with great possibilities for both good and harm.

Like other examples of the exercise of environmental control by Social man, this movement must also be judged by the motives which inspire the conduct in each individual case. If these be unworthy, if the thing aimed at be selfish indulgence, if the satisfaction of individual desires be set before social welfare, then it is a crime against society. If, on the other hand, the end aimed at be better chances of Life for offspring, if due regard be paid to the relative claims of individual and social welfare, then neither the verdict of public opinion nor ecclesiastical disapproval can convert the exercise of foresight and control, when prompted by worthy motives, into an immoral act.

But, however we may judge of this movement, it will eventually be judged by its fruits, by the effect it has on those communities which practise it.

Whether it be destined to bring about the self-destruction or the self-renovation of Human Society will depend on the type of citizen it tends to perpetuate—that is to say, whether it encourages capacity in the individual to appreciate right aims and to exercise self-control in right directions—much also depends on whether Public opinion appreciates in time the magnitude of the movement and directs it along right, that is, along Eugenic lines. For, though at present it is chiefly limited to the Middle and Upper classes of Society, it is gradually reaching the Lower strata and will eventually permeate the whole. And herein lies a possibility for good. The movement may provide a way of escape from some of the greatest of the burdens which oppress Humanity. The warlike nations are those in whom an expanding population is shut up within circumscribed boundaries, and increase of population has a greater influence than peace tribunals on the Peace of the world. Other vital sociological problems, such as the restriction of competition, the possibility of earlier marriage, and the attainment of a higher standard of Life by the working classes, and the reduction of Prostitution are all also intimately related to this question of the voluntary control of the birth-rate. This at any rate is certain, that the voice of Public opinion and the voice of Social custom, if they are fundamentally opposed to true Social welfare, will eventually fall on deaf ears.

Some students of Sociology have sought in this voluntary reduction of the Human birth-rate an explanation of the decay of past civilisations. It is true that Empires and civilisations, like individuals, die from above downwards. But the real cause of the decay of nations, as of families, is growth of environmental control—that is, opportunity for satisfying desires—out of proportion to natural capacity to use these opportunities to worthy and public ends. Material civilisation outstrips ethical civilisation. The fatal facilities afforded by luxury lead to a damping down of effort in worthy directions, and unless innate capacity rises above its surroundings this leads eventually to stagnation and decay.

In so far, then, as this exercise of voluntary control over the increase of the population is exerted for selfish ends, it does constitute a grave danger to Society; if, on the other hand, its aim be the removal of some of the worst results of unrestricted competition and faulty life conditions, it may, if properly directed, prove a powerful means of progress.

The danger lies not in the increased power of environmental control nor in its employment in the field of race culture, but in not using the increased power to right ends; and the remedy is to be sought, not in a return to Natural Selection, but in a further extension of the newer method of artificial selection, under proper control.

The only efficient way of dealing with this important problem of the voluntary control of the human birth-rate is to bring about such social and industrial conditions as will render the fulfilment of the duty of race production and of rearing healthy offspring economically possible, on the one hand,

and to develop by Eugenic methods, and to foster the exercise of an innate love of parenthood and a sense of parental responsibility in the citizens, on the other. We must, in fact, deal with this as with all Social problems, by attacking it on its individual as well as on its environmental aspect. If the social and economic conditions of modern life are such that a high standard of parental responsibility cannot be exercised, the mere substitution of easier circumstances will not evolve a love for parenthood in citizens in whom it is by Nature absent.

This in effect means that the whole attitude of society to these vital problems of sex and parenthood needs revision in the daylight of modern knowledge and testing by modern conceptions of public and private duty. At the same time we must not forget that in thus speaking as though we ourselves were in this way or that solving social problems, what we really mean is that in this way or that these problems are in the course of social evolution solving themselves.

We may now summarise our conceptions of Individual and Communal health by regarding it as harmonious adjustment on the part of the individual citizen and the State to both the good and the bad agencies in the environment, and not merely as the absence of insanitary surroundings and of disease organisms. But Public and Private Health so regarded is under present social conditions unattainable except by a few of the more richly endowed or happily circumstanced members of the community. Like the slaves of ancient Athens, a large part of Society is still disinherited as regards the legacies of Health. Under present industrial and social conditions healthy activities may be over-exercised, and healthy desires may go unsatisfied. Capacity for labour, over-exercised to the point or exhaustion or exercised in monotonous toil, without the relief which comes from change of occupation, or the stimulus of delight in the object toiled for, Capacity for feeling, and action unexercised or exercised under wrong conditions—these things are responsible for much of the disharmony of our artificial city life; these things are incompatible with perfect health.

There are only two ways of righting disharmony in every department of Life. Either the environmental conditions must be improved to allow of the exercise of the larger faculties, or the capacities must be reduced to the level of the narrower environment.

It will not be enough even in the coming time that there will be no waste of infant life, the result of lack of knowledge or lack of care, or that, by the control of accidental, and the removal of preventable causes of disease, the life of the adult citizen will be prolonged to the full span of human vital capacity. The citizens of the Great State will ask for more than this. They will claim to be delivered from the strain on body and soul which comes from disharmony between capacity and the conditions under which capacity is exercised, as well as from the drain on vital energy which now results from suffering and disease. After the satisfaction of the immediate needs of existence they will look for a reserve of energy which may be spent in enlarging the horizon of life, and in this clearer atmosphere they will taste once more the Joy of Living. It is in this way that the problem of Health in the widest sense is linked up with the problem of Education, on the one hand, and the possibilities of social, economic, and industrial reform, on the other.

Among Health-promoting factors two of the most important, at any rate under the depressing conditions of our modern industrial life, are "Healthy Recreation" and "Change of Occupation." Other writers will deal with these aspects of life under the better conditions of the Great State, but when that freer interchange which we all hope for has been brought about between the life of the country and the life of the city, when the fresh air and the freedom and the rest of the country can be obtained by the town dweller, and the means of easy communication and opportunities for social intercourse reach to the country, then some of the lifelessness that results from exhaustion and monotony will be done away with.

We now realise that the biological foundations are the only firm foundations on which we can build

up Health or resist Disease, and in the coming time
we shall also learn that Innate Capacity, the conditions under which it is exercised, and the acquirements that it makes, must also provide the fundamental principles by which the education of the
child, the life and labour of the adult citizen, and the
duties of the State must be guided and controlled.

II

HEALING

WE have now formed some conception of what
Communal and Individual Health in its widest and
best sense will mean under the improved social conditions of the Great State, and we must pass on to
consider some of the ways in which this fuller Life
may be realised.

In the first place, a true sense of the relative
importance of the objects to be aimed at is very
necessary if we are to avoid the error of confusing
mediate with *ultimate* ends. For while the final
aim must be the Health, the fuller life of the community as a whole, the efficiency and the welfare of
the profession of Healing are of fundamental importance as a necessary step towards the realisation of
the goal.

One thing, at any rate, is clear: if Health means
Harmonious Adjustment to environmental conditions, then every one whose business it is to bring

about health must be an adapter and a harmoniser. The Profession of Healing must concern itself with all efforts which tend to bring about harmonious adjustment between the citizens and their environment. It must be occupied, not only with the removal of insanitary surroundings and the promotion of individual resistance to infection, but it must also strive to develop a normal mental and bodily response on the part of the citizens to all kinds of healthy stimuli.

Before we can indicate the lines along which future progress in this direction may be looked for we must first pass in brief review one or two aspects of the relationship which at present exists between the Medical Profession and the Public. To begin with, the service of Health is vital to Society. It is indeed so vital that it has become one of the fundamental concerns of the State that medical and surgical treatment should be available for all, that the healthy life and the means of attaining it, as far as such means are attainable, should be within the reach of every member of the community, poor as well as rich.

How do we stand to-day in regard to this matter? The treatment of disease is now carried on in two ways: by the *Institutional* method and the *Home*-treatment method. Of these two the Institutional is by far the most efficient and the most valuable from the point of view of the cure of disease; but under present conditions it is quite inadequate to meet the needs of the great mass of the working-class population, at any rate in this country in which the General Hospitals are supported by voluntary contributions, and are not subsidised by the Municipalities or the State. It is calculated that Hospital accommodation is only available for from twenty to fifty per cent. of the population it ought to benefit. It touches, in fact, only a portion of the mass of disease amongst the poor.

When we turn to the treatment of disease in working-class homes, we find a still more unsatisfactory condition of things. A great part of the contract medical and surgical practice of Great Britain —at any rate that part of it which is concerned with the Home visiting and the treatment of working people in private surgeries, hospital out-patient departments, and out-patient clinics under the Club system—is suffering from certain serious inherent defects which tend to bring about inefficiency of treatment and a false mental attitude on the part of the patients and the medical attendant towards the whole problem of disease. In the first place, owing to unrestricted competition among medical men themselves, this contract practice is inadequately remunerated. This means that a great number of sufferers from real or imaginary diseases must pass through the medical attendant's hands if he is to make a living, and this means hurried observation, imperfect diagnosis, and inadequate treatment in many cases. Further, it brings about a tendency to make up for lack of thoroughness in investigation by a routine system of drug-prescribing, with the result that a false sense of satisfaction is thereby engendered in the minds of patients who are often ignorant of the real relationship between the administration of drugs and the curing and prevention of disease. An extravagant belief in the necessity for drugs in the treatment of disease has sprung up in the mind of the Public, and an easy acquiescence in this line of least resistance in the minds of some medical men which is demoralising to the Profession.

It thus happens, through the fault of a system rather than through the fault of the individual, that the true function of the "Healer" is obscured and misunderstood, and in many cases a futile attempt to treat symptoms or to remove results has overshadowed the more lengthy and more difficult but more efficient method o᷑ dealing with the causes of disease. The real remedy for this unsatisfactory state of things is a deeper appreciation of the true meaning of "Health," on the one hand, and a clearer recognition of the real function of the "Healer," on the other. If some of the energy which is now being expended by medical men in the routine visiting of long lists of contract and club patients, and in the prescribing and dispensing of drugs for the relief of symptoms, could be directed to the prevention of the beginnings of disease in people's homes, and to the provision of efficient institutional treatment for those persons whose recovery would be materially aided by removal to better surroundings, then not only would the health of the people be more efficiently safeguarded, but the lot of the doctor would be a more useful, a more self-respecting, and therefore a more happy one. But this means two things: it means a great extension of the Institutional system, and it means a reorganisation of the system of Contract and Club Practice, through which the poor now obtain medical assistance.

With regard to the first it is hopeless to look for any great extension of hospital accommodation on the lines of voluntary support. Hospital administration has in this country now passed through the experimental and initiatory stage, during which it is wiser to leave it to the stimulus of individual effort and voluntary support. It has become an absolute necessity of our social and industrial life. General Hospital administration now requires the integrating influence of State control to bring it into co-ordination with Poor Law Infirmaries, Infectious Hospitals, and with other voluntary and municipal health agencies. Moreover, there are many indications that it is in this direction that the problem of Hospital administration will eventually be solved.

Things are also moving in the same direction in the domiciliary side of medical practice. Owing to unrestricted competition among its own members, the profession of Medicine is suffering from lack of co-ordination of effort, waste of energy, and want of control; and owing to the same cause it is also suffering from inadequate remuneration and, as a further consequence, from a lack of appreciation on the part of the Public of the real value of its services and the true position it ought to occupy in the State.

The uncertainty and the obscurity which hung around the methods of the "Healer" in the past still tend to obstruct his vision and prejudice his authority, now that he is called upon to play the part of health adviser to the community. Society forgets that the Profession of Healing has long ago discarded the old garments of magic and superstition, which clothed it in infancy, and that it has almost succeeded in shaking off the fetters of tradition and dogma which still encumber its old companions Theology and Law, and that it is both ready and willing to enter on the duties of mature age and wider experience. On the other hand, the community is also suffering from the imperfections of the present system, but in a different way. It suffers from the inefficiency of service which comes from uncontrolled contract practice, and from the demoralisation which follows a too ready acquiescence in a symptomatic as opposed to a preventive and radical treatment of disease. The eventual remedy for both difficulties can only be a National Health Service in which the conditions of service include adequate remuneration and a reserve of time, money, opportunity, and legislative freedom for progressive development, for the acquirement of new knowledge, and for the application of new and improved methods in the treatment of disease.

The Science and Art of Healing and those who practise it must be protected against unnecessary interference by officialdom, against hampering and restrictive legislation prompted by a sentimental or ill-informed public opinion; and this must be secured by an efficient representation of medical opinion and medical interests on Municipal and State councils.

In the same way the interests of the community must also be safeguarded against undue regimentation in matters of health. False assumption of authority in administrative matters on the part of the Profession must be prevented by Free Trade in the National Health Service, by free choice of doctor on the part of the individual citizen or social groups, and by freedom on the part of the public to decline any special or improved form of treatment, subject always to the important condition that such refusal does not endanger public safety or run counter to the interests of the community.

Now, this scheme of a national health service must be conceived on a well-thought-out plan. It must embrace the Health interests of the individual citizen, on the one hand, and social, municipal, and State interests, on the other. Here, as in all matters of State enterprise and Municipal trading, there are certain things which are best left to individual effort

166

and voluntary support, and there are others which are better done by social co-operation. To the former must be relegated the medical attendance, institutional and domiciliary, of all those more fortunately circumstanced citizens who desire and are in a position to pay for medical services other than, or over and above those provided by the State. For the remainder of the population which embraces the very poor and the small salary-earning and small wage-earning class a National Health Service should in this country develop along the following lines:

Co-ordination must be brought about among existing institutions for the treatment of disease. The voluntary General Hospitals, Convalescent Homes, and Sanatoria must be linked up with the rate and State - supported institutions, the Municipal Infectious Hospitals, the Municipal and County Asylums, the Municipal Sanatoria, the School Clinics, the Poor Law Infirmaries, and the Prisons Medical Service. The present honorary Staffs of the General Hospitals would be paid salaries, they would be brought into relationship with medical officers of health, with the Staffs of Infectious Hospitals, of Asylums, of Sanatoria, and of School Clinics, with Poor Law Officers working in Poor Law Infirmaries, and with Prison doctors. The whole of this great institutional system, with its vast material and wide opportunities for the study of disease, would become available for the purposes of medical education, not only so, but a far larger number of already qualified and practising medical men would be thus enabled to keep in touch with new knowledge and new methods, for it is especially true in a growing science like medicine that for any seeker after knowledge to be satisfied with past experience or to attempt to live on the record of past attainments is woefully to restrict usefulness, even if it does not hinder success. And with this Institutional part of the National Health Service must be linked up a corresponding Nursing Service.

The other or the domiciliary side of the Health Service, the visiting of the citizens in their own homes, would be carried out by District and Divisional Medical Officers. They would treat such cases as could be well treated at home, and such as were too ill for removal, or not sufficiently ill to require institutional treatment, and they would be assisted in their work by an organised District Nursing Service.

One very important part of the duty of these Medical Officers would be the periodic visiting of all households and the reporting on the health and life conditions of the householder and his dependants. This need be neither inquisitorial nor offensive, if there is a proper system of local controls over the appointments of the medical men concerned. There need be no more inconvenience in the visit of the Medical Officer than in the visit of any other Municipal official. In this way the early beginnings of disease would be often detected and the prevention of disease would become a reality, for the health authorities would be provided with accurate statistics and reliable information about disease. In this way, too, the work of the Medical Practitioner would be raised in dignity and in tone. He would be one among many officers occupied in a great national inquiry into the causes of, as well as the best way of treating disease; he would feel that he was being paid for work of value to the community, as well as to the individual.

What are the objections which can be brought forward against such a scheme?

Doubtless those who dread the introduction of so-called socialistic methods into any new departments of human life will again raise the objection which was formerly raised against the introduction of State Education. So-called free doctoring is to such persons on a level with so-called free education: both are equally vicious. But, in both cases, such objectors overlook the fact that in reality neither the benefits of a National Health Service nor the benefits of a State-provided Education are really free; as a matter of fact, that service cannot be truly described as free in which both the expenditure and the effort which are necessary to provide it are shared by all directly or indirectly. It is only free in the sense that it is available for all, just as it is provided by all.

Indeed, a question of even greater importance

to-day is not so much that of the free provision of
medical attendance as of the desirability of the
compulsory adoption of the means of attaining
health by all citizens. If, like the attainment o
knowledge, the attainment of Health is so vital to
national welfare that the State makes it compulsory, then, like the service of knowledge, the service
of Health must be free, too. If the State has learned
to recognise that the uneducated citizen is a source
of national inefficiency, surely the State must also
realise that the unhealthy and the diseased citizen
is a source of national danger. We are only beginning to realise that it is just as wrong to be ill, if
the illness be preventable, as it is wrong to be ignorant if the ignorance can be dispelled. It is not
enough that a small proportion of the members
of any community should be robustly healthy or
highly trained; the whole body of citizens must be
raised up to a certain minimum level of mental and
bodily efficiency: above this average minimum of
Health and Sanity there will always remain plenty
of room for further development. Moreover, and
most important of all, the provision by the State of
the means of attaining Health, if it be also accompanied by care in seeing that these means are adopted,
is, like State education, free from the disadvantage
of producing concomitant demoralisation and relaxation of individual effort; for both the attainment of
Health and the attainment of Knowledge recognise
the biological law of Response, they both presuppose

some effort on the part of the citizen benefited, while the increased efficiency of body and of mind which result lead in their turn to increased capacity for further effort.

It is those well-meant but misguided social efforts to ameliorate the conditions of life among the poor and the sick which do not include the recognition of the fundamental necessity for some responsive effort on the part of the persons benefited, that cause demoralisation of character. The provision of healthier surroundings and opportunities for the exercise of higher capacities does not fall within this category. Let no one suppose that the provision of a healthier and better environment will bring about a less worthy type of citizen.

But there will also be objections on the part of Medical Men. One of the difficulties in the way of reconciling the Medical Profession to the idea of a National Health Service is the suspicion and dislike with which individual medical men regard all forms of contract service and payment per capita, or by salary for whole or part time service. This suspicion and dislike arises largely from past experience of this kind of service at the hands of the Friendly Societies and Clubs under the old régime of unrestricted competition. When we inquire into the evolution of these different methods of remuneration we find that payment by individual patients for individual services rendered is as a rule found in less progressive communities than payment per capita or by salary for whole-time service. In industrial life, piece-work and time-work correspond more or less accurately to payment for services rendered and payment by salary in professional life. Now, it is a significant fact that while in different trades some trade-unions recognise piece-work and some time-work, yet no trade-unions recognise piece-work unless it is compatible with collective bargaining. In fact, both employers and employed adopt either method according as it leads to advantageous bargaining. Of the two methods of remuneration for professional services, payment for whole-time service is far more consistent with collective bargaining than payment by individual patients for services rendered, while payment per capita stands in an intermediate position as a form of bargain, between the State Agreement, on the one hand, and the Agreement between the doctor and his individual patients, on the other. In fact, State or Municipal salary for whole-time service (and payment per capita by Friendly Societies in a less degree) tends to approximate the old basis of agreement between doctor and patient to the modern basis of agreement which obtains between employer and employed in industrial life. It substitutes the newer relationship of one employer (the State) to many employed, for the older relationship of many employers to one employed, as in the agreement between the private doctor and his individual patients, and by so doing if favours the possibility of collective bargaining on the part of the employed; and on this ground it ought to receive favourable consideration by the Profession, or at any rate that portion of the Profession which realises that its relationships with the public in the future will be more and more regulated, as far as remuneration for services is concerned, by trade-union methods of the better kind.

For we know that the average employer constantly seeks to get more work for the same payment, while the average employee desires to get more pay for the same amount of work; and both alike favour time or piece work according as either method seems best calculated to bring about this result. Hence it comes about that it is impossible to prevent the degradation of the standard of Professional Life under unrestricted competition, just as it is impossible to prevent it in competitive industrial occupations, unless the terms and conditions of service allow of some form of collective bargaining between the individuals or the groups concerned. Hence the importance of securing some method of remuneration which allows of collective bargaining.

Owing to a deficient social conscience in many citizens, both employers and employed, and in spite of education and moral training, conduct continues to be directed by considerations of supposed self-interest rather than by considerations of social welfare. It is possible that in a regenerated State, public-spirited conduct, inspired by worthy motives, will allow of a return to the old individual relationships in matters of remuneration for service rendered, and that a fair reward for whole-hearted service will not need to be secured by any form of collective bargaining; but that brighter day has not yet dawned, and we are now concerned with the means by which the end may be attained rather than with the end itself.

The ultimate test of the fitness of any institution or industrial enterprise or profession for municipalisation or nationalisation must be Utility. It must be the relative value to Society of such institutional enterprise or professional service under municipal or State as against individual control, and this will to a certain extent depend on the degree of integration and co-ordination, that is on the state of development of the enterprise or service in question, and on the nature of the service which it can render to Society. Some enterprises are more organised than others, some services are more vital than others to the welfare of Society. As a matter of fact, those branches of the medical profession which are concerned with Municipal and institutional administration, with preventive medicine and public health, have already reached a certain level of organisation. It is the private practice and the domiciliary side of professional service that need bringing up to the same level.

The enormous importance of the problem makes it a matter of vital concern that the ingoing information and the outgoing energy of a National Health

Service should be co-ordinated in one central brain in one department under the control of a Minister of Health, and this Minister must combine in himself, or be able to obtain at first-hand, medical knowledge and a knowledge of biological Sociology; the Health Department will be the most fundamental of all the departments of State. It will be called upon to advise other departments concerning the biological principles upon which education and labour must be founded, upon which the activities of the soldier, sailor, and other public servants must be guided; and upon which the control and reformation of the mentally deficient, the pauper, and the criminal must be carried out.

Having attempted to answer various objections that may be raised against it, having discussed the question of a National Health Service from the point of view of the State, we must now consider the effect of nationalisation on the Medical Profession itself. As soon as we rise above the level of the primitive society, with its impelling desires to satisfy only the primary needs of existence, we come under the control of other motives and meet with other springs of conduct. The desire for the approbation of fellow-citizens, the wish to stand well with society—these are the motives which direct human conduct and sway the actions of civilised mankind on a large scale in the pursuit of worthy and unworthy ends. It is this which leads to the amassing of wealth, the acquirement of power, and it is this which, if conceived in a selfish spirit or moulded by a debased standard of social approbation, brings about the vicious circle in which unworthy conduct in the influential citizen vitiates public opinion; and debased public opinion approves of the un-unworthy conduct. Everything turns on the average level of public spirit and the standard of public duty in every community. The nationalisation of the Health Service, like that of every other service, is undesirable and unsafe until a certain standard of social and ethical development has been reached by the community. Indeed, it is only possible where a civic consciousness is present among both those who render the service and those who benefit by it.

We believe that in Great Britain, at any rate, such a stage of civic evolution has already been reached.

But there are other and important reasons why the relationship between the Profession of Healing and the community should be a State relationship rather than a relationship between individual citizens. So long as medical treatment is concerned with the protection of the individual citizen against outside infection, against those injurious environmental factors which prejudice personal health, it does not run counter to individual inclinations, and so long even as medical advice concerns itself with the present it does not evoke any great opposition. The difficulty arises when we begin to act in the interests of future generations. Now there are sources of disease outside the control of individual doctors, outside the authority of Medical Officers of Health and Sanitary Authorities. As we have already seen in Part I of this essay there are congenital deficiencies, errors of development which are not the result of disease organisms or of insanitary surroundings. It is in regard to these mental and bodily disabilities which arise from the faulty union of deficient natural tendencies that the profession of Healing, when dealing with the problem of race culture, will be increasingly called upon to decide; and, if it is to speak with authority in cases where duty to the next generation does not always coincide with the desires of the individual citizen, then it becomes necessary that the skilled adviser shall be free from ignorant opposition and supported by the general intelligence of the community. This can only be secured by placing the relationship between adviser and citizen on the secure basis of a State-controlled and State-recognised service in a State which is the expression of a highly developed collective mind.

It is only from such a standpoint, too, that the profession of Health can speak with power in matters of immorality and intemperance in those regions of social and individual misadjustment in which the disharmony is the direct or indirect result of a departure from a temperate or moral mode of life.

Moreover, the conspiracy of silence which now envelops the whole subject of sex responsibilities and sex morality must be cleared away, and it will be the duty of the Health adviser to co-operate with the educationist in dispelling ignorance about normal sex functions, and in pointing out the harmful results of immoral conduct in ruined health and in diminished efficiency. The work of the State doctor will be preventive rather than curative, national as well as individual, and educational in a high degree. He it is who will act as guide and counsellor in the coming transition period in the history of the human race, which is now approaching much more quickly than many suppose. For mankind is passing out of the control of its old schoolmaster, Natural Selection, and is entering on the wider career of adult life, when the old evolutionary landmarks will be lost sight of, when preadaptation and instinctive response will be largely supplemented by capacity to profit by experience, and when the power of controlling his environment will enable man to take a large share in the shaping of Human destiny. Those who are called upon to advise the race in these great issues must be public-spirited citizens above all suspicion of self-seeking. Such public spirit as we need demands public service and public recognition; it will flourish in an atmosphere of penetrating criticism efficiently performed, it will languish under conditions both of unrestricted competition and of restricted activity. It perishes in a life of unlimited self-assertion and uncontrolled individualism.

The uncertainty and the obscurity which have in

the past hung about the methods of the Healer in the treatment of disease in the individual citizen still cling to his reputation and prejudice his authority, now that he is called upon to act as the adjuster between the social organism and its environment. But this will rapidly disappear with wider knowledge and increasing experience on his part, and with a broad sustaining collective intelligence and criticism behind and penetrating his specialised authority. Of this much we may be quite certain, that it is only as the Healing Profession responds to the call which will be made upon it by Society for instruction and guidance in the important field of race culture, only as it concerns itself with the causes and the prevention of disease in childhood, in prenatal and germinal life, only as it rises to the full measure of its responsibilities to the Race and to future generations—only as it does these things can it claim to save society from internal decay, as it now claims to protect it from those external factors which produce disease.

When adequately remunerated and thoroughly efficient medical treatment and advice are secured to every citizen, when the unessentials have been cast aside and the energy now expended in the treatment of symptoms and on attempts to neutralise the effects of disease is directed to the detection and the removal of its cause, when Society understands that amateur attempts to apply untrained methods in dealing with disease are bound to fail, when the State recognises the wisdom of following the well-considered advice, as well as consulting the mature opinion of skilled advisers in matters relating to the health of this and the next generation, when the Profession of Healing itself recognises that it exists for the purpose of bringing Society into more harmonious adaptation to its environment and that its only legitimate demands must be for freedom, encouragement, sympathetic understanding, and opportunity to carry on its work of healing under such conditions of service as will lead to greater efficiency on the part of its own members, and greater benefits to the community which it serves, then, and not till then, will the Science and practice of Medicine be worthy of the Great State; and then, and not till then, will the Great State fully recognise the usefulness and the worth of its Health Service.

LAW AND THE GREAT STATE

BY E. S. P. HAYNES

VI

LAW AND THE GREAT STATE

Of Law no less can be said than that her seat is the bosom of God, her voice the harmony of the world.--Hooker.

THIS eloquent sentence is scarcely likely to find an echo in modern sentiment. In our world of to-day law has associations of terror for the poor, of financial jeopardy for the rich, of richly confused legislation for the lawyer. Law makes little or no appeal either to the collective intelligence or to the collective affections of the community. The law, in popular estimation, is a "*hass.*" In the estimation of a growing minority it is (as administered by modern bureaucracy) simply a brutal bully, whose intervention must be avoided at any cost, or an overbearing sharper extremely difficult to evade. There is still, perhaps, for many minds a certain mystical glamour about it. The ordinary man who might make an inte lectual effort to understand the workings of his household cisterns or sanitary arrangements would as often as not flinch from investigating all the possible complications of his own will. To some extent this is inevitable. In a highly civilised community legal machinery cannot be simpler than any other machinery, though, of course, it should not be more complicated than other machinery, if such a state of things can be avoided. Again there is an inevitable tendency to make judges the mouthpieces of our virtuous indignation. All vulgar people love to hear a good scolding properly applied. Many men who resent a peremptory summons, reeking of pains and penalties, to serve on a jury, feel that society is not altogether rotten when they read:

"The Judge then assumed the black cap and addressed the prisoner as follows: 'John Jones, you have been convicted of a dastardly murder by an impartial jury of your countrymen, and the sentence of the Court is that you be taken from this Court . . . and hanged by the neck till you be dead, and God have mercy on your soul.'"

This gratifies all the lingering nursery morality in the common man, and it is none the less pleasing to him that the Judge is attired in a costume exclusively associated with the pronouncement of doom, and is, therefore, invested with a kind of halo, or, as more irreverent persons might say, a kind of tabooing power. The Judge would not be felt to be "voicing" the community if, wearing ordinary morning dress, he said, merely:

"Mr. Jones, the legal consequence of the foreman's remarks is that, unless you succeed in persuading the Court of Appeal to quash the conviction or unless you obtain a reprieve from the Home Secretary, you will be executed as the law directs. I do not wish to intrude into the question of your religious opinions, but, if you desire it, the chaplain shall wait upon you, your solicitor and your intimate friends are at your service, and you shall have every opportunity of settling your affairs in a manner as satisfactory as this unfortunate occasion permits."

No doubt, however, the judges and lawyers of the Great State will feel it less incumbent on them to reproduce the violence and fierceness of the past than they do now. The modern parent can bring up children without incessantly flourishing a big stick, and it is time the law came up a little nearer to the present level of civilisation. . . .

In this connection it is instructive to remember the politeness of the Athenians. Readers of Plato's *Phædo* will remember the civility of the executioner to Socrates when he presented the hemlock and lucidly explained how it would work This is quite an advance on pinioning and blindfolding the victim or preventing him forcibly from committing suicide. On the one hand one observes barbaric insult and a brutish vindictiveness, on the other a dignified appeal to human dignity and citizenship even in a criminal condemned. Still more startling to modern notions is Socrates's expression of attachment to the laws of Athens when Crito urges him to escape. To Socrates the laws appear almost as friendly deities who have watched over him from the cradle, and whom he is bound by the obligation of past benefits not to defy. Mr. Zimmern explains this attitude very well in the masterful chapter on "Law" in his *Greek Common-wealth*.[1]

"We have our Constitution written or unwritten and the ever-changing body of our Statute Law. But they are remote from our daily life. We do not ourselves enforce them or even know them. . . . Between us and the enforcement of law stand the policeman and the magistrate: between us and the making of law stand Parliaments and the government. But in Athens there was no such thing as the 'government' as distinct from the people."

There, perhaps, Mr. Zimmern puts his hand upon the essential difference in spirit between that ancient civilisation and our present confusion. Our modern States—and, so far as the law goes, this is true even of the American republic—derive from bullying monarchs, bullying dukes and earls and barons who bullied their tenants and so down; and we have an enormous traditional *incubus* of vile aggressions to shake off before the Great State will be able to emulate the fine nobility of those ancient cities. It must, moreover, be noted that a mere replacement of feudalism by a sham democratic bureaucracy is not likely to give us any great increase of sweetness and light in our courts—or elsewhere. The spirit of bureaucracy is to distinguish between the official and the citizen, and it is typical of this that the London trams are labelled "L. C. C.," and that the notices in the public parks are signed "By Order L. C. C."—showing that these things are

[1] *The Greek Commonwealth*, p. 125. (Clarendon Press, 1911.)

not the property of the people of London, but of a select and fortunate body of adventurers in control. This is quite alien from the magnificent inscription of "S. P. Q. R." of the Roman banner.

But in the Great State the tram and the post notices will say, and not only say but mean, "This belongs to the Londoners," and the mail-cart or railway signal will say, "This mail - cart or railway signal belongs to the Englishmen"; so, when the prisoner stands in front of the judge, that judge will not only be, but also appear, a reasonable civil gentleman instead of a Minos in miniature.

Such a state of things as Mr. Zimmern describes, of course, necessitated a rotation of citizens in different offices; there were no "officials" because every one had office in turn; the ordinary Athenian citizen was personally familiar with both judicial and legislative work. Such a participation is absolutely necessary for a civilised relation between the law and the ordinary man. The requisite leisure of the Athenian citizen, no doubt, reposed on a foundation of slave labour; in the Great State it will rest on a foundation of power-increasing machinery. The essential point is for every citizen to regard justice and legislation as part of his own work, and the whole apparatus of the State as his possession, instead of as alien things imposed on him by such persons as cabinet ministers and judges. Such an achievement can only spring from a new

harmony between law and custom, order and freedom, and from a local connection in whatever remains localised. I do not mean that such localisa-
tions need necessarily be those of an agricultural
community or the Normal Social Life. I am speaking of local units of thought and administration.
The unit may be that of a township or county, but
clearly much law arising out of local matters must
be administered throughout a number of distributed
circles, and cannot be too rigidly centralised. Now,
the citizenship of the ancient civilised state was
destroyed just in so far as the feudal military system
crushed out civic life, and the feudal or territorial
units of justice were in turn crushed out by the
centralisation of justice as the bigger States of
Europe came to birth in the fifteenth and sixteenth
centuries. Modern citizenship was scarcely likely
to flourish in what Mr. Wells calls the "jerry-built
nationalities" of the last fifty years, or, even where
the nationality already existed, in the welter of
the industrial revolution.

The law of the Great State should, therefore, not
be too highly centralised, and should leave rooms
under its catholic universality for local, and not
merely local, but a certain kind of specialised Justice.
Much admirable work is done by Commercial Court
judges and by magistrates paid and unpaid. By
"specialised Justice" I mean the kind of work that
is done by the Commercial Court or, on a smaller
scale, by the Incorporated Law Society's Discipline

Committee or any Court Martial. I believe that the Great State will develop wide extensions of specialised justice. Subject to the right of appeal, better justice can generally be obtained from men who are well acquainted with the subject-matter before them. Juries often make hideous blunders in civil actions concerning complicated business affairs of which they know nothing. "Judicial ignorance" has become a proverbial phrase. But, were the defeated litigant to appeal from an expert Court of first instance, the subject-matter would have been already well cooked and served up for the purely legal mind.

There is, in all litigation, a curious little conflict between reality and the apparatus that has to deal with it. There is a struggle between the issue and the process. What the lawyer wants is the simplification of facts; what the layman wants is the simplification of law. The layman often has a touching belief in the utility of codes because he is unaware that foreign codes are interpreted largely in the light of past litigation about them. A code cannot altogether do away with the difficulty of forcing facts into the strait-waistcoat of legal definition. What can be done, however, is to increase statutes like the Partnership Act, 1890, which summarise and boil down a multitude of decided cases. If our jurisprudence is to justify the maxim *"Ignorantia legis neminem excusat,"* then it must be thoroughly proof against Bentham's amplification, "Ignorance

of the law excuses no one except the lawyer." If
is to adopt the old equity motto "No wrong withou
a remedy," then it must be so framed and so mad
acceptable to the general understanding that n
wronged citizen can fail to be conscious that he ha
at least some sort of remedy. It should not b
impossible so to simplify the law in its elementar
stages that the necessarily abstruse points are onl
those which have to be decided in the Courts o
Appeal.

Decisions of a court of first instance are accepte
as final more often from the litigant's disinclinatio
to gamble than from his thinking that the decisio
is irrefutable in itself. Such a simplification as
have suggested could be achieved by a series o
statutes which (a) boil down and clarify the cas
law of each preceding twenty years and (b) boil dow
and clarify the crude, or perhaps experimenta
legislation on any given subject during the sam
period, much as excellent soup may be made ou
of bones. In some such fashion the lawyer woul
find his facts more readily pigeonholed in advance
and the layman would find his law less difficult t
assimilate. I do not see why there should not b
some special department of the public service o
the Great State engaged continually in this proces
of stewing a sort of legal stockpot for legislativ
stuff.

If one development is more certain than anothe
in the future, it is the unification of internationa

law on matters concerning marriage, divorce, succession to property, the *renvoi*, etc. The tests of nationality and residence are bound to supersede the vague and inadequate test of domicile to which the United Kingdom and many English-speaking communities so obstinately cling. A doctrine which grew up in the Dark Ages, when there was no nationality and but little travelling as we know it now, cannot but create the boundless confusion and uncertainty that the doctrine of domicile does at present create in English-speaking civilisation. Even if the Great State be not itself international, the development of an international intelligence must surely end those ridiculous anomalies which perplex the layman and enrich the lawyer of to-day.

Beyond these issues I find little to say in the way of generalisation about the law of the Great State. I am not a Socialist, though I have to admit, with all sane men, the manifest necessity of an increasing public control of, and property in, the main social services. Clearly the laws of possession must follow the changing ideas of the nature of what is, so to speak, property-able. With the decline of the bureaucratic movement, and subject to the foregoing proviso, it is not unreasonable to expect a rapid and successful assimilation of the law of real property to the law of personal property instead of its departmental complication by officials. Moreover, the mockery of justice due to the publicity of legal proceedings which are worse than useless, except under conditions of more or less limited privacy will presumably cease to exist. I allude more particularly to cases of blackmail, of divorce, or of libel and slander. I need not enlarge on the effects of publicity regarding blackmail or divorce, but I may add that the publicity of libel and slander proceedings often denies relief to all but that particular class of litigants who seek pecuniary damages rather than the rehabilitation of character. But this is a mere obvious step in civilisation that will be reached long before the Great State can be more than dawning.

It is difficult to anticipate any particular developments of the law governing the *status* of women, either as dependent or independent of men, when the whole institution of monogamy, so-called, that now exists may be fundamentally altered; and the difficulty is even more formidable in regard to children and succession to property. Such matters I will leave to my colleagues with a certain relief.

As to criminals, it is to be hoped that the criminal law of the Great State will be of as little immediate consequence to the citizen of the Great State as it is to the well-to-do citizen of to-day. As Hobbes well puts it:

"Every Sovereign ought to cause Justice to be taught, which (consisting in taking from no man what is his) is as much as to say, to cause men to be taught not to deprive their neighbours, by violence or fraud, of anything which by the sovereign authority is theirs."

LAW AND THE GREAT STATE

To this most men are ready enough to subscribe. Our criminal law, a peculiar blend of barbaric violence, medieval prejudices, and modern fallacies, affects only the more or less submerged portion of the community, whose semi-starvation not only of material comforts, but also of all the higher pleasures that make life worth living, will presumably not continue in the Great State. Where a citizen has everything to lose by violence—to wit, his reputation, his earning power, his liberty—where can the inducement to violence exist? By robbery he actually risks the loss of what he can honestly earn, and he is not likely to rob unless he is a collector—from whom no man is safe—or actuated by some mania for the acquisition of property on a large scale. And as for murder and such like offences, they are nowadays far more often the results of the economic pressure under which we live than of any innate evil in men. It is merely silly to kill a wife or concubine when there are means to divorce the one or to make decent provision for the other. The want of these things manufactures fifty per cent. of our murderers. It is equally absurd to kill an illegitimate child if its birth does not pillory the mother so that her earning power is reduced exactly in proportion to her necessity for more. There again is a class of offence for which the Great State will leave no inducement. Again, there is a large category of crimes demanding medical rather than legal treatment.

In the end I conceive that the Great State will have little more to consider in the way of crime than those inevitable clashes of jealousy, the Crimes of Passion. Sordid crime will disappear; only romantic crime will remain.

1. I mean something far more drastic than the statute revision that is going on to-day, and the recent suppression of discussion in the House of Commons removes the old obstacles to symmetrical reform.

2. Even romantic crimes are peculiar to men or women of no wide intellectual interests or recreations who by reason of their limitations cannot shake off the obsession of a particular person or a fixed idea.

To write on the problem of the law in the Great State is as difficult as to describe a strange country seen from an aeroplane. Only the crudest outlines emerge; all the essential characteristics of colour and scheme and detail remain gray and blurred. I sketch only what I can see. Yet, though it may be difficult to discern a celestial city, the Great State will at least avoid "mistaking memories for hopes," to adopt Hallam's famous sentence about the statesmen of medieval Italy. I mean that the Law of the Great State will be untrammelled by memories of the golden age or a state of Nature; it will seek no inspiration from imaginary theodicies or pedigrees; it will be inviolate by greed or superstition. That Law may, perhaps, in sober fact embody and proclaim the harmony of a better world.

DEMOCRACY AND THE GREAT STATE

BY CECIL CHESTERTON

VII

DEMOCRACY AND THE GREAT STATE

ALL free men feel that the only tolerable condition of Government is Democracy. No such man will tolerate the compulsory direction of his actions by any temporal authority save the general will of his fellow-citizens. This great truism I shall assume as the foundation of all that I have to say in this essay. With those who do not feel its truth, with those who regard a Hereditary Aristocracy or merely the Rich or Experts or Men in Advance of their Age as the proper repositories of political power I shall not here argue. I will argue with them when they have answered the plain question of the Jesuit Suarez, "If sovereignty is not in the People, where is it?"

Democracy, then, we assume as the fundamental condition of the state of society which we desire to create; but it is of vital importance to have in our minds a clear and unalterable idea of what Democracy means. Democracy means Government by the General Will. That is to say, it means that such laws as the mass of the population approves are passed and enforced, while such laws as are obnoxious to the mass of the population are rejected. It is clear that this has on the face of it nothing to do with special devices such as representation, by which modern men have attempted to achieve the end of Democracy. Despotic institutions, hereditary rulers, and representative bodies must alike be judged from the democratic standpoint by whether they do or do not result in a system of Government which accords with the general will of the people.

Democracy, considered in this sense, is not a new thing (as our Moderns suppose), but just about the oldest thing in the world. In what Mr. Wells has christened "The Normal Social Life" practical Democracy has always prevailed in the matters which most deeply affect the ordinary existence of the common man. Now and then, no doubt, a far-off ruler not chosen by him might force the common man to take part in a war which was not of his making. Taxes not levied with his consent would occasionally be imposed upon him. But in the matters that concern his daily life, in his sowing and reaping, in his buying and selling, in his marrying, in the bearing and upbringing of his children, in his religion, and in all other things for which such a man normally cares, his actions would be regulated by the customs of his tribe or commune, and any disputes would be settled by a council of his neighbours. That is to say, these matters would be settled by the general will. He would be living, whether he knew it or not, under the conditions of Democracy.

Now in this, as in other matters, what we must seek to effect is a return to what is wholesome and natural to Man in the Normal Social Life while availing ourselves of the advantages which a more elaborate system of society affords us. We must seek under the conditions imposed by the growth of larger States and the consequent necessity of a more extensive political organisation to obtain that which is obtained so easily in a simple society by the meeting of villagers under a tree.

The matter is the more urgent because so long as our system of government remains essentially undemocratic every step in the direction of Collectivism will be a step away from Democracy. It is no use denying that the "permeation" of our politicians and others with what are called "Socialist" ideas has tended, up to the present, rather to diminish than to increase the power of the General Will. Not only have measures directed towards the regimentation of the poor and tending, not to Collectivism, but to the Servile State been rushed through under the inspiring title of "Social Reform," but even where the direct Nationalisation of capital was involved the rich have known how to turn the Collectivist philosophy to their use. An example at once deplorable and farcical may be found in the extraordinary history of the National Telephone Company, whose monopoly was first secretly created and then ostentatiously bought (at an exorbitant price) by "the Nation"—that is, by the politicians, some of whom had also been directors. I can conceive no state of society—not even a frank plutocracy —more odious than one in which the governing class held all the economic power and administrated everything, nominally on behalf of the public, really on their own. And that plutocratic Collectivism is an extremely likely end to the efforts of a generation of Socialists, unless the machinery of the State can be made really to reflect the General Will.

The method by which most modern societies have attempted to solve the problem of Democracy is the method of Representation. Since it is obviously impossible that all the members of a great modern Nation, still more of the larger federations of men which the future will probably see, to meet together in one place, and there to discuss all the details of political administration, it is thought that the same end might be achieved if certain groups of such men delegated their power to some person chosen by them who should have their authority to speak in their name.

Now it is clear that the success of this experiment depends essentially upon the exact correspondence between the actions of the delegate and the wishes of those from whom his authority is derived. I say this is clear to any one who has attempted to think out the problem of representation. It is apparently by no means clear to a great many writers in the press or to a great many speakers on political platforms. These people are forever drawing an entirely meaningless distinction between "a Delegate" and what they call "a Representative." What this distinction means I have never been able to conceive. A man must vote either according to the wishes of his constituents or against those wishes. If he does the former he is acting as a faithful delegate would act. If he does the latter, he is neither a delegate nor a representative. He is an Oligarch. For how can we say that a man "represents" Slocum when he is in the habit of saying "Aye" where the inhabitants of Slocum would, if consulted, say "No"?

Now it is pretty obvious to most of us that, in England at any rate, there is absolutely no such relation as I have predicated as essential between the "Representative" and the people he is supposed to "represent." With the special causes which make this divorce more complete in England than elsewhere I shall have to deal in a moment. But apart from those special causes there is that in the very nature of the Representative System which tends to render it unrepresentative. In England to-day the Member of Parliament is not really in any sense chosen by his constituents. But even if he were so chosen it would still be true that the very fact of his having been marked out from his fellow-citizens for special governmental functions would give him a point of view which would not be quite an accurate mirror of the mind of those fellow-citizens. Put him in a room with several hundred other men similarly marked out from their fellow-citizens, and this psychological result is indefinitely intensified. It has always been so with political assemblies, however democratic their constitution, and in all probability it always will be so with them.

The divorce between the Politician and the Citizen is, of course, enormously increased when the former takes to politics as a profession.

The Professional Politician is the dominant figure in the Government of all civilised countries to-day, and nowhere is he more dominant than in England, where a large number of innocent persons refuse to believe in his existence.

That Politics should become a profession was perhaps inevitable so soon as the government of the country was no longer the affair of the citizens themselves. At any rate, in all known periods after politics had emerged from the primitive condition of the village community the Professional Politician has existed.

I shall discuss later how far he can be eliminated, but while he exists the important thing is to recognise that he does exist, to recognise that in all Nations which have developed to the point to which England has developed a class has appeared of men who make the government of the people their ordinary means of livelihood.

In moments of high civic excitement it has sometimes been possible to conduct the affairs of state without the payment of Politicians. This was so, for example, in the high hope and anger of the French Revolution. Then men entered politics urged by a passionate desire for social justice and a passionate patriotism, and left Politics (sometimes by the Tumbrils) poorer than they were in the first instance. It is doubtful whether, in any case, such self-devotion could be made permanent in times of comparative quiescence. But one thing is certain: with this intense self-devotion to the common weal inevitably goes an instinct that Politicians should be poor men. The great and determining characters in the revolutionary drama of France boasted that while they administered millions they themselves lodged in the cheapest lodgings and dined at the cheapest restaurants.

Nothing could be more absurd than the present practice in England, the practice, I mean, of rewarding success in politics with salaries varying from £1,200 to £10,000 a year, and then pretending that these sums are of no account at all to the persons who receive them. Such a practice directly tends to produce corruption of the worst kind. A Professional Politician may be, like a Professional House-Agent, a perfectly honest man—that is, he may endeavour to give in return for his salary honest and efficient service to the State. But we all know what would happen if it were a general assumption, which it was "in bad taste" to challenge, that House-Agents were entirely indifferent to their fees and were actuated solely by compassion for persons who found themselves for the moment homeless and by a desire to see them adequately housed. Such a general assumption would be used by really dishonest house-agents to cover their offences, while the honest house-agent, working, no doubt, for money but fairly earning it, would find himself handicapped. And that is exactly the condition of English Politics to-day.

Politics in England, and largely throughout the civilised world, are for the most part a means of livelihood for those who concern themselves with them. No doubt it is true that a large number of men enter the House of Commons without any intention of increasing their income, some from vanity and the desire for an honorary distinction, some (very few) with a desire to express their personal views, and here and there (the rarest thing of all) a man determined to voice the opinions of his constituency. But these are not the men who direct Parliament or really determine the Government of the Country. The men who do this are the Professional Politicians.

These may be broadly divided into two classes. There are the men who belong by birth to what we may call the governing class. These are considered to have a right to co-option into salaried political posts. It is to them that Mr. Belloc's amusing poem refers:

> "It happened to Lord Lundy then,
> As happens to so many men,

DEMOCRACY AND THE GREAT STATE

About the age of twenty-six
They shoved him into Politics.
In which profession he commanded
The salaries his rank demanded."

This is on the whole the most harmless and least
corrupt kind of professionalism in politics. Such
men are apprenticed to politics as a profession (that
is, as a means of making money) just as men of
humbler rank are apprenticed to be Solicitors,
Greengrocers, or Compositors, because their parents
happen to be able to command for them an opening
in these trades. Such men, if they happen to be
honest men, often try to do their best to earn their
money by serving the community to the best of
their ability. This method of choosing governors
is repugnant to Democracy, but is not clearly repugnant to plain morals or to the national interest.
It is the method by which all oligarchical States are
governed. It was the method by which England
was governed during the eighteenth and the greater
part of the nineteenth century.

A much worse form of Political Professionalism
has arisen of late years. Young men, conscious
perhaps of some talent, enter Parliament with the
deliberate intention of getting a salaried place from
those at whose disposal such places and salaries
are placed. Such a man violates, of course, the
essential idea of representation as it has been out-
lined above. His intention is not to serve his
constituency, but to serve those from whom he

14   205

expects his pecuniary reward—that is, the very Executive which he is supposed to check and criticise. If a sufficient number of such men are returned to the representative assembly, it is obvious that such an assembly will exist only to ratify the decisions of the Executive; that is to say, from the democratic point of view, it will not exist at all. And that practically is the state of the case at the present time.

Men—that is, the men that count—enter Parliament with an eye to a professional career. This career can only be obtained by leave of the small co-opted group which constitutes "the Government" and "the Official Opposition"—that is, those who, though not at the moment in receipt of public money, expect to receive it when a change of government shall take place. He knows very well that certain votes and speeches will hurt his chances of ever making any money in politics, while certain other votes and speeches will help him to do so. Naturally, like any other man pursuing his trade, he desires to ingratiate himself with his customer; and he speaks and votes accordingly. Add to this the fact that in England the Executive has the power at any moment of ordering a dissolution of Parliament, that Elections are very expensive, that only very rich men can afford to finance their own candidatures, that a vast secret fund exists to finance such candidatures, and that this fund is readily placed at the disposal of those—and of those only—

who are ready to act as the subservient retainers of the successful professionals, and you have an adequate explanation of the undemocratic character of English politics to-day.

I have already said that it is dubious whether we can ever dispense altogether with the Professional Politicians under ordinary conditions. But one thing is clear. If Politics are to remain a profession, that profession must in the public interest be most strictly safeguarded. That is to say, every temptation to which the politician may be subjected to act against the interest of those who employ him must be most carefully provided against; and any disposition on his part to prefer his private interests to his duty of obedience to the general will must be immediately and rigorously punished. It is to this end that I now propose to devote some consideration.

One necessity stands out manifest and incontrovertible. If politics are to be a Profession, *the profession of Executive Administrator must be kept strictly separate from the profession of Delegate to the Legislature.* If this is not so, the Legislature can never in the nature of things be really independent of the Executive, and can, therefore, never really act as an effective check upon it. Every member of the Legislature body will be on the lookout for the more profitable administrative posts. These posts will of necessity be in the gift of the Executive. They will necessarily be bestowed upon those of whose conduct the

Executive approves. The Executive will naturally approve of the conduct of those who do not oppose or even criticise it. Therefore there will be (as in fact there is to-day) an immense pressure upon members of the Representative Body not to act in a representative fashion, but rather to use all the power and influence they possess to support, not those who have elected them, but those from whom they expect benefits.

It is obvious that in any state of society some one or other must be intrusted with the business of practical executive administration. It is equally obvious that no man can reasonably be expected to take on such a task as a mere hobby. He must be paid for it; it must be his means of livelihood, in a word, his profession. To that there is, in the abstract, no more objection than there is to the profession of Doctor, House-Agent, or Butcher, provided always that the employer of such a man—*i. e.*, the Community—has as full a control over him as a man has over the tradesmen he employs. A butcher does not supply you with such meat as *he* may think will suit your health or personal efficiency, but with such meat as *you* demand. So long as the expert administrator confines himself to endeavouring to satisfy his clients as the butcher does and makes no pretence to an authority superior to that of his clients, he is harmless and may be exceedingly useful. It is impossible to deny that the details of administration in a modern state are so complex that the sheer routine work of administration does, and must, involve a degree of special knowledge to which the ordinary citizen cannot and would not choose to attain. So does the trade of a bootmaker. I cannot make a pair of boots. I have to ask a bootmaker to make them for me. But—and this is the essential point—I am the judge of the pair of boots when made: if they do not fit me I reject them and dismiss my bootmaker. I am in no way deterred from following this course by the assurance that the bootmaker is "an expert" or that he is "more advanced" than I, or by any other of the pretences by which oligarchy is being once more foisted upon the people.

The great problem, then, is that of the control of the necessary professional administrator by the General Will. It is, I admit, an exceedingly difficult problem, and for the present I can see no solution save the old expedient of a representative assembly—defective as I know that expedient to be. I have often wondered whether some one would not one day hit upon a method of extending to general politics the much more really democratic method of the Common Jury. I have often had a fancy, for example, for a Second Chamber constituted upon that principle—a name chosen by lot from the voting list of every constituency, attendance to be compulsory, and a reasonable and equal remuneration to be granted to every person compelled to attend. I am quite confident that such a chamber would represent the General Will a great deal better than either the House of Lords or the House of Commons has done in the past, and would make very short work (to the great satisfaction of the mass of the population) of much legislation that has passed with ease and with "the consent of all parties" through our present Parliament.

But I do not pretend to have any such scheme ready for practical advocacy; and so for the present we must rest content with the representative system, doing, at the same time, all that we can to prevent its abuse, to mitigate its inevitable failings, and, above all, to keep it continually controlled by the direct expression of the General Will.

Let us first draw as clear a distinction as we can between the inevitable defects of representation and the accidental evils to which it does make it quite intolerable in this country.

Take the latter first.

In England to-day representative government suffers from two prime evils. First, the representative assembly is not independent of the executive, and therefore cannot control it. Secondly, it is not freely chosen by the people, nor does it derive its effective mandate from the people; but its composition is selected and its programme devised by those very professional politicians upon whose actions it is supposed to exist as a check.

I have already adumbrated my view of the first necessary step in dealing with the former of the two evils. The members of the representative assembly should in no case whatsoever be allowed to become administrators paid by the Executive. Let them be paid, by all means, for the services they render as representatives to the people by the people whom they represent, and let the people who pay them see that they are really represented. But let them all be paid exactly alike, whether they support or oppose the Executive, and let there be a strict rule that no one shall within, say, ten years of sitting in the legislature receive public money in any form from the Executive. In that case, if commercial motives enter in any way into their calculations, they will find that their interest lies primarily in standing well with their constituents. Their constituents can deprive them of their salaries; the "Government" cannot. On the lowest motive, therefore, it will be better for them to please those who elect them than those whom they are elected to control.

What, then, will become of "the Ministry"? It will disappear. The professional head of a department—strictly excluded from the assembly—will remain. The popular assembly elected to control that permanent head will remain. Probably the assembly will find it convenient to divide itself into Committees for this purpose, though such Committees should have no more than investigatory and advisory powers. The decision must rest with the assembly itself. But the "Minister"—that is, the Professional Politician who has entered Parliament by pretending to represent some body of electors and has consented for a salary not to represent them, but to represent instead the Caucus that pays him—for him the new Democracy will have no use.

But when you have liberated the Representative Assembly from the control of that little group of Professional Politicians which is commonly called "The Government," but which I have always preferred to designate more accurately as "The Two Front Benches," you have not, therefore, necessarily made it really responsible to the people. That is, you have not achieved Democracy. It must be insisted upon again that, though the present political régime in England intensifies all the evils and dangers of Representative Government while depriving it of all its uses, yet there are evils, there are dangers which are not created by the régime, and which would not necessarily cease with the overthrow of that régime. They are found in America and elsewhere where that particular régime is unknown. They are inherent in the nature of Representative Institutions themselves. Every body of men cut off from the ordinary life of their fellow-citizens and vested with special powers tends, unless popularly controlled, to become an Oligarchy. We can see both in history and at the present time examples of assemblies internally free but irresponsible, and governing according to their own interests or prejudices, without regard to popular mandate. The Grand Council of Venice was such an assembly, and the

English House of Commons in the eighteenth century; to a certain extent the French Chamber is such to-day.

Against this peril the only real security is a vigilant and instructed popular opinion. With such an opinion always goes an extreme distrust of the representative, a feeling that he will always cheat you if he can, and a determination that he shall not be allowed to do so. Walt Whitman saw very far indeed into the truth when he set down as one of the conditions of his ideal State that the people should be "always ready to rise up against the never-ending audacity of Elected Persons."

The chief change needed, then, is, it must be admitted, a change in the popular psychology. Nevertheless, there are changes in machinery which would be the necessary accompaniments of such a change, and which may do a great deal to make it easier. And here I come to methods which the peculiar independence of the several States of the Union has already enabled America to put to the test, in certain cases, upon which an American writer may be better qualified to write than myself.

Chief among these is the re-creation of the electoral unit as a thing capable of political initiative. What I mean is this We say that Slocum sent Sir Josiah Gudge to Parliament to carry out a certain "programme." As a matter of fact, Slocum had nothing to do either with choosing Sir Josiah or with framing his programme. It could have nothing to do with either as things stand even if the special corruption incidental to the English political system was removed, for Slocum has no organised and articulate political existence. In a word, it has no initiative, and has to take its programme from Sir Josiah, and Sir Josiah from whatever Unknown Powers may have decreed his candidature. It is obvious that if we are to have democracy this state of things must be ended. Whatever body of men elect, our representatives must be organised for collective action, must be articulate, must be capable of framing their own demands, of choosing, controlling, and, if need be, punishing their servants.

I am inclined to think that it will eventually be found that a better system of representation can be obtained by representing men by their guilds or trades rather than by their localities. The geographical method of election really dates back to a time when small local units, still essentially in the phase of the Normal Social Life, had a natural homogeneity. They have no such homogeneity to-day. The State no longer consists of a collection of village communes; nor is the type of State the government of which we are here discussing conceived as being organised in such a fashion. But the State must always consist of groups of citizens co-operating for certain necessary social purposes, and it is to the Guilds, which will naturally, under a system of co-operative production, spring up throughout industrial worlds, that I should look to find the Electoral Unit of the future.

I do not wish to trespass upon the subject of industrial organisation, which is dealt with in this volume by other and abler pens; but it is so essential to Democracy that the Electing Body should be one with large powers of control over its own affairs that I should be very glad to see these Guilds invested with considerable powers of self-government under the general supervision of the National Executive. Of course, it would not do to give the coal-miners, for example, irresponsible control of the coal-fields. The coal-fields must be national property; on that we agree. But I do not see why all details of management, such matters as the hours of labour, provision against accident, and the like, should not be settled directly by the organised workers concerned. If such powers were vested in these Guilds, you would start with the immense advantage, from the democratic point of view, of an electing body accustomed to debate, to decisive action, and to the control of its own affairs, which would be able to thrash out the instructions to be given to its delegate, and to send him to the representative assembly with a real mandate derived from themselves.

Incidentally it should be remarked that such an infusion of reality into the operations of the electoral unit would go far to meet such cases as that of the United States, where the evils arise, not from the oligarchical control of a small clique, but rather from the omnipotence of a political Machine subject to no real popular control. And a further check upon the development of a two-party system in which there is no wider alternative than the chances of two candidates may, perhaps, be found in some such method of voting as Proportional Representation affords. Of course it is essential that the control of the Electing Body over the delegates should be absolute. Two checks on their action would greatly help to accomplish this.

The first check is the Recall. Not only should elections be reasonably frequent, but a certain proportion of the Electors should at any time have the right to demand a general poll on the question of whether the delegate was or was not carrying out the mandate of his constituents. Should the vote go against him, the delegate would have to resign, and another would be elected in his place. The mere threat of this action would probably be enough in most cases to prevent the delegate from shamelessly and continually violating his trust, as is so often done to-day.

The second check is the Referendum accompanied by the Initiative. How powerful a weapon even under the present degrading political conditions is the popular *plébiscite* may be perceived by noting the horror with which the Professional Politicians regard it, and the panic which seized them when one of their own number was imprudent enough to mention it a couple of years ago. But for the Referendum to be a really effective democratic weapon it must be capable of being put into force, not merely on the initiative of the legislature itself or on any section of it, but on the initiative of a fixed proportion of the Electors. Indeed, for my part, I am disposed to think that under the freer political system such as I have sketched no substantial alteration of the laws should be passed without a direct appeal to the popular will. To those who are incapable of looking beyond the corruptions and futilities of modern politics such a pronouncement will doubtless seem absurd. But we are presupposing that those corruptions and futilities are at an end; and when they are at an end there will be no need whatsoever for all this plethora of legislation which we have come to think of as something inevitable. When one comes to consider it in the abstract it is really rather absurd that a nation should have to keep some six hundred men busy for nine months in the year at the interminable task of continually altering its laws. If just laws can once be established, it is reasonable to suppose that for some considerable time at any rate they will prove adequate Doubtless from time to time some unforeseen change in economic or other conditions may necessitate modifications, but I do not look forward in the Great State to the unending legislation of our own time—a legislation which owes its necessity at best to the need for patching up a system in process of active decay, and at worst to the requirements of the Party "Programme" and, what is much more important, the Party War Chest   No doubt the change from the present basis of society to a juster and healthier one will mean a good deal of drastic law-making—and I suspect a good deal of law-breaking also—but, once the change accomplished, I should expect a vital alteration of the laws under which citizens are to live to be almost as rare a thing in the State of the Future as it was in the settled and happy communities of the past.

Such are a few of the comparatively rough and crude suggestions that I would make for the democratic organisation of the State of the future.   They pretend to be nothing more than an outline, and even as an outline they will doubtless require much modification.   Every democrat must feel a certain disinclination to lay down hard-and-fast conditions for the future, if only for this reason, that, if his democratic faith be genuine, he desires that the people should have, not the form of government *he* likes, but the form of government they themselves like.   That is what has always made me dislike answering detailed questions as to how this or that would be done "under Socialism."   I may have thought of a very ingenious answer, but it does not follow that it is the answer that my fellow-citizens will give.   And it is for them, not for me, to pronounce the ultimate decision.   *Securus judicat orbis terrarum.*

WOMEN IN THE GREAT STATE

BY CICELY HAMILTON

VIII

WOMEN IN THE GREAT STATE

In forecasting—or rather in making a tentative endeavour to forecast—the position of woman in the Great State, one wrestles from the outset with difficulties; whereof the first and most obstinate is the practical impossibility, under present conditions, of coming to a definite conclusion as to how far the traditional and still existing inferiority of woman—with its resultant dependence, mental and economic, upon the other sex—is the product of natural demands and forces, how far the artificial creation of the class distinctions of the Normal Social Life. That is to say, of a society which, for countless generations, has looked upon its female members merely as the breeding and love-making class—the wives or mistresses of its male members and the mothers of its children. It would be comparatively easy, of course, to launch out into a prophecy of inevitable improvement in the position of such a class, in the shape of amended conditions of wifehood and motherhood and so forth; but such considerations would leave the essential point untouched. Amended conditions and improve-

15

ments are bound to come; but whether, when they do come, they raise woman in general to a relatively higher level in the community than she occupies at present; whether, when they do come, they endow her with freedom, real as well as nominal, or leave her adorned and shackled with comfortable chains, is a question to which, at the present moment, it might be rash to return too absolute an answer. One has hopes, of course, encouraged by the obvious trend of the Woman's Movement of to-day towards independence—independence at any cost, mental, economic, and moral, as well as political; but aspirations equally fierce and far-reaching have been stifled before now, and may be stifled again, by the gift of material benefit. Equitable marriage and illegitimacy laws, for instance, the endowment of motherhood, and the prevention of sweating are quite compatible with continued masculine confusion of the terms "woman" and "wife," and with continued feminine acquiescence in such masculine confusion of ideas. A parasite is none the less a parasite because fed well, housed well, clothed well, and generally made much of.

If we suppose—as I think we are entitled to suppose—that the danger I have indicated is in the end surmounted, and that woman in the Great State is recognised as an individual with capacities apart from domesticity, love-making, and child-bearing, with an existence independent of husband, lover, or son, her position in the State will, as in the case of the male citizen, be determined by two factors—what the State has the right to demand of her, and what she, on her side, as individual and citizen, has the right and the energy, or power, to demand of the State. . . . What the State has the right to demand of her will be that she, like her father, her husband, her brother, shall conduct herself decently and in accordance with its laws. What it has not the right to demand of her—either directly or indirectly, by bribe or by indirect pressure—is that she, in return for its protection, shall consider herself under any obligation to produce its future citizens.

This distinction in the Great State must be made absolute, clear, and emphatic; since, without it, the position of woman, however improved materially, however safeguarded by law, will remain fundamentally unaltered and fundamentally unsound. Unaltered—and therefore, essentially undignified — because perpetuating the hoary but active tradition that woman does not count except as a wife and the mother of children; unsound, because artificially restricting her energies and possibilities by confining them to the channels of sexual attraction and reproduction of the race. Once admit such a principle into the conduct of any State, however great—the principle that women in general can deserve well of the social organism not directly as individuals, as workers and citizens, but only indirectly through their husbands and the children they bear them—and you reopen the door to all the abuses of the past: to the grossest forms of tyranny and sex dominance on the one side, and, on the other, to degradation spiritual as well as bodily.

It is to be hoped that the woman of the near future will have the power, as she will certainly have the right, to demand—in her own interest as in that of the community at large—that this distinction shall be made. (For instance, to take a concrete case, it is to be hoped that she will be energetic and clear-thinking enough to insist that such a needful and inevitable measure as the State Endowment of Motherhood shall not take the form of a bribe to bear children or an economic stimulus to her sexual instincts.) I may be wrong; but, as I see it, the future and progress not only of womanhood, but of the race in general, depends largely upon whether or no woman is able to insist that the satisfaction of her sexual instincts and the consequent bringing of her children into the world shall be an entirely voluntary—in other words, an entirely natural—proceeding on her part. Until the satisfaction of these instincts and the consequent bearing of children do become entirely voluntary, entirely natural; until no compulsion, social or economic, drives women into marriage or prostitution, it is practically useless to imagine that you can really and permanently raise the level of the mothers of the race. (And in this connection I

224

would remind those who still cling to the belief that we exist only for sexual attraction and motherhood that if they are correct in their estimate of the over-powering strength of our natural instincts, these natural instincts can surely be left to themselves— no additional or artificial stimulus being needed in order to induce us to fill our destiny.)

I may possibly be misunderstood when I say that the first duty of an enlightened community towards its women will be to secure to them the right to refuse marriage and motherhood; but I say it, and say it with emphasis. The common sense and civic view of marriage and motherhood is that in themselves, and, as far as the community is concerned, these natural relationships are neither good nor bad, desirable nor undesirable, moral nor immoral; that whether they are desirable or undesirable, moral or immoral, depends upon the kind of marriage and the quality of the parents and their offspring. Any system that encourages indiscriminate commercial marriage on the part of women—marriage for the sake of a home or breadwinner, marriage as the only alternative to the social stigma of spinsterhood, and the bearing of children for the same reasons—is to be deprecated and, in the Great State, will be deprecated as much in the interest of the child as of the mother. It is, of course, impossible to regulate the workings of human passion and attraction as you regulate the workings of a watch; men and women will mate for foolish, fleeting, and inadequate reasons as long as the world goes round. But it ought to be possible to insure that the social system should not, as it does at present, encourage marriage and child bearing from mean and inadequate, if entirely excusable motives; shall not, as it does at present, force its women into motherhood through the pressure of poverty or the insidious cruelty of closing to them every other avenue to activity and advancement. It ought to be possible for a sane and clearthinking society, by the simple process of securing to women alternative means of livelihood, alternative careers, to make of marriage for women what marriage for women never yet has been—a voluntary institution.

The entire question now at issue, not only between Woman and the State, but between Woman and Society in general, can be narrowed down to this: has she, like the other half of the race, a primary, individual, and responsible existence? or is she what may be called a secondary being—such value to the community as she possesses being derivative only and arising out of her family relations to other persons? Is she, in short, a personality, or merely the reproductive faculty personified? . . . So far—roughly speaking and allowing for a certain number of exceptions—she has counted in the world's history and progress in the secondary sense only; as the personification of the reproductive faculty, as wife, as mistress, and as mother of sons. It remains to be seen whether she is able to establish and maintain a right to count as an actual personality, an individual and direct member of the social organism. That right, once established, would bring with it inevitably the further right to select her own manner of living as freely as a man does; and to resent legislative or other attempts to induce her to support herself or serve the State in one particular fashion, legislative or other attempts to make the sacrifice of mother-hood anything but a purely voluntary sacrifice.

One realises the difficulties of so complete a change not only in the attitude of man to woman, but in the attitude of woman towards herself. Two of these difficulties at the present day loom promi-nently; the economic and the sentimental. The Great State, one takes it, would deal trenchantly with the first—the economic—difficulty; even its sourest spinster would not need to starve. But the stodgy mass of false sentiment on the subject of sexual relations and children that has come down to us through the ages—the glorification of mother-hood, however compulsory, however stupidly un-thinking—that is a more insidious and more deadly matter. It is through that stodgy mass of false sentiment that the woman of to-day and to-morrow has got to wade if she is ever to attain to anything like moral and intellectual equality with her brother and her mate. And be it noted that, in order to overcome false sentiment and false idealism, she must refuse most steadfastly to take advantage of it. If the Great or any other State is once permitted to look upon its women with a sentimental eye, the last condition of those women will be even as their first. Once more they will sink back into the class of wives and mothers, and found their claims to consideration solely upon their position as the breeding factor of the race; whereupon the Law, like the society from which it emanates, will pet them and kick them by turns. Once more they will slide back to the position of parasites living by sexual attraction and finding favour in the eyes of husband or lover on the express condition that they do not presume to compete with husband or lover in intellect.

It is not, I think, generally recognised how largely —one may hope entirely—the undoubtedly low level of intelligence in woman, as compared with man, is the direct result and product of dire economic necessity, the need for bread or the need for success in life. It has paid woman in the past—in some walks of life, notably marriage, it still pays them—to be stupid; intelligence in woman has been an obstacle to, not a qualification for, motherhood. The consciousness of superiority is a pleasant thing; and it is a sober fact that for countless generations the human male has taken real and active pleasure in despising the mental attainments of the human female; has insisted with emphasis that the wife of his bosom, the mother of his children, should be a creature he could look down upon as well as love. Standing in the position of capitalist—of employer in a compulsory trade—the average husband was able to dictate terms, to bargain for and obtain in his helpmeet the low level of intellectuality which he considered necessary to his comfort and self-esteem. With the bitter result for the human race that the mothers thereof have been, to a great extent, selected for their lack of wisdom and encouraged to be greater fools than nature intended to make them.

I have already taken it for granted that the State of the future will deal with this economic temptation to stupidity on the part of woman by assuring her bread and by opening to her other careers than marriage, many of them demanding the use of intelligence. Certainty of bread alone will not provide her with brains; but, by automatically removing the need to cultivate stupidity for a livelihood, it will place her in a position to make use of such brain as she possesses; with probable results of importance to herself as well as to the race.

It may possibly be urged that the placing of the average woman in a position of economic equality with himself would not necessarily remove the deep-seated desire of the average man to despise the partner of his joys and sorrows. Under present conditions it is impossible to speak with certainty on the point; and it may be, of course, that the said desire is instinctive and inherent rather than artificial and acquired. But, whether instinctive or acquired, there can be no doubt about its evil results on the race in general; and the duty of a far-sighted community is to control, as far as possible, such instincts as are dangerous to its health and progress by the provision of an adequate system of check and counter-balance. Human nature, unfortunately, tends to despise and take pleasure in subjecting its economic as well as its intellectual inferiors; thus, with the removal of general economic disability, it is more than possible that the masculine estimate of, and consideration for, woman will rise to a higher level. So far as I can make out there are few grounds for the supposition that the sex instinct in man is so faint as to run serious risk of extinction through loss of contempt for its object; but, even in the rather unlikely event of a considerable diminution in woman's power of sex attraction, society in general would have no right of complaint against her. On the contrary, society in general owes her a heavy debt for the sacrifice of all those qualities and pos-sibilities of her life which, according to its narrow judgment, interfered with her primary duty of attracting the opposite sex.

I have not the faintest doubt that the motive power underlying the present and growing revolt of woman against her traditional conditions of en-vironment is the strengthening consciousness of her own degradation—a degradation which is the direct result of her environment, the direct result of gen-erations of cramped intellectuality and concentra-tion of all powers of mind and body upon sexual attraction and child-bearing. The usual justifica-tion for a state of things which has resulted in the undesirable inferiority of woman to man, in mind as well as in body, is the welfare of the race. (In this connection one concludes that the word "race" is used to denote only the masculine half of the species.) The welfare of the race, we are given to understand, demands that a woman shall live only through and by her husband and her children; the sacrifice to them of all her other interests and energies is a sacrifice demanded of her by Nature in the interests of the species. . . . It is obvious that Nature does demand a sacrifice from the mothers of the race; the sacrifice of physical suffering; but, with regard to the other disabilities imposed upon her, there are two or three questions which woman is beginning to ask, and to which she has a right to demand plain answers. They run something like this:

How far has Society the right to increase the burden that Nature has laid on her?

How far has Society the right, hitherto exercised, to insist on a training and environment which encourages bodily weakness and moral and intellectual dependence in women?

Is it possible to enfeeble one-half of the race and leave the other half free to fulfil its destiny of progress, or does man born of woman have to share in the end the degradation he has allotted to others?

Roughly speaking, it is expediency that will answer in the end. If, in the long run, it be proved

that the race cannot get on without sacrificing in
the process the individuality and independence of
its women, without crushing them into one mould,
without confining their energies to one channel—
then in the long run the race will have to insist in
the future, as it has insisted in the past, on the dependence mental, moral, and physical, on the
virtual subjection of its women. If, on the other
hand, it be proved and realised — as the modern
feminist believes that it will be proved and realised
—that woman, as an integral part of the species,
cannot be brutalised and retarded in her personal
development without, in her turn, brutalising and
retarding Society in general; that the excessive
sacrifice demanded of her is not paid by herself
alone, but that her consequent inferiority reacts
upon the son of woman who desires and encourages it;
that the consistent policy of regarding her as nothing
but the breeding factor of the race has actually im-
paired her value as the breeding factor of the race—
then it will be manifestly the interest as well as the
duty of Society in general to reconsider its attitude
towards woman and seek not to increase but to allevi-
ate and counteract the burden of weakness laid on
her by Nature. If it be proved to the satisfaction of
Society that woman as a parasite condemned to live
by sexual attraction, by marriage and prostitution,
is a source, not of strength, but of weakness to the
State, not of strength, but of weakness to the race,
Society, as a matter of course, will do all in its

power to discourage parasitism and encourage independence in women. For the simple reason that, in casting up its accounts, it will have discovered how high a price it has paid for sex dominance, on one hand, and sex subjection, on the other—how high a price in blood and brain and money and hopeless confusion of issues.

Let me condense, then, into as few words as possible the root principles which I conceive will actuate the Great State in its endeavours to deal justly with women as a class.

1. Having recognised parasitism as an evil, the Great State will discourage that form of feminine parasitism which gains a livelihood through the exercise of sexual attraction. That is to say, it will render it unnecessary for any woman to earn her livelihood by means of her powers of sexual attraction.

2. Having recognised women as citizens and individuals—with a primary instead of secondary existence, a place in the world as well as in the house—the Great State will permit and encourage them to employ their energies and abilities in every direction in which they desire to employ such energies and abilities. That is to say, it will throw open to them every department of work at which they desire and can prove their fitness to occupy themselves; thereby insuring, so far as it is humanly possible to insure, that marriage shall not be made by women, and children brought into the world by

them, merely because there is nothing else for women to do but make marriages and bear children. The Great State, in short, will hold it better that a woman whose tastes do not lie in the direction of maternity should be a good spinster instead of an indifferent mother.

It may be urged that from my point of view the Great State is an institution for the promotion of the celibate life and the more or less rapid extinction of the race. To which I can only reply that marriage, as it affects one party to the contract—man— has existed for a considerable period of time as a purely voluntary institution, and that it does not appear to be any less popular with him on that account. I fail to see, therefore, why the modification of the compulsory character of the institution, as it affects the other party to the contract—woman —should make it any less popular with her. Unless, indeed, and in spite of all that has been sung and said and written about woman's love and need of motherhood, the sex instinct in us is so feeble a thing that it will only work on compulsion—the pressure of hunger, the lack of other occupation or interest. . . . If that should turn out to be the case, I admit with all frankness that I see no particular harm in leaving the sex and maternal instinct in woman to die out of its own feebleness, to perish in its own inertness; but, speaking personally, I see no reason to suppose that so the world's troubles will shortly be brought to end.

WOMEN IN THE GREAT STATE

If I refrain from prophecy concerning the particular direction in which the influence of women who have attained to complete recognition as citizens and individuals will make itself felt in the State of the future, it is, honestly, because I find such prophecy not merely difficult, but impossible. There are certain things it is fairly safe to say: as, for instance, that women in the main will always concern themselves intimately with such legislation as affects the conditions of motherhood and the health and education of children. But the point of view from which the absolutely free woman will approach legislation affecting the condition of motherhood and the health and education of children is a point of view at present non-existent, or, at best, only struggling into being. Enactments framed for the protection of workers at a compulsory trade—as marriage still is to a great extent, for women—will necessarily be very different in character from enactments framed to suit or improve the conditions of workers who have a wide field of occupation and livelihood to choose from. It is quite within the bounds of possibility that workers with a wide field of occupation and livelihood to choose from might be unable to see why conjugal affection should be interpreted as a desire to enter domestic service without wages. It is quite within the bounds of possibility that they might be unable to see any necessary connection between conjugal affection and domestic service, between the frying of bacon and the bearing of the future citizen; and that, regarding domestic service and conjugal affection as entirely separate departments of human life and effort, they would draw a sharp line of distinction and division between housekeeping and marital love. . . . The above is not intended as a prophecy; it is a suggestion merely, a simple example of an every-day problem which has not yet been approached by women sufficiently independent in mind and in pocket to attempt their own solution of it. It may be that, when such women do attempt it, their solution thereof will be the present, or masculine, solution; but, on the other hand, it may not. . . . The only thing we know with certainty concerning the attitude of the human race towards housework is that men dislike it. Women, if asked, might be of the same opinion. So far they have not been asked.

In the same way we can surmise with safety that the present terms of the contract of marriage will undergo considerable modification; but it would be rash to attempt an indication of the precise nature of such modification. A bargain struck between economic and social equals who desire to unite their lives will, of necessity, be an entirely different affair from a bargain struck, as at present, between a member of a superior male class and a member of an inferior female class. Further, the requirements of a woman who merely desires a husband will differ to a considerable extent from the requirements of the woman who is endeavouring to secure not only a

husband, but a means of livelihood, a home or a
refuge from the despised estate of spinsterhood.
For both parties to the contract the situation will
be simplified enormously; between them will lie
the clear issue—under present conditions obscured—
of mating and the rearing of children. . . . There
will be a foundation to build upon; rock-bottom
to work from.

If I have expressed my meaning with any degree
of clearness it will be understood that I consider the
best service the Great State can render to its women
will be to allow them to find their own level. That
is to say, to allow them to discover by means of
education and experiment the precise point at which
the real disabilities imposed on them by Nature can
be distinguished from the traditional and artificial
disabilities imposed on them by Society. And in
this connection nothing should be assumed, nothing
should be taken for granted.

It should not be assumed, for instance, that
because a woman has married a husband and borne
him children her entire existence—her hopes and
her pleasures and ambitions—are bound up in wifehood and maternity. Any more than it should be
assumed that a wife and mother has an unaccount-
able, instinctive preference for forms of labour
heartily disliked by other persons; forms of labour
which bring her in neither personal advancement
nor monetary reward. It should not be assumed

16   237

that the longing for and love of children exists in every woman; it should not be assumed that it is unnatural or abnormal for a woman to vary from the accepted type. It should not be assumed that woman is a childlike barbarian guided only by her instincts, by the promptings of sex and maternity. . . . All these assumptions, of course, may be perfectly correct; but, under present conditions and without experience and experiment, I maintain that we have no right to regard them as anything but speculative guesses. Under present, and still more under past conditions all these assumptions, these speculative guesses, have not only been acted upon by the masculine half of humanity, but instilled, from its infancy upwards, into the feminine half of the race. With the result that a good many of us are in the humiliating position of not knowing what it is we want. All we do know is that, for some mysterious reason, we don't want the things we are told we ought to want, don't like the things we are told we ought to like. . . . And the Great State will have to give us leave to find ourselves.

It is possible that the process of finding ourselves may take time. We have the accumulation of generations of artificiality to throw off—of artificially induced virtues as well as of artificially induced vices. Submission and humility are not always compatible with self-respect; complete absorption in the life of another with progress in "fine thinking." "Love and fine thinking," one takes it, will not always be demanded, as now, in separate consignments from the separate sexes. The woman's point of view will be asked for, not snubbed out of existence, by the social organism of the future; hence, the woman will have to fight her way to a point of view essentially her own.

That she will hate doing so goes without saying. In all ages man, in the mass, has hated the trouble of thinking, has paid, implored others to do his thinking for him: and it has never been enjoined upon man, as it has upon woman, in the mass, that he had no need to think, that ignorance was another name for virtue. So much and so often has stupidity been enjoined upon us, and so completely have we obeyed the injunction, that out of our compliance there has grown up the legend that nature has designed us as creatures incapable of connected thought. It is said and believed of us that the mental processes by which we arrive at conclusions are essentially and radically different from the mental processes whereby the same conclusions are arrived at by our men-folk; that, in short, we are instinctive —or, as it is more courteously called, intuitive—not reasoning beings.

The legend has this truth in it that, in deference to the wishes of our men-folk, we have made small use of our reason. . . . And, that being so, fine thinking may not come easy to us.

One of the essential differences between the attitude of the Great State towards its women and the corresponding attitude of the Normal Social Life will be that the former will permit and encourage variety, where the other has insisted on uniformity of type. So far the atmosphere of the social organism has been favourable to the production of but two species of woman: the wife and mother, and her equivalent outside the law. Custom and education alike were strenuous and unceasing in their efforts to run all womanhood into the same mould, to make all womanhood conform to the same standard of domesticity and charm. (It is, by the way, really pitiful to think of the amount of energy wasted th ough the ages and still wasted by countless women in the vain endeavour to make themselves what Nature never intended them to be—charming.) Any variation from the above type has usually been received with anything but a sympathetic welcome; on the contrary, its customary greeting was a derisive hoot. Woman, in fact, until our own times has been judged, measured, and condemned by a prehistoric standard requiring of her uniformity of temperament, taste, and attainment, a standard which has not been applied to man since the days when the entire male population of the earth earned its meat by the only trade it knew—the chase. It is a curious proof of persistent masculine failure to recognise in woman a humanity as complete as his own, this absolute refusal of man (while himself progressing along the lines of differentiation marked out for him by Nature, becoming agriculturist and

240

townsman and a thousand things besides) to perceive in his partner and dependant any fitness or capacity save fitness and capacity for the two occupations of sexual attraction and homekeeping. Had he ever realised that his partner and dependant was indeed as human and complete as himself, it would surely have been borne in upon him that nature and civilisation would work in her humanity after much the same fashion as they worked in his—by the production of numerous variations from an original uniform type. Instead, therefore, of assuming that all variations from the accepted idea of woman were unnatural, freakish, and out of place in the scheme of Nature, he would have realised that the really unnatural and abnormal feature about womanhood in general was its unfortunate lack of such variation, the artificially unhealthy uniformity of type produced by generations of economic pressure and restriction of opportunity. After all, it is only when the normal number of variations from the type are permitted to appear that you can say with certainty what the type really is and to what extent particular qualities are essentially characteristic of it.

There are, it seems to me, good grounds for believing that the common basis of human character is very much wider than has hitherto been supposed. Given the same influence and environment, the customary difference between the desires and behaviour of the sexes lessens perceptibly, swiftly, and automatically, thereby often proving itself to be more customary than natural. Warfare, for instance, has seldom been looked upon as a feminine business; on the contrary woman has usually been shielded from contact with actual bloodshed. Yet, over and over again, when brought into contact with actual bloodshed woman has proved that such contact acts upon her in much the same fashion as it does upon man; that the hardships of a siege or the fury of hand-to-hand fighting produce in her symptoms of wrath, desperation, and hatred which are in no way essentially different from the corresponding symptoms in her brethren. Again, it has been assumed that the power of combination for a common purpose is a characteristic essentially male; those who took the assumption for granted forgetting that it was the military tradition—the need for standing together in the face of a common enemy—that first taught combination to men. The political tradition was but the same lesson repeated in other terms—a lesson for men only; and so was the male industrial system, the habit of working together in numbers. . . . Only on comparatively rare occasions in the history of the world has warfare or political activity entered directly into the lives of women except in so far as they suffered or advantaged passively from the effects of both. While the home industries at which for centuries the great majority of women were accustomed to earn their keep, if little else—brewing, baking, spinning, child-tending, domestic labour of every sort and kind—were, in the very nature of things, isolated industries, carried on in separate households on a small scale and without co-operation or combination. The home industry kept its workers apart; it did not bring cooks, housewives, nurses, and weavers together in their tens and their hundreds and unite them by the tie of a common interest in their common labour. It was not until many of these isolated industries began to dwindle and vanish with the general introduction of machinery and consequent reorganisation and centralisation of the means of production; not until the home ceased to be a self - supporting institution and became merely a place to dwell in, that women began to learn, outside the home, the lesson of combination they had never learned inside it. When the weaving trade, the spinning trade, the brewing trade, the pickling trade, and half a dozen others had removed themselves bodily from the kitchen or parlour to the factory, drawing after them inevitably the workers who depended on those trades for a living, then, practically for the first time, women were steadily and systematically thrown together in large numbers, with the tie of a common work between them, with similar aims and hardships, and similar causes of resentment.

When we remember how very recent is the introduction of women to the organised collective life of the community, it seems remarkable that they have so quickly responded to its appeal and assimilated its influence. Collective labour outside the narrow confines of the home is already working upon them exactly as it has worked upon their brothers; informing them with the spirit and power of combination and a sense of class, as distinct from individual and family, need. The insistent and growing demand of women for a share in political power is the direct and inevitable result of the revolution in industrial conditions which has driven them out of the isolation of their homes to earn their bread and rub shoulders with others in the process.

To take another instance of a human quality hitherto considered masculine: not the least interesting feature of the Woman Suffrage movement in England is the fact that the excitement of political struggle has produced in a certain type of healthy young woman exactly the effect which it often produces in a similar type of healthy young man—the excited mental condition which expresses itself in acts of rowdyism. I would not be understood to mean that all the women who, of late years, have taken part in what are known as militant suffrage demonstrations belong to the rowdy type; on the contrary, I should say that the proportion was small indeed compared with the numbers of those who are actuated by a sense of duty, self-sacrifice, and loyalty. But no one who has mingled observantly with the demonstrators can doubt that the rowdy type amongst women exists—the girl who, like her

244

brother, is at the same time thrilled and amused by the idea of actual conflict and whose high spirits find natural vent in noise and vehement action, usually destructive. I see no reason why the fact should be denied: first, because it is a fact; secondly, because it does not seem to me a fact to be greatly ashamed of. A touch of rowdyism has always been taken for granted in the youthful human male; the militant suffrage movement has shown us that we must henceforth take it for granted in the youthful human female—and thereby demonstrated that a characteristic hitherto deemed the peculiar property of the male was only awaiting an opportunity to reveal itself as the common possession of both sexes.

If I am right in supposing that the present undoubted superiority of man over woman is less a sex than a class superiority, and that the essential differences between naturally developed man and naturally developed woman are fewer than is commonly supposed, it follows that those legislative enactments in the State of the future which affect women as a class apart will be comparatively few in number. Motherhood, of course, will always place a woman in a class apart for a certain length of time, a class demanding special provision and undertaking special responsibilities. But in dealing with women in general the State of the future will be mindful of the fact that it is dealing with a class whose interests are varied and multiple; it will not assume that all the members of that class are or ought to be in a perpetual condition of pregnancy, and try to regulate their existence accordingly.

It is, of course, one thing to give freedom; it is quite another to induce the recipients of freedom to make use of it. I believe that the conscience of Society will insist in the very near future that woman shall be granted every opportunity of proving herself the equal of her brother in fact as well as in name; it will rest with herself, therefore, whether she takes full advantage of such opportunity. The real difficulty in her way, I take it, will be at first the weakness and instability of purpose common to every class that has been accustomed to exist without personal responsibility and need for independent thinking. It is because they have been composed of such a class that newly enfranchised democracies have so often proved lacking in intelligent capacity for self-government. They have failed because they were stupid; because the enlightened democracy has so far scarcely existed outside an election address.

As I have pointed out, no other section of the community has been encouraged to be stupid to the same extent as women. No influence could have been better calculated to weaken moral fibre in a human being than the long-accepted tradition—accepted even by herself—that woman apart from man was a creature half alive; that, as the cant phrase goes, she was "incomplete." You cannot expect independence of judgment and sense of responsibility

246

from a being to whom you deny the elementary right and fact of separate, independent existence.

Women, one imagines, will attain to liberty of thought and action in much the same way as other subjugated classes have attained and are attaining it—by degrees more or less slow, and after passing through what seems to be the inevitable process of revolting against one tyranny only to put another in its place. In those long habituated to submission and control the habit of dependence is, as a rule, too deeply rooted to be swept away by the first uprush of the desire for freedom; and, having overthrown one idol, decrepit and despised, they are as apt as not to set a new one in its place—one rigid dogma for another, a new narrow loyalty in place of an old blind one, a sovereign people in place of a sovereign lord. . . . Watching the process of seemingly retrograde stumbling, the hearts of many who desired freedom for others as well as for themselves have grown sick even to despair of their ideal. A despair not justified, save in the case of those who have never revolted at all. For the habit of revolt against injustice grows, like other habits, by the exercise thereof; so that those who have overthrown one despotism, material or spiritual, will, in the end, remember a precedent and turn on the oppressor themselves have set up in its stead. It is the first forward step, the precedent for revolt, in a subject class that counts; since what has been done before can always be done again.

THE ARTIST IN THE GREAT STATE

BY ROGER FRY

IX

THE ARTIST IN THE GREAT STATE

I AM not a Socialist, as I understand that word, nor
can I pretend to have worked out those complex estimates of economic possibility which are needed before
one can indorse the hopeful forecasts of Lady Warwick,
Mr. Money, and Mr. Wells. What I propose to do
here is first to discuss what effect plutocracy, such as
it is to-day, has had of late, and is likely to have in
the near future, upon one of the things which I should
like to imagine continuing upon our planet—namely,
art. And then briefly to prognosticate its chances
under such a régime as my colleagues have sketched.

As I understand it, art is one of the chief organs of
what, for want of a better word, I must call the
spiritual life. It both stimulates and controls those
indefinable overtones of the material life of man
which all of us at moments feel to have a quality
of permanence and reality that does not belong to
the rest of our experience. Nature demands with
no uncertain voice that the physical needs of the
body shall be satisfied first; but we feel that our real
human life only begins at the point where that is
accomplished, that the man who works at some

uncreative and uncongenial toil merely to earn enough food to enable him to continue to work has not, properly speaking, a human life at all.

It is the argument of commercialism, as it once was of aristocracy, that the accumulation of surplus wealth in a few hands enables this spiritual life to maintain its existence, that no really valuable or useless work (for from this point of view only useless work has value) could exist in the community without such accumulations of wealth. The argument has been employed for the disinterested work of scientific research. A doctor of naturally liberal and generous impulses told me that he was becoming a reactionary simply because he feared that public bodies would never give the money necessary for research with anything like the same generosity as is now shown by the great plutocrats. But Sir Ray Lankester does not find that generosity sufficient, and is prepared at least to consider a State more ample-spirited.

The situation as regards art and as regards the disinterested love of truth is so similar that we might expect this argument in favour of a plutocratic social order to hold equally well for both art and science, and that the artist would be a fervent upholder of the present system. As a matter of fact, the more representative artists have rarely been such, and not a few, though working their life long for the plutocracy, have been vehement Socialists.

Despairing of the conditions due to modern commercialism, it is not unnatural that lovers of beauty should look back with nostalgia to the age when society was controlled by a landed aristocracy. I believe, however, that from the point of view of the encouragement of great creative art there is not much difference between an aristocracy and a plutocracy. The aristocrat usually had taste, the plutocrat frequently has not. Now taste is of two kinds, the first consisting in the negative avoidance of all that is ill-considered and discordant, the other positive and a by-product; it is that harmony which always results from the expression of intense and disinterested emotion. The aristocrat, by means of his good taste of the negative kind, was able to come to terms with the artist; the plutocrat has not. But both alike desire to buy something which is incommensurate with money. Both want art to be a background to their radiant self-consciousness. They want to buy beauty as they want to buy love; and the painter, picture-dealer, and the pander try perennially to persuade them that it is possible. But living beauty cannot be bought; it must be won. I have said that the aristocrat, by his taste, by his feeling for the accidentals of beauty, did manage to get on to some kind of terms with the artist. Hence the art of the eighteenth century, an art that is prone before the distinguished patron, subtly and deliciously flattering and yet always fine. In contrast to that the art of the nineteenth century is coarse, turbulent, clumsy. It marks the beginning of a revolt. The artist just managed to let himself be coaxed and cajoled by the aristocrat, but when the aristocratic was succeeded by the plutocratic patron with less conciliatory manners and no taste, the artist rebelled; and the history of art in the nineteenth century is the history of a band of heroic Ishmaelites, with no secure place in the social system, with nothing to support them in the unequal struggle but a dim sense of a new idea, the idea of the freedom of art from all trammels and tyrannies.

The place that the artists left vacant at the plutocrat's table had to be filled, and it was filled by a race new in the history of the world, a race for whom no name has yet been found, a race of pseudo-artists. As the prostitute professes to sell love, so these gentlemen professed to sell beauty, and they and their patrons rollicked good-humouredly through the Victorian era. They adopted the name and something of the manner of artists; they intercepted not only the money, but the titles and fame and glory which were intended for those whom they had supplanted. But, while they were yet feasting, there came an event which seemed at the time of no importance, but which was destined to change ultimately the face of things, the exhibition of ancient art at Manchester in 1857. And with this came Ruskin's address on the Political Economy of Art, a work which surprises by its prophetic foresight when we read it half a century later. These two things were the Mene Tekel of the orgy of Victorian Philistinism. The plutocrat saw through the deception; it was not beauty the pseudo-artist sold him, any more than it was love which the prostitute gave. He turned from it in disgust and decided that the only beauty he could buy was the dead beauty of the past. Thereupon set in the worship of *patine* and the age of forgery and the detection of forgery. I once remarked to a rich man that a statue by Rodin might be worthy even of his collection. He replied, "Show me a Rodin with the *patine* of the fifteenth century, and I will buy it."

Patine, then, the adventitious material beauty which age alone can give, has come to be the object of a reverence greater than that devoted to the idea which is enshrined within the work of art. People are right to admire *patine*. Nothing is more beautiful than gilded bronze of which time has taken toll until it is nothing but a faded shimmering splendour over depths of inscrutable gloom; nothing finer than the dull glow which Pentelic marble has gathered from past centuries of sunlight and warm Mediterranean breezes. *Patine* is good, but it is a surface charm added to the essential beauty of expression; its beauty is literally skin-deep. It can never come into being or exist in or for itself; no *patine* can make a bad work good, or the forgers would be justified. It is an adjectival and ancillary beauty scarcely worthy of our prolonged contemplation.

There is to the philosopher something pathetic

in the Plutocrat's worship of *patine*. It is, as it were, a compensation for his own want of it. On himself all the rough thumb and chisel marks of his maker—and he is self-made—stand as yet unpolished and raw; but his furniture, at least, shall have the distinction of age-long acquaintance with good manners.

But the net result of all this is that the artist has nothing to hope from the Plutocrat. To him we must be grateful indeed for that brusque disillusionment of the real artist, the real artist who might have rubbed along uneasily for yet another century with his predecessor, the aristocrat. Let us be grateful to him for this; but we need not look to him for further benefits, and if we decide to keep him the artist must be content to be paid after he is dead and vicariously in the person of an art-dealer. The artist must be content to look on while sums are given for dead beauty, the tenth part of which, properly directed, would irrigate whole nations and stimulate once more the production of vital artistic expression.

I would not wish to appear to blame the plutocrat. He has often honestly done his best for art; the trouble is not of his making more than of the artist's, and the misunderstanding between art and commerce is bound to be complete. The artist, however mean and avaricious he may appear, knows that he cannot really sell himself for money any more than the philosopher or the scientific investigator can sell himself for money. He takes money in the hope

that he may secure the opportunity for the free func-
tioning of his creative power. If the patron could
give him that instead of money he would bless him;
but he cannot, and so he tries to get him to work not
quite freely for money; and in revenge the artist
indulges in all manner of insolences, even perhaps in
sharp practices, which make the patron feel, with
some justification, that he is the victim of ingrati-
tude and wanton caprice. It is impossible that the
artist should work for the plutocrat; he must work
for himself, because it is only by so doing that he
can perform the function for which he exists; it is
only by working for himself that he can work for
mankind.

If, then, the particular kind of accumulation of
surplus wealth which we call plutocracy has failed,
as surely it has signally failed, to stimulate the
creative power of the imagination, what disposition
of wealth might be conceived that would succeed
better? First of all, a greater distribution of
wealth, with a lower standard of ostentation, would,
I think, do a great deal to improve things without
any great change in other conditions. It is not
enough known that the patronage which really
counts to-day is exercised by quite small and humble people. These people with a few hundreds a
year exercise a genuine patronage by buying pictures
at ten, twenty, or occasionally thirty pounds, with
real insight and understanding, thereby enabling the
young Ishmaelite to live and function from the age

of twenty to thirty or so, when perhaps he becomes known to richer buyers, those experienced spenders of money who are always more cautious, more anxious to buy an investment than a picture. These poor, intelligent first patrons to whom I allude belong mainly to the professional classes; they have none of the pretensions of the plutocrat and none of his ambitions. The work of art is not for them, as for him, a decorative backcloth to his stage, but an idol and an inspiration. Merely to increase the number and potency of these people would already accomplish much; and this is to be noticed, that if wealth were more evenly distributed, if no one had a great deal of wealth, those who really cared for art would become the sole patrons, since for all it would be an appreciable sacrifice, and for none an impossibility. The man who only buys pictures when he has as many motor-cars as he can conceivably want would drop out as a patron altogether.

But even this would only foster the minor and private arts; and what the history of art definitely elucidates is that the greatest art has always been communal, the expression—in highly individualised ways, no doubt—of common aspirations and ideals.

Let us suppose, then, that society were so arranged that considerable surplus wealth lay in the hands of public bodies, both national and local; can we have any reasonable hope that they would show more skill in carrying out the delicate task of stimulating and using the creative power of the artist?

THE ARTIST IN THE GREAT STATE

The immediate prospect is certainly not encouraging. Nothing, for instance, is more deplorable than to watch the patronage of our provincial museums. The gentlemen who administer these public funds naturally have not realised so acutely as private buyers the lesson so admirably taught at Christie's, that pseudo or Royal-Academic art is a bad investment. Nor is it better if we turn to national patronage. In Great Britain, at least, we cannot get a postage stamp or a penny even respectably designed, much less a public monument. Indeed, the tradition that all public British art shall be crassly mediocre and inexpressive is so firmly rooted that it seems to have almost the prestige of constitutional precedent. Nor will any one who has watched a committee commissioning a presentation portrait, or even buying an old master, be in danger of taking too optimistic a view. With rare and shining exceptions, committees seem to be at the mercy of the lowest common denominator of their individual natures, which is dominated by fear of criticism; and fear and its attendant, compromise, are bad masters of the arts.

Speaking recently at Liverpool, Mr. Bernard Shaw placed the present situation as regards public art in its true light. He declared that the corruption of taste and the emotional insincerity of the mass of the people had gone so far that any picture which pleased more than ten per cent. of the population should be immediately burned. . . .

This, then, is the fundamental fact we have to face. And it is this that gives us pause when we try to construct any conceivable system of public patronage.

For the modern artist puts the question of any socialistic—or, indeed, of any completely ordered—state in its acutest form. He demands as an essential to the proper use of his powers a freedom from restraint such as no other workman expects. He must work when he feels inclined; he cannot work to order. Hence his frequent quarrels with the burgher who knows he has to work when he is disinclined, and cannot conceive why the artist should not do likewise. The burgher watches the artist's wayward and apparently quite unmethodical activity, and envies his job. Now in any Socialistic State, if certain men are licensed to pursue the artistic calling, they are likely to be regarded by the other workers with some envy. There may be a competition for such soft jobs among those who are naturally work-shy, since it will be evident that the artist is not called to account in the same way as other workers.

If we suppose, as seems not unlikely, in view of the immense numbers who become artists in our present social state, that there would be this competition for the artistic work of the community, what methods would be devised to select those required to fill the coveted posts? Frankly, the history of art in the nineteenth century makes us shudder at the results that would follow. One scarcely knows whether they would be worse if Bumble or the academy were judge. We only know that under any such conditions *none* of the artists whose work has ultimately counted in the spiritual development of the race would have been allowed to practise the coveted profession.

There is in truth, as Ruskin pointed out in his *Political Economy of Art*, a gross and wanton waste under the present system. We have thousands of artists who are only so by accident and by name, on the one hand, and certainly many—one cannot tell how many—who have the special gift but have never had the peculiar opportunities which are to-day necessary to allow it to expand and function. But there is, what in an odd way consoles us, a blind chance that the gift and the opportunity may coincide; that Shelley and Browning may have a competence, and Cézanne a farm-house he could retire to. Bureaucratic Socialism would, it seems, take away even this blind chance that mankind may benefit by its least appreciable, most elusive treasures, and would carefully organise the complete suppression of original creative power; would organise into a universal and all-embracing tyranny the already overweening and disastrous power of endowed official art. For we must face the fact that the average man has two qualities which would make the proper selection of the artist almost impossible. He has, first of all, a touching proclivity to awe-struck admiration of whatever is presented to him as noble by a constituted authority; and, secondly, a complete absence of any immediate reaction to a work of art until his judgment has thus been hypnotised by the voice of authority. Then, and not till then, he sees, or swears he sees, those adorable Emperor's clothes that he is always agape for.

I am speaking, of course, of present conditions, of a populace whose emotional life has been drugged by the sugared poison of pseudo-art, a populace saturated with snobbishness, and regarding art chiefly for its value as a symbol of social distinctions. There have been times when such a system of public patronage as we are discussing might not have been altogether disastrous. Times when the guilds represented more or less adequately the genuine artistic intelligence of the time; but the creation, first of all, of aristocratic art, and finally of pseudo-art, have brought it about that almost any officially organised system would at the present moment stereotype all the worst features of modern art.

Now, in thus putting forward the extreme difficulties of any system of publicly controlled art, we are emphasising perhaps too much the idea of the artist as a creator of purely ideal and abstract works, as the medium of inspiration and the source of revelation. It is the artist as prophet and priest that we have been considering, the artist who is the articulate soul of mankind. Now in the present commercial State, at a time when such handiwork as is not admirably fitted to some purely utilitarian purpose has become inanely fatuous and grotesque, the artist in this sense has undoubtedly become of supreme importance as a protestant, as one who proclaims that art is a reasonable function, and one that proceeds by a nice adjustment of means to ends. But if we suppose a state in which all the ordinary objects of daily life—our chairs and tables, our carpets and pottery—expressed something of this reasonableness instead of a crazy and vapid fantasy, the artist as a pure creator might become, not indeed of less importance—rather more—but a less acute necessity to our general living than he is to-day. Something of the sanity and purposefulness of his attitude might conceivably become infused into the work of the ordinary craftsman, something, too, of his creative energy and delight in work. We must, therefore, turn for a moment from the abstractly creative artist to the applied arts and those who practise them.

We are so far obliged to protect ourselves from the implications of modern life that without a special effort it is hard to conceive the enormous quantity of "art" that is annually produced and consumed. For the special purpose of realising it I take the pains to write the succeeding paragraphs in a railway refreshment-room, where I am actually looking at those terribly familiar but fortunately fleeting images which such places afford. And one must remember that public places of this kind merely reflect the average citizen's soul, as expressed in his home.

The space my eye travels over is a small one, but I am appalled at the amount of "art" that it harbours. The window towards which I look is filled in its lower part by stained glass; within a highly elaborate border, designed by some one who knew the conventions of thirteenth-century glass, is a pattern of yellow and purple vine leaves with bunches of grapes, and flitting about among these many small birds. In front is a lace curtain with patterns taken from at least four centuries and as many countries. On the walls, up to a height of four feet, is a covering of lincrusta walton stamped with a complicated pattern in two colours, with sham silver medallions. Above that a moulding but an inch wide, and yet creeping throughout its whole with a degenerate descendant of a Græco-Roman carved guilloche pattern; this has evidently been cut out of the wood by machine or stamped out of some composition—its nature is so perfectly concealed that it is hard to say which. Above this is a wall-paper in which an effect of eighteenth-century satin brocade is imitated by shaded staining of the paper. Each of the little refreshment-tables has two cloths, one arranged symmetrically with the table, the other a highly ornate printed cotton arranged "artistically" in a diagonal position. In the centre of each table is a large pot in which every beautiful quality in the material and making of pots has been carefully obliterated by methods each of which implies profound scientific knowledge and great inventive talent. Within each pot is a plant with large dark-green leaves, apparently made of india-rubber. This painful catalogue makes up only a small part of the inventory of the "art" of the restaurant. If I were to go on to tell of the legs of the tables, of the electric-light fittings, of the chairs into the wooden seats of which some tremendous mechanical force has deeply impressed a large distorted anthemion—if I were to tell of all these things, my reader and I might both begin to realise with painful acuteness something of the horrible toil involved in all this display. Display is indeed the end and explanation of it all. Not one of these things has been made because the maker enjoyed the making; not one has been bought because its contemplation would give any one any pleasure, but solely because each of these things is accepted as a symbol of a particular social status. I say their contemplation can give no one pleasure; they are there because their absence would be resented by the average man who regards a large amount of futile display as in some way inseparable from the conditions of that well-to-do life to which he belongs or aspires to belong. If everything were merely clean and serviceable he would proclaim the place bare and uncomfortable.

The doctor who lines his waiting-room with bad photogravures and worse etchings is acting on exactly the same principle; in short, nearly all our "art" is made, bought, and sold merely for its value as an indication of social status.

Now consider the case of those men whose life-work it is to stimulate this eczematous eruption of pattern on the surface of modern manufactures. They are by far the most numerous "artists" in the country. Each of them has not only learned to draw but has learned by sheer application to put forms together with a similitude of that coherence which creative impulse gives. Probably each of them has somewhere within him something of that creative impulse which is the inspiration and delight of every savage and primitive craftsman: but in these manufacturer's designers the pressure of commercial life has crushed and atrophied that creative impulse completely. Their business is to produce, not expressive design, but dead patterns. They are compelled, therefore, to spend their lives behaving in an entirely idiotic and senseless manner, and that with the certainty that no one will ever get positive pleasure from the result; for one may safely risk the statement that until I made the effort just now, no one of the thousands who use the refreshment-rooms ever really *looked* at the designs.

Now what effect would the development of the Great State which this book anticipates have upon all this? First, I suppose that the fact that every one had to work might produce a new reverence, especially in the governing body, for work, a new sense of disgust and horror at wasteful and purposeless work. Mr. Money has written of waste of work; here in unwanted pseudo-art is another colossal waste. Add to this ideal of economy in work the presumption that the workers in every craft would be more thoroughly organised and would have a more decisive voice in the nature and quality of their productions. Under the present system of commercialism the one object, and the complete justification, of producing any article is, that it can be made either by its intrinsic value, or by the fictitious value put upon it by advertisement, to sell with a sufficient profit to the manufacturer. In any socialistic state, I imagine—and to a large extent the Great State will be socialistic at least—there would not be this same automatic justification for manufacture; people would not be induced artificially to buy what they did not want, and in this way a more genuine scale of values would be developed. Moreover, the workman would be in a better position to say how things should be made. After years of a purely commercial standard, there is even now, in the average workman, left a certain bias in favour of sound and reasonable workmanship as opposed to the ingenious manufacture of fatuous and fraudulent objects; and, if we suppose the immediate pressure of sheer necessity to be removed, it is probable that the craftsman, acting through his guild organisations, would determine to some extent the methods of manufacture. Guilds might, indeed, regain something of the political influence that gave us the Gothic cathedrals of the Middle Ages. It is quite probable that this guild influence would act as a check on some innovations in manufacture which, though bringing in a profit, are really disastrous to the community at large. Of such a nature are all the so-called improvements whereby decoration, the whole value of which consists in its expressive power, is multiplied indefinitely by machinery. When once the question of the desirability of any and every production came to be discussed, as it would be in the Great State, it would inevitably follow that some reasonable and scientific classifications would be undertaken with regard to machinery. That is to say, it would be considered in what process and to what degree machinery ought to replace handi-work, both from the point of view of the community as a whole and from that of the producer. So far as I know, this has never been undertaken even with regard to mere economy, no one having calculated with precision how far the longer life of certain hand-made articles does not more than compensate for increased cost of production. And I suppose that in the Great State other things besides mere economy would come into the calculation. The Great State will live, not hoard.

It is probable that in many directions we should extend mechanical operations immensely, that such things as the actual construction of buildings, the mere laying and placing of the walls might become increasingly mechanical. Such methods, if confined to purely structural elements, are capable of beauty of a special kind, since they can express the ordered ideas of proportion, balance, and interval as conceived by the creative mind of the architect. But in process of time one might hope to see a sharp line of division between work of this kind and such purely expressive and non-utilitarian design as we call ornament; and it would be felt clearly that into this field no mechanical device should intrude, that, while ornament might be dispensed with, it could never be imitated, since its only reason for being is that it conveys the vital expressive power of a human mind acting constantly and directly upon material forms.

Finally, I suppose that in the Great State we might hope to see such a considerable levelling of social conditions that the false values put upon art by its symbolising of social status would be largely destroyed and, the pressure of mere opinion being relieved, people would develop some more immediate reaction to the work of art than they can at present achieve.

Supposing, then, that under the Great State it was found impossible, at all events at first, to stimulate and organise the abstract creative power of the pure artist, the balance might after all be in favour of the new order if the whole practice of applied art could once more become rational and purposeful. In a world where the objects of daily use and ornament were made with practical common sense, the

18   269

æsthetic sense would need far less to seek consolation and repose in works of pure art.

Nevertheless, in the long run mankind will not allow this function, which is necessary to its spiritual life, to lapse entirely. I imagine, however, that it would be much safer to penalise rather than to stimulate such activity, and that simply in order to sift out those with a genuine passion from those who are merely attracted by the apparent ease of the pursuit. I imagine that the artist would naturally turn to one of the applied arts as his means of livelihood; and we should get the artist coming out of the *bottega*, as he did in fifteenth-century Florence. There are, moreover, innumerable crafts, even besides those that are definitely artistic, which, if pursued for short hours (Mr. Money has shown how short these hours might be), would leave a man free to pursue other callings in his leisure.

The majority of poets to-day are artists in this position. It is comparatively rare for any one to make of poetry his actual means of livelihood. Our poets are, first of all, clerks, critics, civil servants, or postmen. I very much doubt if it would be a serious loss to the community if the pure graphic artist were in the same position. That is to say, that all our pictures would be made by amateurs. It is quite possible to suppose that this would be not a loss, but a great gain. The painter's means of livelihood would probably be some craft in which his artistic powers would be constantly occupied, though at a lower tension and in a humbler way. The Great State aims at human freedom; essentially, it is an organisation for leisure—out of which art grows; it is only a purely bureaucratic Socialism that would attempt to control the æsthetic lives of men.

So I conceive that those in whom the instinct for abstract creative art was strongest would find ample opportunities for its exercise, and that the temptation to simulate this particular activity would be easily resisted by those who had no powerful inner compulsion.

In the Great State, moreover, and in any sane Socialism, there would be opportunity for a large amount of purely private buying and selling. Mr. Wells's Modern Utopia, for example, hypothecates a vast superstructure of private trading. A painter might sell his pictures to those who were engaged in more lucrative employment, though one supposes that with the much more equal distribution of wealth the sums available for this would be incomparably smaller than at present; a picture would not be a speculation, but a pleasure, and no one would become an artist in the hope of making a for-tune.

Ultimately, of course, when art had been purified of its present unreality by a prolonged contact with the crafts, society would gain a new confidence in its collective artistic judgment, and might even boldly assume the responsibility which at present it knows it is unable to face. It might choose its poets and painters and philosophers and deep investigators, and make of such men and women a new kind of kings.

THE PRESENT DEVELOPMENT OF
THE GREAT STATE

BY G. R. STIRLING TAYLOR

X

THE PRESENT DEVELOPMENT OF
THE GREAT STATE

I

IT is possible that some of the readers of this book of essays may find the ideas involved in the conception of the Great State altogether detached from the facts of contemporary life and present social construction. They may rather hastily assume that, however desirable and pleasurable these ideals may be, they are beyond the reach of human attainment, and not in the line of any possible social development. It will be the endeavour of the present writer to consider the connecting-links which, he believes, bind the ideal of the Great State into an intimate union with the facts of the social order (or disorder) of to-day and to-morrow.

The use of the term "development" in the title of this essay may be expanded by an initial explanation. There will be no assumption here that a period of Transition will be followed by a time when the Great State can be said to have arrived as an accomplished fact. The evidence before us seems to forbid any such distinction between a period of travelling and a moment of arrival. The serious social reformer is wise enough to hope that he will never arrive; he is optimistic enough to believe that there will always be something better beyond. He does not visualise himself as one of a party of excursionists who will be disembarked at the Millennium, as it might be at the end of his favourite sea-side pier. The conception of continual travelling is innate in the ideal.

The Great State will not be a spontaneous creation or a sudden accomplishment. If it come at all, it will be by a development of the human affairs which make up the States of to-day. This essay will endeavour to analyse these existing social phenomena, in order that it may be shown how, in the opinion of the present writer, they are already tending in the direction of the Great State, which is the ideal of the other essayists in this book.

II

THE ELEMENTS OF DESTRUCTION

IT will be generally admitted that there is no static condition in social organisation. It is one of the chief virtues of human nature to be eternally discontented. The healthy mind is continually striving for something which it does not possess. And this demand for change seems especially insistent at the present moment; the constructive statesman of the day is faced by a more or less coherent chorus of demands which will not be satisfied by any trivial reform. For the purposes of clarity, it will be convenient to group these elements of discontent round three main points.

There is, first, that chaotic manifestation of unrest which the newspaper headlines very fitly name The Labour War—the struggle between the wage-earners and the masters who buy their labour. The wage-earners are demanding a higher wage, shorter hours, and better conditions; in fact, they ask for a larger share of the good things of life. This is no new fact in history; it has been a very general human demand all through, wherever masters and men have confronted each other. The new note in the situation is the fact that there are indications that the demand is now so united and insistent that the present system of industrial organisation cannot long continue to stand the strain. While the profits of capital become smaller and more precarious, the workers are continually demanding that their share of the profits shall be larger. We seem to be nearing the point when it will no longer be possible to pay a dividend to shareholders and employers when the wages bill has been paid. Moreover, the workers are being impelled towards revolutionary thoughts and deed by the higher prices which are encroaching on their already scanty wages. It also seems obvious that, by continual strikes, the workers can insist on their case being dealt with first. In other words, whatever may have been, or whatever are the advantages of the present industrial system under the control of the capitalists, it is now on the point of breaking down, becoming impossible. Profit-making is its imperative end, and this is rapidly becoming more difficult to reach.

But the Labour War is not merely between master and man. The capitalists are not only at war with their workmen; they are at equally deadly war with each other. The reformer can claim that he is trying to save them from destruction instead of trying to destroy them. The smaller capitalists, the smaller wholesale and retail producers and distributors are wearing each other out in a fierce war waged to get control of the market. Circling round these smaller men are the great financiers (for they are now men with the banker's mind, rather than experts in the intimate processes of their trades); these greater capitalists are gradually extinguishing the weaker members of their class; the small workshop is being shut because it can no longer do its work as quickly and cheaply as the large factory. Even in distribution, the independent shopkeeper is being supplanted by the "multiple-shop" system, where often the retention of the individual name only covers the position of the commissioned agent of the combine which is working in the background.

So this term "Labour War" really covers something wider than the ghastly struggle of the manual labourers. It is a competition for the right to a tolerable living wage, fought out between all those human beings who are not in possession of sufficient capital to allow them to look over the battle-field as non-combatants—that is to say, as persons possessing a "private income." There are comparatively few capitalists, however, who are not also themselves engaged in the struggle, which, indeed, is the general basis of life in all the present great communities.

It seems clear that a further development of this struggle will bring about an impossible situation. To a believer in the advantages of the Great State, it is illuminating to observe that this Industrial War is crushing out that wasteful competition which the collectivist reformers have long condemned. The smaller men, even the smaller states, are being eliminated by the Pierpont Morgans, the Speyers, the Rockefellers, the Rothschilds, the Harrimans, the Beits. It begins to appear that one of these days, if the present process continues without a change of direction, we may get the Great State, indeed;[1] but it will be under the autocratic control of the final survivors of this terrific industrial struggle. It is possible, by a happy chance, that these victors might be benevolent despots, who would provide for all their subjects a sufficiently generous living. But such a state as this would be incompatible with the possession of that individual liberty which is

[1] See Wells's *When the Sleeper Wakes* for an anticipation of this.

one of the fundamental desires of the healthy and well-developed mind. It is, on the whole, only the cramped mind that can submit to domination or can look forward with pleasure to a plutocrat-appointed bureaucracy, however benevolent.

One turns from the discontents of the Labour War —the distress of wage-earners and bankrupt masters —to another huge mass of revolutionary ferment— the Revolt of the Women. It is scarcely less widely spread than the revolt of labour; and its basis is not very different. Like the wage-earner, the woman is demanding a fuller share of the good things of life. In so far as she is a worker already, she is conscious that she is getting even a lower wage than the men who are working beside her. The great majority of the sweated workers are women. Again, take the case of the Civil Service as an example: the woman clerk gets a lower salary when she does the same amount of work as her male companion. That it is often the same amount of work has recently been illustrated by the fact that the British Postal Savings Bank Department has been put on a more economic basis by the substitution of women for male clerks. Presumably the same amount of work has to be done by these clerks—the saving comes from the fact that the women are paid less than the men.

But there is another element in the women's demands. Not only do they demand an equal wage for equal work; they are also claiming that they shall be allowed to share in the responsibility of the intelligent work of the world—in the organisation of their community as politicians and voters, in the professions, in the arts. They ask that the sex barrier shall be removed from the door to these things: they ask that their success or failure shall, at least, be fairly tested: that the distinction of sex shall not be considered in the field of work. The merits of this demand are not in question for the moment; they are the subject of another of these essays. We have now merely to register this discontent as one of the factors of the present situation.

Beyond this demand for the removal of the sex barrier in affairs where, they claim, the distinction of sex has no place, women are also insistently asking for a wider freedom in that relation of lover and child-bearer wherein their distinctive sex attributes are concerned. In the relationship of marriage and parenthood, the women claim that they must be on an equality with men. This demand will be discussed later on in this essay.

There is a third classification of present-day discontent, which perhaps cuts through all the other classes of discontent; but it is such a definite thing, and a demand which is so bitterly threatening the present social structure, that it deserves tabulation by itself. It is that wide-spread desire, common to all classes except the very narrow ones which are in possession of ample means of living, that there shall be some fuller realisation of the enjoyment of life. Not only the wage-earners, but also the salaried men, the struggling professional classes, the smaller traders with their back to the wall against competitive stress—all these are becoming conscious that there is no organic necessity in social structure why life should be a frantic driving for the supplying of mere physical needs. The thoughtful younger members of the middle class are especially getting impatient when they see all these possibilities of a generous and dignified career submerged in a chaotic muddle of social mismanagement and easily avoidable economic errors. They are thrown, side by side with the more cruelly crushed weekly wage-earners, into the pit of social anarchy; and they are coming to see that their salvation lies along the same road. And the root of this restless discontent is that desire for the sweeter things of life, the consciousness that it may be something more than ceaseless toil; it is that vague, impulsive longing to have time to feel "the wind on the heath" that Borrow's gipsy knew. The most insistent things of life—the driving force behind revolutions—are often most vague. Perhaps it can be expressed as the desire to protect that individual freedom which is being crushed out by the present system of capitalist domination.

The present social organisation does not seem able to offer any satisfaction to the three-noted cry of discontent which one has attempted to sum up briefly in the above passages. It is clear that a way out must be found. The ideal of the Great State, expressed in this volume, is one offer of a solution. Having seen the elements which are making towards the end of the present social organisation, one now proceeds to pick up those lines of existing developments which make it possible and even, one suggests, inevitable that our social affairs should lead in the direction of this Great State.

III

THE ELEMENTS OF CONSTRUCTION

THE first thought that occurs when one considers the Great State is that such complex social machinery could only be worked by a highly educated people. It is almost as much beyond the intelligence of the present citizens as it would be beyond the intelligence of a bushman to administer a municipal constitution. The vast stretches of country, both physical and intellectual, which would be controlled by the machinery of the Great State will need for their handling a knowledge of facts and a power of logical judgment which is certainly not possessed by the present electorate, or even by its statesmen and bureaucrats.

It is not so much the good-will that is lacking in the average citizen of to-day; he is, take him all round, neither vicious nor anti-social. He is not a grasping person who desires to rob his fellow-men of everything that he can take. His desire for gain is usually a perfectly healthy and legitimate wish to have a full life; he is only made brutal in its pursuit because, under the laws of the present industrial organisation, one must often be brutal or go under. It is not his instincts that are far wrong; his chief fault is his ignorance. The average man of to-day is a light-hearted person who does not trouble to think out the whys and wherefores, or the precise method by which the largest amount of happiness and comfort can be obtained. He prefers to enjoy himself rather than to think. This is, perhaps, not altogether an unhealthy state of mind.

We shall not get much further in the perfecting of our social organisation until the normal citizen has been educated to think more quickly and more accurately. The wise community will consider that no sum is too high to spend on making the education of its citizens as full as possible. It is the basis of every other reform, it is the investment which pays higher interest than any other enterprise. Just as a manufacturer knows that it pays to have the best machinery, so a wise statesmanship will maintain that it pays the Nation to have the finest human machinery. It is scarcely realised what an enormous waste in productive power is caused by inefficient and niggardly education. To send the children from the schools to work as we send them, imperfectly equipped, to-day, is little better than sending a man to dig with a wooden spade when we might give him an iron one. A highly educated citizen will be the basis of the Great State; for only from such material can come a sufficient volume of demand for intelligent reform, and only by the hands and brains of such people will it be possible to produce all that wealth which is necessary for a civilised life; at least, only by efficient workers will it be possible to get this work done without wearisome toil.

This improvement in education has already made a definite advance during the last half-century; and it is probably the cause of the increasing insistence of the discontent analysed above. This advance is produced not merely by the formal school; it is being accomplished by our newspapers, by the vast supplies of books, by every instrument which tells the citizen something about the world in which he lives. It is useless for the conservative statesmen (whether Tory or Liberal) to try to resent great change if they allow the halfpenny paper and six-penny novel and the shilling classic to exist; and these agencies are already working for the Great State. That is the first development which one can claim to be going in the right direction.

Closely linked with the extension of information, the widening of horizons, this improvement of mental education, goes the improvement of the physical health of the community, which again has only to continue to develop on lines already laid down.

For example, there is the plan of providing meals at the public elementary school. By that system two immediate ends will be attained: first, the children's food will be better in quality and in quantity, and there will be economy by the cooking on a large scale instead of the senseless waste of hundreds of repeated operations; secondly, the mothers will be relieved of an appreciable amount of their present serious overwork in the home. School meals will thus benefit the health of the mother as well as the health of her child. At first, perhaps, a charge will be made for this food; but when it is realised that healthy children are a State asset, and that the parents are the tax-payers, then it will soon be held ridiculous that they should, as parents, pay themselves as citizens. It will not be worth the bother of book-keeping such a simple circulation of money.

The preventive side of public-health administration will get unlimited funds when it is realised, as is rapidly happening that it costs less to prevent disease than to cure it. The recognition of this fact will mean the more energetic development of a whole group of reforms which are already on the statute-books of most civilised states. The sweeping-away of the slum areas has already been linked to the beginning of a system of municipal housing and town-planning; which, in its train, is bringing the possession of public land and the ousting of the private landlord. Again, considerations of public health will be the utilitarian motive behind the probable development of municipal bakeries and municipal milk farms, which will be followed by the public town farm for the production of the vegetables and fruits which will not stand carriage from a greater State farm. Instead of bearing the worry of inspecting private cow-sheds and pouncing on private milk for analysis, it will dawn on the most classical of Town Councillors that it would be better to have the whole process under their control from the beginning, with the added advantage of the larger profits or cheaper prices which will follow the larger-scale production. On all matters of this kind there will be a simple-minded, even if sincere, attempt to defeat the schemes by quoting the abstract philosophy of "private enterprise." But the majority of the people will see no advantage in defending abstractions if they have to risk an early death from contaminated milk and pay a higher price as the sequence of their philosophy. And it will be the same common-sense practice, rather than abstract reasoning, which will initiate most reforms of the collectivist kind we are now discussing.

The department of curative medicine will decrease in importance as the preventive side succeeds in its work. For the sake of the whole people, even if no motives of pity intervened, an intelligent community will continue to provide a fuller series of hospitals and convalescent homes. Of course, there will be no charge made on the individual patients. One would no more ask a fee for the opportunity to stop the spread of dangerous disease or the loss of a working member of the community, than one would demand a fee from a tiger if it called at an Indian village with the request that the headman would draw all its teeth. Besides, it is almost impossible to trace the disease to its responsible source. Why charge A with the cost of curing his children of consumption when the infection came from B's children, who caught it from C's? Only those who have a morbid interest in private detective agencies could be bothered to work out the problem to its end.

While the citizens are being trained to a higher standard of mental and physical fitness the machinery of the State will be developing; the process is coincident, partly cause and partly effect. The development towards the larger industrial organisations which are inherent in the Great State ideal has already begun. Alike on the employer's side, in the form of Companies and Trusts; and on the wage-earner's side, in the form of Trade-Unions and Federations; this process is working itself out before our eyes. In the shape of the vast co-operative Societies, productive and distributing, we have a kind of cross between the two; which, however incomplete and undemonstrative, is still an admirable object-lesson in social machinery. The present tendency is for these organisms to grow greater every year. Although as yet the process remains based on the capitalist-wage-earner system, the machinery itself is not very different from the

288

machinery which may conceivably be used in the Great State. It is, indeed, possible to conceive of the machinery of the embryo Great State being in a fairly complete condition, while the resulting wealth is still credited to the banking accounts of a group of capitalists. For example, if things went on as they are at present tending, the railways of England would soon be under the control of one central private Railway Board. The same tendency shows itself in many industries and distributing agencies: centralisation and a common control are becoming the normal state of affairs. For example, we read of Meat Trusts, Cotton-Thread Combines, Tobacco Trusts, Shipping Amalgamations.

A very slight rearrangement of affairs might change this capitalist industrial machinery into Central Departments of a Great State. The essential change would be that the resulting wealth would no longer be allotted to the capitalist as such; though it may well be that the Great State will continue to pay large salaries or commissions to the "captains of industry." But that is an open question: it will choose the method which gives the best results in the production of social wealth and human character.

This attainment of economy in industrial processes by large organisation must not by any means be accepted as an invariable rule, inherent without exception in the structure of such an ideal as the Great State. Economy of time and labour will only be sought by that method when the large organisation does not encroach on the pleasure which the human mind (in many cases at least) takes in the more direct personal process which is conveniently described as handicraft, as distinguished from machine production. If it so happens that the raising of the standard of education and the decrease of boisterous competition shall produce a majority of citizens approximating to the type of William Morris, then it is probable that there will be a general agreement to sacrifice a part of the time that might be economised by the machine, and return to hand labour in some processes, if it gives a definite return in pleasure to the craftsman.

But in all such departments as transit and distribution, and in a large number of the industrial processes (such as the manufacture of raw material, the making of steel and leather, of uniform cloth and linen goods, and so on), the claims of the craftsmen will scarcely be advanced. The general point to note is that each question of this kind will be decided on its merit as it arises, on the principle that the methods of labour must give way to the rational desires of man, not man to an autocratic demand for cheap and rapid production. On the other hand, the human being of the future may decide that it is better to produce necessities as quickly as possible, and use the economised time in some manner which does not yet appeal to the present mind. The human mind is a subtle thing;

it would be unwise to dogmatise as to what it will or will not want. The citizens of the Great State may crave every possible moment for work with the hands; or, again, for the contemplation of mysticism; or, still again, for the unpremeditated delights of sport and play. Who knows? Why not some of every kind?

There is one possible development of industrial organisation which must be just mentioned before leaving the subject, though it is impossible to amplify it here, for it is a very debatable subject of which the facts are by no means yet clear. It is possible that the function of the State as an organiser of industry may take the form of sub-contracting work to trade-guilds which are, in fact, Trade-Unions of the trade concerned. Thus, it is possible that the State may get its railways built by a guild or Trade-Union of Railway Engineers; or a town may get its municipal houses constructed by a guild of builders; its concerts may be provided by a guild of musicians, and so on. It may be by some such method as this that the problem of the relations of the craftsman and artist to the State may be solved in certain trades. Under the shelter of a publicly recognised guild the craftsman may be able to protect himself from that public dominance which he dreads, not altogether without sound reason. But here the subject can only be dismissed by this hint of a possible solution.

So far, we have been discussing possible developments in the organisation of industrial machinery. As we have seen, this does not in itself settle the question of the distribution of the products. It is scarcely necessary to say that the Great State will not tolerate the present injustice of this distribution. In a condition of society where all will have equal chances of education and opportunity, it is probable that the resulting work will be more equal than it is to-day; and there will certainly be a realisation that every citizen has an innate right to a minimum share of the social products, which will be handed over to him without excessive bargaining as to return duties.

This development towards a communal minimum has already begun in England and most civilised states by the provision of such things as old-age pensions, free elementary education, free roads, free street lighting, free police service, public parks, and municipal bands to play therein. If roads are free, there is no possible argument against free railways; if the turnpike gate has been swept away, it is idle to think that the railway-ticket barrier will remain eternally sacred. In England free meals at the public schools have been already provided in urgent cases; the process is extending, and it seems almost inevitable that the provision of all meals for all children is only a matter of time. From that to the provision of clothes is a development of practice and not of principle. Again, the basis of a free communal medical service is already firmly laid down by our school inspection, medical officers of health, and public hospitals, even if all these departments are at present woefully inefficient. The Insurance Act recently adopted in Great Britain is not altogether communal; but the principle of a State subsidy to insure against sickness and unemployment has been thereby admitted, although the immediate result to the workers is probably no present advantage, and they would have been well advised in this case to wait a little longer for a completely communal system of general insurance.

It is probable that this communal system may extend until it covers all the elementary necessities of life. It is probable that a full minimum of food, clothing, housing, and travel may, within a comparatively short time, become the right of every member of the Great State. But it does not necessarily follow that Communism will carry us beyond this minimum. It is not an ideal which covers the whole case of the distribution of wealth. It must never be forgotten that the end of social organisation is to give the greatest amount of freedom to the individual. We will not make out a case for the Great State unless we show that it will make the individual freer than he is under the Capitalist system. It will be an advantage to give the citizen as much as possible of his wages in the form of money which he can exchange as he pleases, rather than payments in kind, which he must take, to a certain extent, as it is offered by the State. At least, he must have a generous margin for his free use, over and above his expenses in bare necessities. So the problem of distribution of wealth will continue further than the solution by communism. Here again, the future development is already foreshadowed by the existing custom. The graduated income tax, with its super-tax on all incomes above a determined figure, has already laid down a system by which the distribution of wealth can be manipulated in any manner that the community desires.

It is by no means probable that even the most democratic Great State will insist on equality of income; those who look forward to this Great State are not necessarily in conflict with those who say that personal gain is the most powerful incentive to work. It will be quite possible, by the method of a graduated income tax, to pare down the excrescence of undue wealth and still leave its legitimate inequalities. It will almost certainly be by the graduated and super-income tax that wealth will be most fairly distributed during the transition period which we are now considering. The clumsy methods of taxing land values and liquor, tobacco and tea, will be dismissed as ineffective, as not taxing the super-rich, but, on the contrary, allowing them to escape in the confused complexity of the national budget.

But the most radical way to distribute wealth in a fairer manner is, of course, to pay it out at the start in fairer wages and salaries. It will be recognised that if there is any departure from the line of crude equality, then the decision of what is fair will remain a problem of detail which will need continual readjustment and cannot be solved by any hard-and-fast principle. It is probable that it will work itself out on much the same lines that it is already being approached. There probably will be a statutory minimum wage; and the maximum will be won by some kind of bargaining between the State Departments and the organised workers in these trades; there will, in short, be trade-unions, as there are now.

There is one other already urgent matter of social organisation which covers a vast field, and yet has not conveniently come under any of the previous heads of structure of industry or the distribution of wealth or the promotion of the public health. In truth, it could be discussed under all these heads, but it will be clearer to give it a place by itself. One refers to the position of the Mother. Stated in cold economic terms, detached from all the true and false glamour that clusters round her, the Mother is, as such, a worker engaged in the industry of producing that most valuable of social wealth, children. The problem which arises is that under present conditions she is not paid that independent wage, secured by a contract, which is the legal distinction between the position of the free worker and the slave. The Mother, in all normal cases, has merely her maintenance according to the standard of her husband's position, and in some cases an indeterminate sum, over and above, at her own disposal beyond house-keeping. This analogy with the position of a slave does not necessarily involve the statement that the mother is treated with cruelty or inconsideration, in the ordinary sense of the words. But it does involve the statement that she is not an independent unit in the social system. The same might be said, in a sense, of every worker in a factory or government office or a shop. But there is this radical distinction: however badly the ordinary worker be paid, she gets a definite wage for more or less definite hours of service; and this is the basis of an independent life, however insufficient. Whereas the position of the mother is indefinite, and decided by sentiment, not contract.

As it is an essential part of the problem of the Great State to find the method which will loosen the units of the community from unnecessary restrictions on their individual freedom, it is, therefore, logical that we should attempt to discover a method by which the largest class of workers, the mothers, should be given a just and substantial independence. And no amount of beautiful sentiment will be a substitute for a definite wage enforceable by law. The question follows: Who is to fix and pay that wage?

We are not concerned here with the sex relationship, except in so far as it results in a child, the only point where the community seems to have any right to interfere. A calm consideration of all the facts leads one to believe that the State as a whole is far more concerned in the production and control of children than either the father or the mother, and that it will be the State, not the father, which will in future pay the mother the wage due for the work she expends on the child. The endowment of motherhood (which has already become the usual term to denote this idea) will be, in brief, the payment to the mother of a sufficient wage to support herself and her children during the period she devotes to their birth and rearing, and any further period during which she is incapacitated by her previous specialisation in child-bearing. It will be sufficient to cover the necessary outgoing expenses, and, over and above this, provide a profit to herself, at her own free disposal, just as her husband may have a profit over the expenses of his trade or profession. In short, it will give mothers a definite wage for a social service, on exactly the same grounds that any other work is rewarded.

This system of payment for mothers (which may be established much sooner than many of us imagine) would be the longest step towards the collectivist community that the world yet has seen. It will be the more easily carried into practice by the fuller development of that system of collective housekeeping which has already begun, and is another development in the direction of the Great State. The large co-operative blocks or squares of dwellings, with common dining-rooms, libraries, playrooms, nurseries, and kitchens, will revolutionise the position of the mother and, incidentally, tend to a freedom from excessive domestic work, a freedom which will do more than anything else to give women that place in the general work of the world which they are at present demanding. It is not good that an intelligent woman should give up her whole time to the care of a single house or of two or three children, who would be far better in the more varied society of a larger group, which could be more economically and efficiently tended by a professional nurse who chose that work by preference. All these developments, eventually, may lead to the disappearance of the family as a social unit. There will probably be no place in the larger-thinking Great State for the narrow autocracy of the father, controlling the individual rights of either the mother or the child. Such a unit will only hamper the individual, without assisting in the wider work of the State.

Here one must end this brief summary of the elements of the present social organism which are tending in the direction of the Great State.

These have been grouped, for convenience, under the four heads of educational and physical development; the collective organisation of industry; the distribution of excessive wealth; and the development of communal rights; while the case of the public endowment of motherhood has been treated as a special example which illuminates the whole principle. The growth of internationalism might be added to the list. All these tendencies will, on analysis, be found to result from the common-sense fact that it is more satisfactory to accomplish the work of the world on the co-operative basis of organised effort than on the lines of anarchical impulse. It may be far more difficult to organise the former than to permit the latter; but the manifest possibilities of the former will continue to stimulate the human imagination until every difficulty is overcome. The organisation of that "collective mind" which will be the basis of the Great State needs an educated people—a people who will work in unison with the next-door neighbours, the next parish, the next county, or the next nation, whenever there is any advantage to be gained by so doing. The vague, instinctive, childish antagonisms of class and race, and the sentimentalities that would veil the essential brutality, are giving way, generation by generation, before the more precise and larger-spirited thinking of the new time.

A PICTURE OF THE CHURCH IN THE GREAT STATE

BY THE REV. CONRAD NOEL

20

XI

A PICTURE OF THE CHURCH IN THE GREAT STATE[1]

At last I came upon the Cathedral, as we must now call it, for every group of parishes has its bishop who is in more than name a "father in God" to his priests and people, and not, as too often in the past, a feeble person remotely overlording a vast area and following instead of forming public opinion, his mind a tangle of concessions and his days a round of trivialities. The people themselves are nowadays consulted in the election of the clergy, a custom which recalls the choice of Ambrose to the

[1] This paper takes the place of a projected essay upon Religion in relation to the Great State. The general editors of the book were unable to arrange for a comprehensive discussion of this important aspect of human life because they could find no writer at once interested and impartial; and the Rev. Conrad Noel has very obligingly, and under a considerable pressure of other work, sketched a Catholic ideal of religion in the Great State. Unlike our other contributors, he has not seen fit to adopt the form of a reasoned essay, but instead he has made an imaginative description of a visit to a cathedral in the year 2000 or so, the basis for his forecast of the future catholic teaching. It is his personal forecast, from his individual standpoint as a priest of the Church of England; but many will agree with his spirit who will not approve either of his doctrine or of his ornaments.

Archbishopric of Milan by acclamation of men and women, and even little children, and replaces the intrigue and secrecy of the past. Many "Congregationalists" welcomed the change, and now exist within the Church as a guild, with particular methods and a standpoint of their own. But although there still remain certain small and independent coteries of the pious—and perhaps not illogically, for their forefathers became separatists from the Unity of Christendom not so much in protest against the private patron as in championship of the private congregation, holding no brief for the common people, but only for the "people of God"—modern sectarianism has lost point and vitality, for the people believe that the Church is an army for the quickening and confirming of a Kingdom of Righteousness, and that through the comradeship of arms men and women attain a gracious and eternal personality.

To the majority the idea of "free" and competing churches has therefore become meaningless, and is only upheld by the sects themselves on the assumption that Christ did not found a Fellowship, but a number of sky-seeking cliques or comfortable "homes of the spirit," which do business as drug stores and insurance companies for a restricted clientèle.

Within the Church itself, however, there exists a great variety of ideas and a greater variety of worship. There are to be found within its organisation many companies whose members before the great changes had been dissenters; each has its shrine or oratory, and emphasises some one or other aspect of truth, but without breaking away in thought or emotion (heresy) or in organisation (schism) from the bond and proportion of the Catholic Religion. In the Cathedral, for instance, there is an oratory dedicated to Wisdom, containing a library of books, where people come for study and contemplation; no public service is held here, but it is the favourite meeting-place for a Guild of the Friends, who use it for purposes of silent adoration.

The common worship of the Church is elaborate, for it is the people's tribute to the Supreme Ritualist who is making a rich and complex and visible world with its pageantry of days and nights, and of the varying seasons. But to many of the guilds the ceremonial worship makes no special appeal. They are present at it as an act of Fellowship from time to time, but find their particular satisfaction in simpler exercises of the spirit, in which, indeed, the whole people frequently join.

As to the position and temporalities of the Church, a controversy is raging. I hear that only last week a passionate appeal against Establishment was made from the pulpit of the Cathedral by one of the younger canons. The Church had been disestablished, and to some extent disendowed for many years, and at the present time the churches are maintained and the Clergy supported in different ways. In some parishes the priests work "productively" for an hour or so every day, giving their ministry freely. In others they are supported by a voluntary levy. In others again some small endowment exists. Now, a great number of people, including some of the most lively and public-spirited, are in favour of complete establishment and uniform State endowment; but the preacher of last week, who voiced a vigorous minority, had passionately warned the people against the proposed official union. The price of just government was alert criticism and eternal vigilance, and this criticism had hitherto been encouraged by a vigorously independent Church. I have no notion how this particular controversy will be settled, but it seems possible for people to hold opposite convictions on the subject of temporalities, and, indeed, on many others, without breaking the bond of Christendom.

The Cathedral Church of All Saints was the old Tudor structure of my childhood, but where was the Society for the Protection of Ancient Buildings? For there had been added a new Chapel towards the east, a Council-room to the north, and I noticed innumerable other alterations, each showing decision and individuality. These acts of "Vandalism" are defended by the present architects, who point to the audacities of style in successive periods of the Middle Ages, a daring clash of individualities and a supreme harmony. It was as if a Great People, in regaining some secret spring of life, had fulfilled the Unities by becoming as unconscious of them as an athlete is unconscious of a good digestion.

The old niches had their saints restored to them, and many new shrines were peopled with a strange medley of figures: St. Catharine of Siena, and her namesake of Egypt; the Blessed Thomas More and John Ball, of St. Albans; St. Joan of Arc; the Blessed John Damien, and hundreds more, many of them unknown to me, but likely enough images of martyrs who had fallen in some recent struggle—artists, artisans, poets, priests, and statesmen. The inclusion among these shrines of pre-Christian and non-Christian heroes seemed to me extraordinary, but the principle of this People is to accent the vitalities of tradition and let the rest go; I was reminded that one of their greatest theologians, St. Thomas Aquinas, had woven Aristotle into the Catholic fabric, and that St. Augustine had claimed Plato as a Christian, and that the Catholic Church had baptised images, temples, ceremonial, gods and goddesses, into Christ, laying the whole world under contribution in the building of an Universal Faith, and adoring an everywhere present God from whom all good things do come. Even the very Christmas-trees, with their gleaming tapers and gaudy colours, which decorated the aisles, reminded one that the peculiarly Christian Feast of December was pagan in origin. Inclusiveness with them springs from no mere toleration born of indifference; but from an adoration of that one Spirit who has not left Himself without witness in any corner of the earth. They borrow freely and absorb into their own religion elements the most distant and varying; and the more they borrow, the more unique does this religion become.

The old gargoyles remain untouched, and new monstrosities leer down upon the passers-by. Among them are the faces of pharisees and sweaters of a past régime. So vividly do certain encrustations of the structure record the struggles of a darker century that they seem like some furious battle suddenly arrested and turned to stone.

The principal porch was draped in deep-rose velvet girdled with golden cords, and against the rosy background stood dark branches of the yew in wooden tubs. On entering the carved doors, I was at once impressed with a sense of warmth and incense and worship. One could not imagine such a building deserted; it must always have its groups of devotees; it was surely the temple of a perpetual adoration.

Everywhere were chapels and pictures and shrines, gay with flowers and glittering tapers pointing like spears towards the vast roof. Fixed by small black chains to the benches and the base of some of the images were prayers framed in carved wood with wooden handles. In one such frame was shrined the saying: "I give nothing as duties. What others give as duties, I give as living impulses. Shall I give the heart's action as a duty?"

Many are attracted to the Chapel of "Our Lord of Health." Round its walls are pictured scenes of healing from the Gospels and the lives of the saints, and from the Annals of "secular" medicine. Crutches and other memorials of past feebleness adorned its pillars as trophies of divine healing. A guild for the preservation and spread of health meets here, and its members include doctors and nurses and healers of every kind.

The Chapel of Santa Claus is the largest in the building, and belongs entirely to the children, who have this Christmas-tide decorated it with artificial flowers made by themselves and with sprigs of holly and laurel. The altar was hidden behind a Bethlehem crib roofed with yellow thatch and lighted with a hundred candles. Here is held the daily service of the Catechism, the children choosing their monitors, and even having some say in arranging the details of their worship. They are encouraged to think for themselves, and as much praise is given for a question well put as for a question well answered.

In my wanderings about the Cathedral I came upon a certain oratory with many kneeling figures rapt in prayer, penitents awaiting their turn to make confession; for the new People is intensely practical, and their religion is not merely an affair between the private soul and the private God, but between the individual and a God-penetrated Society and its minister. They believe that Man has not only power on earth to commit sin, but power on earth to forgive sin, and they glorify God

Who has "given such power unto men." They think in terms of fellowship: goodness is that which helps; evil is that which injures the community. The most secret vice by decreasing or deflecting the energies of service is a sin against the whole family of God, and requires the forgiveness not only of God, but of man. In an anti-social age everything from religion to business had become distorted, neurotic, excessively introspective, but now the sacraments were again the witnesses and effectual signs of social grace. The people generally has regained a robust conscience, genuinely sorry for its stupidities, its cruelties, and its egomanias; but ready to make a clean breast of them and shake them off. Religion nowadays is more deeply rooted in the eternal realities of human nature than ever before, and has inspired people with the paradox of humility and audacity which one sees in adventurous lovers and all who drink deep of the fountains of life. They feel the things eternal underlying the things temporal, and are in close converse not with a Jesus and Saints of a dead past, but with a Jesus and Saints who, by their heroic struggle as recorded in the past, have won to that heaven which is close at hand. Far from denying a future beyond death, they hope for it, and already by their friendship with those who have passed through its gate live in "the rapture of the forward view." They laugh good-humouredly at the sick people of the twentieth century who blamed the Church of their day for not lusting for life, and themselves were so little in love with it that they rejoiced at the prospect of annihilation. But when convalescence came, there came back with it the lust of everlasting life. To work for the good of the race is excellent enough, but the work will gain in vigour and enthusiasm when it is no longer the service of a race of summer flies who are to perish in a few moments, but devotion to enduring human beings with the infinite possibilities of infinite worlds.

Had this People developed a new ethical sense, or to what extent are they merely reverting to an earlier standpoint for a time engulfed in the abysses of Christo-Commercialism? Two or three things stand out clearly: they worship no barren and abstract deity called Morality; morality was made for man, not man for morality. They love and worship people, and not principles; their religion is the intimacy and fellowship of friends; their casuistry springs from the fount of worship.

Their teaching of the children is firm and simple, and meets with swift response, for it rings true to some natural grace in childhood, which is always present in some degree or other, however deflected or overlaid or intermixed with alien elements. It was through my presence at the daily "Catechism" that I began to see that they are convinced of the fundamental soundness of human nature and of the divinity of every human birth. Centuries back this conviction had been acknowledged as an essential doctrine of the Christian Church, after the long battle between Apollinarius and S. S. Hilary and Athanasius. And for all this, they do not minimise the distortions of mind and soul. Evil and grace are both acknowledged, but the generosities of grace are suggested as natural to man, and evil is regarded as the inhuman interloper. This is well illustrated in their use of the word "lust," which has recovered its original significance of the natural bodily desires, hunger, thirst, sex attraction, energy, rest, recreation. Lusts are dark and distorted only when uncontrolled and indulged to the injury of the community or the self; hunger becomes gluttony; thirst becomes drunkenness, and physical desire unchastity. In this connection they tell the old story of the shipwrecked swimmer encumbered by his sack of gold, asking if the drowning man owned the gold or the gold owned him. The Church rejects the doctrine which would treat the gold, or the hunger, or the sex need as inherently evil, and children are thus taught to distinguish between the use and abuse of those natural desires which are, in fact, believed to have in them some positive element of goodness. The physical appetites are likened to high-spirited horses, valued for their very lustiness: the business of the driver is not to destroy, but to control them, and this is also the business of life's charioteers. The Church has thus reverted to and is now developing a healthy and more adventurous element in its tradition. Complete suppression of some one or other desire is counselled in exceptional cases, and such a policy is illustrated from the anti-Oriental standpoint of the New Testament.[1] This essential but exceptional abstinence is believed to have its attendant danger, because the converted sensualist may invite into the temple of his soul seven other demons more deadly than the first, for drink has slain its thousands, but pharisaism its tens of thousands. The puritan convert too often devoted the remainder of a maimed[2] life to preaching the gospel of dismemberment among the sound and healthy. The leader in so un-catholic a crusade should surely have been the fox of the fable who, wisely exchanging a tail for a life, is forever counselling total abstinence from tails as the duty of all members of his magnificent species. The present casuistry does not discount the discipline of pain; but no road is either to be chosen or avoided for its painfulness, the way of the cross being sacred, not because of its difficulties, but because of its purpose. Neither pain nor pleasure is regarded as an end in itself, and it is pointed out that the Christ said of Himself not, I am come that they might have pleasure, nor, I am come that they might have pain, but "I am come that they might have life." They often quote the story of the artist whose soul's desire was to paint a joyous picture and bequeath it to posterity. But he lived in a Calvinist city, and the government threatened him with crucifixion if

[1] Matthew v: 30.   [2] Mark ix: 43.

he dared to paint it. If there be any other way out, the artist will take it, and he cries: "If it be possible let this cup pass from me"; but he cannot play the traitor to that joy within him, which he is to scatter among men, and for its sake he is content to go the way of the cross; and the blood of the martyr becomes the seed of the Church.

Deliberate effort towards fulness of life is counted praiseworthy and necessary, for the convalescent must take his exercise, however painful and ungainly the effort may be, though this very ungainliness should remind him that he is still in some measure under the dominion of disease. When eventually the convalescent soul by conscious effort has regained health, actions spring spontaneously from a rich and genial human nature, and he understands the meaning of the light burden and the easy yoke.

This naturalness and spontaneity they see in the saviours of men, but everything they think and feel about the saviours, they think and feel as a possibility for themselves. Jesus Christ seems to them more human than humankind; so they call Him divine. He is supposed to hold the key of an overmastering (eternal) life which is to be the heritage of men as they emerge from the half-formed, malformed sub-human life with which they are often enough content, and become Man. They speak of Jesus Christ as the first fruits of the human harvest, and as the first-born from the dead.

There was a good deal of controversy in the

twentieth century about the "finality" of Jesus; but this doctrine is no longer obtruded, possibly not even believed, not at least in the paralysing sense of past centuries. They do not separate him from mankind, nor from the heroes of men; it is men who, by their lack of life, separate themselves from Man.

They feel that the life of Christ, as contained even in their written fragments, is baffling in its many-sidedness, its richness, and its ferocity, its geniality and its austerity, its tenderness and its audacity; but rather is it His life as a present God illustrated in that localised and limited life of the past, which is adored. The orthodox theologians, both past and present, have not expected to find everything in the written pages, but look for the extension of a life once manifest in Galilee in the subsequent lives of the family of mankind. They look to the life of the good time coming, the life of the golden age, "the world to come." Some writers have spoken of this consummation as "The Second Coming." They point to certain sayings in the scriptures as containing in germ the later doctrine of the Catholic Church on these points of faith.[1]

They do not pretend to find in the written gospels of the Christ after the Flesh, the God-life of mankind drawn out, extended, illustrated in every detail and from every angle. For they have never been bibliolaters. They have never thought that

[1] Luke vi: 40; John xiv: 12.

315

ink or parchment or written words could possibly give full expression to the Word, Who Is God. Nor do they conceive it possible that Jesus of Nazareth, the Very Man of Very Man and Very God of Very God, in a ten months' ministry, or at most three years, could live the long life of the perfect dramatist, the perfect artist, the perfect singer, the perfect agriculturalist, the perfect bricklayer, the perfect dancer, the perfect statesman, the perfect mother.

All art is not only self-expression but self-limitation, and the art of God the Creator implies a restriction, in which may possibly be found the key to the problem of evil. They believe that God the Word or the "God Expressed" limited Himself within the strong channel of a forcible life narrowed to a particular purpose, but that as he lay a babe in his mother's arms he filled and still fills the world with his presence, ever striving to express himself within the limitations of this or that heroic being; hence the importance of seeing God in men and women, and of the worship of the saints, no mere copies, but originals, distinct and multitudinous facets of that jewel of great price which is God.

But the historic Christ is the norm and illustration of the life of God and Man, the ever-present God inspiring men with the same secret of vigour and originality. The saints are taken as illustrations of the million-sidedness of God, latent and suggested in the life of Jesus Christ. As to images and pictures, their scriptures suggest that the idol

316

is in itself a thing indifferent, for it may be the splendid representation of some heroic god, or the dark fashioning of a devil, whose service is that "Avarice which is Idolatry." What gods of wood or stone you make matters not; the God that matters is the god you set up in your heart. The Calvinists never made a stone image of the thing they worshipped. If they had, the children would have run shrieking from its presence. None the less were they idolaters. It is hardly necessary to record the difference between the paintings and images in the churches of to-day and the "religious art" of the Dark Ages.[1] The gentlemanly drawing-room Christs, the simpering Madonnas, the feeble self-immolating saints are things of the past, for the portraits and images are brave and heroic, and the prevailing conceptions have revolutionised religious art.

In the huge nave Matins was being sung. Many of the Jewish psalms had been retained in the Liturgy, but to the Christian psalter had been added blank verse and free rhythms of later date. The chanting by men's voices sounded to me archaic, and I was better able to appreciate the hymns set to folk-melodies and sung by children. It seemed strange that the first lesson should be selected from a modern writer, but the second was from the New Testament. People were still coming into the nave, bringing their chairs from a stack by the west doors,

[1] Eighteenth, nineteenth, and early twentieth centuries.

and sitting where they liked, except that a pompous-looking beadle, gorgeously arrayed, kept a wide alley for the great procession. The decorations presented a daring scheme of colour. The tall pillars were wreathed with evergreen and many-coloured silken materials; between them stood the bright Christmas - trees, and over the entrance to Chancel loomed the Rood with its Calvary. But for the figure of the Crucified, and for the processional Cross, I saw neither crucifix nor cross throughout the building. It was through the grave and gate of pain, as represented on the Calvary screen, that we passed into the joyous life beyond. The wearying repetition of the same symbol was held to mark the impoverishment and decadence of the Catholic idea. At each festival an appropriate image would be placed upon the high altar, or some picture hung above it. But for this image flanked by two candles spiked in candlesticks of crystal and silver, the long altar-table was bare of ornament and the eye was attracted not to the lights upon and above it and clustering at its sides, but to itself, enfolded in a sun-like frontal blazing with jewels. The chancel was hung with flags, faded and tattered trophies of brave crusades. On these flags were painted various emblems, the wheels of Catharine, the gridiron of Laurence, the lions of Mark, the spears of George. I could see, from my seat by one of the pillars, a side chapel with a simple stone altar with two candlesticks of ebony, and

between them an ivory Christ, like a young Greek
shepherd, bearing on his shoulder not a lamb, but
a goat, a symbol of the final restitution of all things.
Before this altar, priests and laymen were vesting,
and here were congregated boy and girl choristers,
acolytes, taperers, robed, some in white, others in
purple and blue and gold. A surpliced priest approached the lamp hanging before the high altar
and brought light down among the crowd, the men
and women in front lighting the tapers they held
in their hands and passing on the light from neighbour to neighbour, from row to row, until the whole
building was a swaying forest of fire. This cere-
mony symbolised the fulgent enthusiasm of comradeship, kept ablaze by the handing-on of the torch
from neighbour to neighbour and from one generation to another. To have witnessed this wonderful
sight almost compensated me for the midnight mass
of Christmas Eve that I had missed, the mass at
which nearly the whole district made communion,
and which opened with the procession of wise men
with their gold and incense and myrrh and shepherds
with their lambs. This function had been pre-
ceded by a drama of Bethlehem, acted under the
huge vaulting of the Middle Tower by people of
the town and their children, a drama in which
humour and solemnity jostled one another in strange
congruity.

The Communion Service was in many respects
like the service of my childhood, but instead of the

negative commandments of the Jews had been substituted the positive commandments of the Christians, and in the prayers for the Great State there has been inserted a memorial of the Confederacy of Nations composing it. The doctrine of the Blessed Trinity, or of the One-in-many, runs through their whole conception of life, suggesting not only the complex personality of the individual, the trinity of the holy family in father, mother, child, but the international and composite unity of the State, the many nations gaining and not losing individuality by each generous advance towards World-fellowship, by every casting-off of insularities and parochialisms.

Just as the many nations are confederate in the State so are the parishes confederate in the national church, and the national churches in the international Catholic Church, sending representatives to the great assemblies at which presides the supreme pontiff, the President of the Eucumenical Councils of the Catholic Democracy. In the prayer for the Whole Church, mention was made of all its officers chosen and consecrated for various functions and administrations in the same.

Beautiful as is the singing of the Gospel from a lectern down among the people, and the little procession which precedes it, I was more impressed by the procession of the Offertory or Offering of the Fruits of the Earth, a procession which, winding in and out among the people, gathers some of them in its train; the laity bringing the offerings of Nature and the works of man's hands towards the altar; following them comes the deacon, his hands muffled in a long silk veil, bearing the sacred bread and wine, universal emblems of the products of art and nature.

Although this People insists on the eternal values of the present life, it seems to be inspired by a conviction of an after life transformed beyond the capacity of our present apprehension. They do not believe that the dissolution of death either destroys personality or with miraculous suddenness transmutes it. The majority of men undergo a process of purification, being cleansed by the fires of conscience fanned in the furnace of the terrible God of Love. They do not think that this process necessarily takes place in the arena of this earth; reincarnation is only one of many legitimate speculations, and by no means a popular one, for theologians realise that this earth is in size a mere speck of dust in the vast network of worlds that form the Universe. They no longer dogmatise as to place, but as to process. They teach that a few pure and courageous souls pass after death into the overmastering life of God's Omnipresence, and find their heaven in co-operation with Him in the work of creation. Our entrance into this heaven is barred by stupidity and corruption, and for all there exists as a dread possibility, the outer darkness and the weeping and gnashing of teeth, though of not even the Judases of the earth are we to think of that possibility as a certainty. The presence of the whole company of heaven seems to pervade and invigorate the people, and prayer to all saints and for all souls is a never-ending fount of energy in the life of the Nation.

From the moment when the Child is initiated by Baptism into the life of the Fellowship until the last rites of the Church are administered in the hour of death, the sacraments of friendship are his nourishment, and the graces of fellowship uphold him. Present at mass from earliest childhood, he makes his Communion only after having received the Sacrament of Confirmation, that effectual sign of the royal priesthood of mankind, "The Coming of age of the Christian." In the Sacrament of "Holy Order" some are consecrated as delegates and spokesmen of the whole human priesthood, and in this parish Mass of Christmas one felt that the Consecration of the bread and wine at the hands of the bishop was not the act of a sacerdotal caste, but of all the people; for, as the great bell tolled at the supreme moment, not only the congregation, but the whole country-side was linked together in that act of adoration, when the everywhere present God is made manifest in the friendship of those who eat and drink in common, and in the nourishment and energy, the gaiety and intoxication of life, as symbolised by the life-giving bread and the genial wine.

THE CHURCH IN THE GREAT STATE

In spite of what might be called the pantheistic, or more accurately the polytheistic, elements in the religion of the Great State, it all roots down into an intense conviction of the Being of the One God. The ethics are lively and practical, because Morality is not worshipped as a fixed and abstract divinity, but is looked upon as dependent on and in relation to people. It is kept from becoming static and stagnant by the Communion of Saints. Behind these innumerable personalities of sinners and saints, personalities ordinary and extraordinary, there is believed to exist the ever-present and personal God. The term "personal" is bravely used, not because His Being does not escape the net of all language, but because He is felt to be in converse and communion with men. Transcending personality, He must yet be appropriately expressed in the highest terms they know, the terms of their own humanity in its most human moments. For the Word became flesh, and dwelt among us, and we beheld His glory, as of the only begotten of the Father, full of grace and truth.

THE GROWTH OF THE GREAT STATE

BY HERBERT TRENCH

XII

THE GROWTH OF THE GREAT STATE

Is the existing form of state certain to transcend its borders? Let us survey, by a fragmentary glimpse over history, the ancient majestic process of polity-making; examine what one form of polity bequeaths to another; and take account also of the profound underlying and unifying force that the whole process implies.

Next; is there a test of true growth, in that process of human societies; a touchstone and assay of their prosperity, a check on false values and on inhuman changes? Yes, there is the Family, the first glowing germ-cell. By this cell, as I shall show, the health of the polity stands, to live or die.

I

WE do not know why the universe is what it is. We do not even know Man as he is; his nature is only being gradually unfolded. But two centres of being, Life and Mind, jut out with incomparable clearness. In the human body, they emerge as heart and brain. All hangs on the interaction of these. In men dying, the pulsation of the muscle of the heart will starve all other organs—feet, hands, organs of generation, stomach—in order to feed, with its last exhausted flutter, the consciousness of the brain. But these two centres are but surface-indexes to profound universal forces, acting through human society. Therein we see Life and finite Mind, moving in the region of Anangke—that is, Nature unguided by finite Mind. Now Life and Mind we judge to be different stages in the growth of an "omnipotential principle, which draws its whole growth and content from its environment."[1] The two forms of Life and Mind are both always being urged by the pressure of this principle to frame wholes, totalities. Life and Mind have jointly the remarkable power of successively crystallising, as it were, round haphazard points, into organisms, selves, families, polities of all kinds. By polity I mean any human group organised by finite Mind.

II

THE aims of civilisation, or polity-making, may seem confused, but are not so. They are the preservation, in reservoirs of ever-increasing group-consciousness and range, of Life and Mind, in a steady relationship to each other, and the training of them both to increased force and completeness. Three reservoirs have been successively organisms, families,

[1] Driesch, quoted by B. Bosanquet.

polities; which may dissolve, but always leave behind them spheres or basins of civilisation, out of which polities emerge and re-emerge, like bubbles from the moist ground round a spring.

The central principle of things requires a ceaseless effort after whole-making; and this ultimately implies, I believe, soul-making. For this purpose a ceaseless interaction goes on between the two centres, Life and Mind, as they move, oscillating, in age-long northward and southward rhythms as well as in eastward and westward rhythms of fertilising invasion over the surface of the globe. The moist ground-area of the spring, we shall see, goes on enlarging.

III

FIRST, towards polity-making, from cave, marsh, lake, move Life and Mind, possibly out of promiscuous or matrilinear group-forms, into the Cyclopean patriarchal Family, the main human unit, with its naked primal economic necessities—food, shelter, warmth, procreation; Life always creeping ahead, always to be followed by wellings-up of Mind, intensifying the Life of the unit—the Family.

It is in an apparently spiral vortex-whirl that Life and Mind, the kindred and antagonistic allies, acting through the sex-lore and jealousy of a sire, create the Family, and thence the Polity.

In the sea octopus, found at a depth of fifteen

thousand feet, shines an eye. The upper half of this eye is an organ of vision, the lower half an actual lamp, projecting light on external masses. Both halves radiate backwards and inwards currents of consciousness within the creature. These are the triple functions of Mind. Mind reflects the ramifying movement, the fern-like expansion of the fibrils, veins, tendrils, and armours of its precursor and fellow-centre. It intensifies consciousness, defensive and formative. In the human, Mind embodies Life in preservative habits, customs, morals, totem food-societies, by co-operative magic and religion. Next it adds the great step, Record; and this Record, tide-mark of life, scored in material more enduring itself, Mind learns perpetually to diffuse.

To diffuse, to interpenetrate, to absorb the outward and project the inward—this is the special power of Mind. True inwardness is thus the complete grasp and absorption of the outward, and the projection of so much as may be of the inward. Mind renders all things transparent, as the soak of essential oils renders transparent, for the operating surgeon, the tissue and cellular structure of bone. And as Life moves forwards in its shell-forming and polity-making it is not only quickened in its pace by Mind; it is affected deeply in its own nature. And therefore the polities which Life and Mind jointly create are more and more thoroughly suffused with Mind. Mind in its turn grasps and intensifies more and more of Life. There follows in the polity, therefore, increase of the brood-care which we call education; increases of self-guidance and group wisdom; and, since the very principle of Mind is diffusion, there is an increase in the range of the external structure of polity. Man does not invent the State only to satisfy the impulse of the Family. He feels the impulse because his natural destination is the State, as Aristotle said. This majestic process thrusting up from some source unknown, but whose unity we fragmentarily apprehend, more and more numerous centres of nerve-consciousness to the surface of the globe, appears to be the expansion of some profound universal root of Self-dominion.

This is the open secret of the world.

IV

In this process the Life-centre and the Mind-centre in any polity are not allowed by the omnipotential principle to fall far apart. Where they do not interact the polity-forming current ceases, a light vanishes, some low form of organism, of which all we know is that it has innumerable nervous centres and some of the philosophy for a brain, crumbles and disappears. There is a decomposition into smaller forms; the bubble of the polity relapses into inferior communities, the germ-cells of scattered families; and soul-making by that reservoir stops. Yet the reservoir has bequeathed something: the bubble of the Polity has relapsed, but the moist ground of the spring, the diffused sphere of Civilisation, remains larger than it was before.

Next observe that, although a vast latitude is allowed as to conditions of Life, and a vast tolerance as to the scope, products and activities of Mind, yet the making of the organised reservoir, the Polity, ceases when either Life or Mind receives mortal injury. The law is that Mind may extend and ramify its universalisings from basin to basin of civilisation, provided that no fatal injury is done to Life, its basis in forming the Familial Unit. The final criterion of the health of the polity is found in the health of that Family for which society came into being. It is obvious that where the primal necessities of this unitary cell are not satisfied, there must follow a dwindling, a kind of cancerous break-down of the cellular tissue of the reservoir, as penalty for the infringement of the law of interaction of Life and Mind. If the area of harm be wide enough, the reservoir perishes; and reservoir-making is begun outside, round fresh foci. And clearly the reservoir may perish in another way: it may fail under the impact of intenser Life outside. But these impacts usually infuse fresh blood; are absorbed and revitalise the reservoir, as the southern Chinese polity in its *cul de sac* was revitalised by Turki, Mongol, and Manchurian blood from the north, Gaul by the Frankish tribes, or Britain by the Saxon invasion.

But the point to be observed is that, whether the

reservoir or polity decays from internal or external causes, it bequeaths greater consciousness to the globe. Its inventions have always overflowed its borders and remained in the common heritage. The result, therefore, on the whole, during the recorded history of the last twelve thousand years, from the time when Nippur drew into a village of reed-huts among the marshes of Euphrates, has always been the formation of larger spring-areas of civilisation, which contain small sparsely-sown communities with a tradition of finer Mind. Out of these spring-areas arise larger polities of coarser structure, in which the small communities with traditions of finer Mind have a gradual influence of permeation; so that the ultimate level of civilisation and the ultimate level of Mind, of the new large polities is higher than in the old; the two main diffusing forces being Trade and Thought, issue of the Life-centre and the Mind-centre respectively. For Mind has the property of never forgetting its own old communal levels; it to-day remembers the level, for instance, which it had in the Athenian polity. Therefore in the new polity of larger area formed by Trade and Thought there will be a steady tendency for Mind to rise in the polity. There will be ultimately, after an interval of relapse, a more comprehensive survey and level of conception than in the old. Life is ever being sheltered by wider intercourses and under an ampler roof; and behind both Life and Mind there is no long pause in the motion

22   333

of the Omnipotential Principle. Stagnancies, fluctuations, delays, recessions of the tidal force, it is true, there always will be; black retrograde periods such as that of the fifth century of our era, when the Eastern and Western halves of the Roman Empire were a prey to Goths, Vandals, and the Huns of Attila. Yet, looked at broadly, if the tidal force has receded out of one reservoir, it has generally been to advance farther and higher elsewhere in another. From climax to climax, crest to crest, of the eight known civilisations, the wave-length period seems to be about fifteen hundred and thirty-five years. But the main depth and body of Mind in its commonalty, upon and out of which these waves are formed, seems steadily to deepen over the world.

v

THUS the first foci of Life in Families crept out of the mists round the common Fire of a village. Through hundreds of thousands of years, from periods pre-glacial and pliocene, human life had risen to the cave-life of the Veddahs, and then the village. Nomad peoples tended to fail, as the hairy forest peoples tended to fail, in comparison with agricultural and settled tribes. Why? Because the settled folk could more effectively guard and feed the Family. Outside the village were the formative pressures of Anangke, duress of famine and fear. Next protection is afforded to the huddling villages by the City, of which the root-idea is Fortress. But the Fortress, larger than the village, requires more food. Fortress becomes Market. The City requires a larger catchment-area of produce or of prey. It needs also roads through the region of Anangke. But primitive waters are roads ready-made, and easier roads than land-roads. River-dwellings on piles also afford protection from wild beasts. The first civilisations are therefore the three River Civilisations, Babylonian, Egyptian, and Assyrian, in the valleys of Euphrates, Nile, and Tigris. Their polities are monarchies, pyramidal also in religion; and their Kings, sole ultimate intermediaries between the families of the people and their god. In each of these River Civilisations the Polity, in the fostering hot current between Life and Mind, swells—hive-like—honeycombed marvellously within into intricate galleries of crafts and castes. But even in remotest stages of early civilisation we find the stability and size of the Polity proportionate to the rank it accords to Mind. The three-staged Ziggurat, or mountainous stage-towers of unburned brick (faced with kiln-dried bricks laid in bitumen), and bearing on their summits the abode of the Babylonian god, had always, in a great outlying building, their attendant Library. These Babylonian libraries, certainly far more than six thousand years before Christ, like the subsequent Egyptian libraries, contained text-books, school exercises, tables of mathematical formulæ, as well as archives of temple and kingdom. In those

River monarchies it was Mind that irrigated the desert. Mingling with the Life-centre, it fused and threw up the great composite structures Art and Religion. Religion, at first a mixed fear of ghosts and a hope in the power of ancestral spirits, finally expressed Man's sense of the relation of his polity and of his own soul to the Infinite power. Religion also now lifted the old local tribal gods into their niche in a system; into their footing in a hierarchy; reflecting the shape of the hive in the spiritual dome of a Pantheon for the gods. The River Polity thus helped to spread the conception of *one* God. For instance, the unifying of the forty-two nomes, or transverse river provinces of the Nile, under the cobra - headed Pharaonic crown, tended to draw their various tribal animal cults into a theocracy of one King-God who was supreme.

Neter, the supreme God, remote and Almighty, indifferent to man, deputed the management of human affairs to a crowd of minor deities, Sky, Heaven, Nile, Earth, Sun, and so on; with a myriad of Spirits. But, at least three thousand five hundred years before Christ, out of this crowd of animal and physical deities a unique company of five gods and goddesses emerged, with the good culture-hero and king, Osiris, at their head. But what is the peculiar distinction of this divine group? It is precisely that they are *human*, incarnate, a sort of holy family. Isis is the sister and devoted wife of Osiris, coveted by Set, his evil brother, who murders Osiris, and poisons his son, Horus, begotten after death by Osiris. Osiris, risen again victorious, becomes God of the Moon, of the Dead, of Justice, Truth, and Immortality. Isis is the perfect woman, ideal wife and mother, a kind of Virgin Mary. Thus the most enduring, lofty, and central form of divinity among the Egyptians appealed to the affections and the domesticity of the people, and took, it will be observed, the form of a family.

Art, the other mixed structure, also arose (like Religion, expressing the whole emotional Man) in poetry, painting, and sculpture; while pure Mind, in experiment and Record, sowed the germ of the sciences. Record, in the shape of law, ramified with the honeycomb; human status was slowly exchanged for contract; the ancient familial blood-rank of a child, class or estate, was slowly exchanged for specialised relationships between individuals, defined for practical purposes on clay tablet or papyrus. At last all the streamlets of these specialised relationships are channelled in the spreading arteries of coded Law, as of Khammurabi's Code. Simultaneously, disciplines of all kinds necessary for ritual, caste and craft and war, appear and are recorded. Every social channel has to be lined against the inner friction of its stream. Every repugnant task which is necessary must be enforced. Every thrust outward of human growth must have a hardened surface, armoured as the drill of tunnelling. Thus, through the efforts of countless centuries, are born the inward and outward *indurations*—each a sign of social growth, inward or external. And, of course, added to religious and labour-class disciplines appears, when the state strikes, the massed discipline of its armies.

Of the whole ancient Polity, as Richelieu said later of the modern, the apparent essential is Finance; collection and distribution of taxes for protection of the worker's means of livelihood, and for the larger livelihood of the King, symbolic father and priest, chief worker and apex of the Polity.

VI

BUT, with the size, wealth, and complexity of the State Polity, its group of wants must expand; its tentacles of ship-and-caravan traffic are pushed farther afield to gather new luxuries in new seas, outer lands, beyond the area of self-sufficiency and self-guidance. We know, for instance, that in the third century A.D. a certain Chinese outpost frontier-officer, near Khotan in East Turkestan, was using Greek gems to seal his official documents. Just so a thousand years later, Marco Polo found China, under the Mongol Kublai Khan, even in her signal isolation behind the Gobi desert, the sea and the Pamirs and highest mountain ranges of the world, yet flooded with Persian luxuries and Greek ideas.

And so, far earlier, even the River-civilisations found themselves diffused. Impelled by the omnipotential principle towards greater completeness, the River-civilisations, by the traffic of their many-mouthed deltas, overflowed and are suffused into the larger Sea civilisations—those of states grouped round the Mediterranean, Phœnician, Cretan, Hellenic, the last a shifting league of free democracies and oligarchies. Athens arises, shining exemplar for our times, served by all her citizens, not by deputy or merely by earning a livelihood in special trades, but by personal service in folk-assembly; all citizens acting as judge and jury; all citizens as soldiers, with no relationships to the state discharged by proxy, so that each man's body and sense allied in loyalty actively to create her beauty and sustain her glory.

Next the Roman central energies radiated, round a Mediterranean turned Roman lake, and spread undulating power round the Capitol, as far as from the Tyne to the Tigris.

To-day the Sea civilisations are being succeeded by the Ocean civilisations; federations extending around the Atlantic and Pacific basins, inevitably to be knitted by the interpenetrations and dependencies of trade and thought, by labour, science, and the intercourse of universities (forming a complex of Life and Mind centres under the pressures of Anangke) into one richer civilisation; even utilising the Negroid and enveloping the globe.

Yet in the Greater Polity, towards which we tend, all the old intermediate forms of polity, with most of their internal class and craft disciplines, harmonised

339

by synthesis, will probably remain as absorbed and subordinated forms, national and municipal. These intermediate forms will contribute structural stability; and, preserving, each in its rank, ancient ideals of perfection (as Liverpool might take Athens for pattern), may long and nobly thrive, utilising the personal service of all our citizens.

VII

But to turn back for a moment. Why, if Mind renders Polity stable through its gift of Record and consciousness, did the Mind of Athens form no empire? Why did the Hellenic leagues fail to endure? The Greeks seemed specially to have come into existence to intensify and express what I have called the Mind-centre in polity-making. They are our masters in polity-making still. They wrote its very grammar. They made Athens a walk of free, probing, analytic, experimental mind; washing into the inlets of all life, disengaging the ideal and essence under all appearance. Their greatest plays are sheer rebellions of the ironic protagonists of Mind against Anangke and the settled status of the Olympians. The very decadence and rhetorical deliquescence of their famous schools of discussion coldly furnished forth later an organisation for that Alexandrian university which became the prototype of all mediæval universities, and of our own splendid foundations in that kind, where we alone enjoy something of the free communal delights of Athenian democracy. For Mind the Greeks stood. Even in the conquests of Alexander, when, urged India-wards, by the omnipotential Principle, whispering "Totality! totality!" he spread his Greek colonies as garrisons far eastward as the Indus. For in time these made the Greek tongue the polite and learned language of the whole East. So that, as everybody knows, when the wreck of the Roman Empire left western learning in darkness, Arabic translations of Aristotle's Ethics and Politics were being commented on by Mussulmans in Timbuctoo. Greeks also, though as mere provincials, supplied the language and bureaucracy of the Byzantine Empire; and bequeathed their own popular democratic spirit to the eastern form of Christianity, itself a great Greek polity. But it is true that Hellas failed to form an enduring federation; perhaps because, always colonising and centrifugal, Athens failed as a political centre; perhaps partly because the age-long rivalry of Sparta would not admit the supremacy of Athens. But chiefly, I think, because larger, lower, and coarser forms of Polity, owing in their making more to Trade than to Thought, were required, at that moment, by the peoples round the Mediterranean basin. For the Greeks, Mind was more than Life. The Roman polity, coarser in texture and at a lower spiritual level than that of Athens, emerged, instead, to meet those wider economic needs. Perhaps the Family stood for less to the Greeks than to the Latins. Certainly the Greeks gathered round no Osirian religious myth, in which the Family becomes divine. The Roman system took as its core rather the Life-centre than the Mind-centre; it stood for the hearth of the Family, the *patria potestas* of the remotest Aryans. It radiated afresh through all the craft or communal forms derived from Egypt, Crete, the Hellas, and the East, the energy of the primitive hearth-fire and Life force. These practical, hardy Latin farmers founded a republic and an empire on a farmsteading. Their colonies were not, like Alexander's colonies. mercantile, but agricultural garrisons. Their Polity grew crystallised, creeping from town to town, from tribe to tribe, throughout five hundred years round a rude life at its roots agricultural.

But by the roads, the colonies, the system of Cæsar's legions and the Pandects of Justinian, the Roman system would not have endured alone. The imperial system of force and law derived from Sulla and Cæsar became aware that it lacked that reinforcement of kindly brotherhood which, after all, the ancient and the barbarian had known in his tribe and phratry. Therefore the Roman system supplemented and allied itself with the Christian religion; a faith of which the very core was the apotheosis and lifting-up of a human Family, as the form and symbol of the divine. The infant Christ was worshipped lying before the hearth-fire of Vesta. The Christian church, thus supplementing the *patria potestas*, was the resurgence of the Family ideal applied to polities. The Vestal orders became, in lineal succession, the sisterhoods of Christ. Scattered ascetic hermits were gradually gathered from their Thebaid desert cells, to form communal families of the spirit in Monasteries. Later, monks and friars of later Christianity undertook to deal, in kindly confraternity, with the outcast and weaker elements of society; to deal with them, that is, as a Family. For the Family is the only sphere in which it is precisely the *weaker* members who receive the greater love and care. Thus the Christian system repaired and supplemented the natural defects of the commercial and military State. The Christian system dealt with the childish scholar, the born wastrel-beggar, the defective, the imbecile, the sick, the enfeebled through age or infancy. It not only created Hospitals, but revived Universities. So, by the co-operation of strength and spirit, the civil and religious systems of the Roman Empire formed the wide basin of European civilisation. The Roman system, assimilating in Cæsar and Marcus Aurelius much of the Greek culture, had assimilated also the new Christian culture, and projected mightily and far, in this joint worship of the hearth, the discipline and the affection of the Family.

Now, despite the rise at the time of the Renaissance of the new modern nationalities, we still live under the shadow and amid the fragments of this double Roman system of law and morals; coloured only, throughout Europe and South and North America, by the local custom, common law and climate, of each country.

THE next main contribution to group-wisdom was made by England. Her special contribution was Representation—the Representation of localities by deputy. It is true that all forms of community were historically in a sense delegations thrown off by the Family unit; but they were delegations that in turn became themselves castes, bureaucracies, or sub-polities between Family and ruler. These skilled specialisations were apt to become alien and impervious to the appeal of the unit that had given them birth; and with the increasing size of the polity the problem has always been to refresh the central executive with the counsel, and control it by the will, of the Family; as well as to gather the Family's taxes. Now all ancient polities, even democratic polities, require the personal *presence* of their tax-payers, if consulted at all. No systematic employment of deputies was known to Egyptian, Greek, or Roman. But England (which had devised already the jury system, in which twelve men of the locality represent and stand for the communal sense in doing justice), from Saxon times, applied the same principle to polities; that is, applied the principle of representation instead of presence, to tax-

344

paying and counselling and controlling the King.
Herein again, as always, we observe the economic
need creating and forecasting the trend of the constitutional growth. The Saxon Township was the cell
from which the whole organic structure of our House
of Commons, or communities, has expanded. Each
township sent a reeve and two or more elected men to
the hundred-moot. The hundred-moot or meeting
in turn sent a reeve and four men to the shire-moot.
Next the shire-moot sent (1275 A.D.) two knights
to the Parliament, while two burgesses were sum-
moned from every borough. The House of Commons was thus itself created by extremely cautious
and slow steps, gathering at last, after three hundred years, the chosen men of the shire-moots,
borough-moots, and townships. So, by representation, the Township was put in touch with the
Crown, and the whole English polity grew up knit
into a marvellously solid structure, astonishing by
its unbroken series of cellular connections between
the people and the executive. But this most ancient word "Township" first meant nothing but
the enclosure of a homestead. England, thus, in a
manner, taught modern Europe how to bring the
Family to bear on law-making, in the extended
modern Polity. It was a device merely due to the
increasing size of nations. All modern constitu-
tions, including those of Latin South America and
Japan, in this have copied hers. But it will be
observed that Representation was a projection of

the Family by deputy; a plan of which the defect is that it does not require direct personal service from every English citizen to the State. Hence the signal lack of state loyalty in modern England.

But largely to extend the size of the polity, beyond the range of direct personal service, tends at first invariably to lower its central ethos and moral *tone*. Further, the sexes lose the balance of their numbers. To the far new frontiers, to the fighting-lines of the pioneer against Anangke, disperse the younger, the more valiant and vigorous men. At home remain the weakly, the street-bred, the commercial, the sedentary, and above all that great surplusage of unfertile women who increase either dulness, luxury, or the mass of prostitution.

At all costs, it is from the group-wisdom of the Family that the modern state, absorbing and replacing the supplementary humanitarianism of the churches, has still to learn. As the organ of the collective conscience it must replace the Church, and must include and co-ordinate all the chance humanitarian philanthropies hitherto left to religious societies. Poverty and unemployment must be utterly done away with, or else the starved and maimed families of our present terrible devitalised town areas will degrade into ruin the unthinking state that has bred them. This process must plainly be reinforced by the endowment of motherhood; for it is not through the facile service of the mother in the factory, to which she is forced by hunger, even during child-bearing, that the greater home functions of the Family, on which all depends, can be healthily maintained.

What mockery is it, that the sheer weight of armaments of modern nations, threatens, through the weight of taxation, to crush the households of humble livelihood, and to deform the Family, which the polity was originally created to protect and to subserve! For, if we seek Wisdom and Life, where do we find Wisdom and Life at their purest?

IX

INDIVIDUAL man has to move in two regions, and to draw wisdom from each. Two teachers only he has, the Family and Anangke. First from the Family he learns, and then from extended activities in the Polity which is a flaking-off from the Family. Secondly, from Anangke he learns; that is, from the hard and bracing Universe, unguided by Finite Mind, whence the Family itself first issued.

From direct and solitary contacts of the mind with Anangke all the mystics (and every man is in part mystic) can draw, by intense and controlled meditation, a sense of cosmic consciousness and fellowship with the roll of the world; a joy of free kingship with the elements themselves; an ecstatic union with that undifferentiated Spirit lying within the soul, to which all can have access, and which the

Indians call Brahm. The solitary contact with Anangke culminates in Death, supreme Necessity.

But the finest, most subtilised, and most delicate forms of wisdom Man derives from the Family. This is the school of all judgment; fount of political measure and sense of proportion. The Family lies upon the breast of Anangke, but differs in law. It is the forge of all the loves. Here reside the central Wisdoms and Fires of life. Only in the Family do we find Ordered Love, the perfect combination of the two centres, Life and Mind. Its sheltered atmosphere of the passions and affections introduces conscience, and alone renders morality intelligible.

Love such as that between Man and Wife, Mother and Child, Child and Mother, is not emotional only, but also the supremest kind of intelligence—an intelligence that feels forth after the past and future of its object, grasping and enswathing it with a memory and foresight, and a tenderness absolutely limitless in its dreams and reaches of intuition. To the depth and quality of this kind of understanding, all other understandings are as nothing. In such almost silent and selfless Love, the blindly moving omnipotential Principle surges everywhere out of the ground of the world, and is seen disengaged, glowing, naked, pure, and at play. Created by and round that life-glow one discerns the true Family; group of the four wrinkled and elder persons nearing the subsidence of death, the two central and mature, the three or four young;

and beyond them, in twilight, the outer kindred.
All political thinking has been obscured by taking
the individual as the human unit. There are no
abstract social truths about individuals. Could our
custom-blind vision pierce the physical surfaces of
society to behold its real shaping forces, it would see
cells, cup-like shapes, of group-consciousness and
emotion, floating perpetually, invisibly, over the
globe, like thistledown over grasses; their childish
edges touching other groups, then mingling and
floating off; while the parent centres shrink, continue a while, subside and disappear, making room
for other cellular forms. Social truth is what is
true for this invisible group of nine Persons of both
sexes and all ages. It is by this group, this glowing
organic cell of nine persons (each no mere numeral
of the statistician, but a fountain of passions,
dreams, and hungers) that the nature of all Polity
is dictated. For them Polity is formed, and if the
common heart and will of that cell is not satisfied,
the polity fades, as the European kingdoms of
Napoleon faded. Its fostering warmth of affection,
playing on the child, is that which forms character,
but it forms more than character—brain. For that
glow has not only an emotional effect. Where affection is absent, the *whole* growth of the child's nature
is stunted. True growth is secret, shy, and free.
The child, highly sensitive, is absolutely defenceless.
Therefore, there must be absence of fear. Where
the mother warmth is not turned on the naked ten-

ᴄ erness of the young child the fibres of its whole
frame and being, frozen into timidities, shrink,
stunted. The strange effect of fear, then, is that it
cancels the free joys and curiosities of the newly
searching brain, and causes it to withdraw its feelers.
The child's being is thereby impoverished not only in
emotions, but in all its faculties. Where no strong
familial and emotional glow has been early felt I
have observed in later life a poorer, thinner, flightier
quality of brain evolved. It is the quick flimsy
brain of the gamin. If the child be deprived early
of the fusing and tempering effect of feeling and response to maternal love, there follows also a permanent loss of equipoise. Even Natures as gifted as
those of Ibsen, the younger Mill, and Ruskin were in
consequence peculiarly apt in advanced age to lose
emotional balance, at the shock of unaccustomed
sexual and emotional explosions. Such often become the prey of sudden attachments, insane and
disastrous, because belated.

Let no exceptional bias of that embittered outcast,
the writer or artist, mislead us in this matter. If
a man has not in childhood, and for years, watched
in their interactions the steady group of the Family,
surmising in his child mind the thousandfold
subtleties of their invisible intercourse and growth,
he has missed the core of all the humanities, and
lost the scale of values which must be learned in
childhood or not at all. Such an one can only
deal purblindly with the fragments of the families

of others. Compared to the childish experiences of love and intelligence felt and returned, all other experiences are shallow. They bear the same relationship to the man's later acquirements and experience as the enormous submerged achievements of bestial Man, in ascending to the successive levels of speech, fire, pottery, and the arrow, bear to all his later inventions. To this Vision and feeling for the group on which he is dependent, and from which all the skilled polities extend, we owe all real education. The nobler thoughts and emotions are group-thoughts and emotions. Effective religion and ethics are results of familial thinking, not of individual intelligence. At this source are felt the play of the very essences of Joy, Sympathy, and Discipline; and these three combined are Wisdom. Therefore, it is in the inmost sheltered ring of the mother's tacit insight and provision, and the outer ring of provision by the father, that the child learns in the cross-currents of the cell the whole complex of Life; with its food, toys, ceremonial magic, exercises and battles, its folk-lore read out by the fire, the wordless comment of the eye felt observing, the reluctant thrashing held in reserve, the trade and barter of childish property, the joys of exploration, the intoxication of carnival and mere riot. All these enter into the judgment, and absolutely and finally *create* it, and all its later values.

The political economist merely darkens counsel by pretentious technicalities of language. The economy of a State differs in nothing, save scale, from the housekeeping of a household. The child also knows more—that its mother is the economist of spiritual forces, shielding and directing and turning souls this way or that. We are deceived by mass and scale. What are the wars of States more than the bickerings and bouts of children? The average natural man acts on three criteria of conduct, in three successive concentric circles: the familial, the equitable, and the predatory. He applies the outermost and last to all strangers and the uncivilised. And yet, and yet . . . seer, prophet, poet, and philosopher have had to die in legions merely to drive home the bare fact that, if the world is to improve, it is solely by projection through it of the Family, with its subtler and more intimate values and its atmosphere of love and personal service. The State has to learn from the home—and not the home from State—that by the "kingdom of God" was meant the spirit of the Family, propelled through myriads of undulations and resistances, to the end of the world; there destined to create a meeting and equipoise of forces, and thence to undulate backward, through the structure of all polities, spreading internally its strength, its discipline, and its enlightenment of life.

X

SINCE War will certainly continue so long as there are tracts of the world not effectively occupied or supervised by civilised states, because till then there must be collisions between states rushing to occupy, common sense would seem to dictate to the stiff and snarling Chancelleries of Europe to lay aside their canine dignities, and, calmly, by international committee, to plot out and assign the virgin soil or the fallow areas. Men will shortly see the costly armaments of modern nations left stranded high and utterly extinct; hulks empty and abandoned as those jutting ruins and mammoth castles that dominate the passes of the Alps. Till then all polities will be arresting their own growth by delaying the cure of poverty, owing to the weight of competing defences.

And it would also seem clear that some new neutral kind of International Power should be called into existence (as the Universities were called in the Middle Ages). Of what nature should this new Power be? It should provide a point of rest, in neutral zones, for the due economy, in the common interest, of all those influences which transcend national boundaries and for which frontiers have no meaning. The following universal interests certainly imply a universal bond. There is a common need of food and fear of death. There is a common delight between nations in all the arts, especially in music. The intercourse of distant universities, the congresses, and co-operative records of all scientific bodies, the sweeping collective influences of emigration, the implied fundamentals of all high systems of ethics, of all the great religions and the missions they send; the ever-expanding network of travel and communication in world-wandering; the nets of electricity and steam. Above all, the overwhelming unities of commerce and banking. All these things imply a streaming mass of universal interests, a world-force which may be gathered and utilised, framed into a new International Power, modelled perhaps on Universities combined with Chambers of Commerce; and given, as seats, enclaves of territory or neutral spheres, in the southern and northern hemispheres on each continent.

XI

THE omnipotential principle tends blindly to enlarge the size of the polity, seeking universal stability and fertilisation of the globe by life and mind. But outward peace and stability once attained, the size of the polity should again diminish to Attic limits, as of the small republics, within range of direct personal service, and of the powers of the Family to purify. And if War between nations vanishes, it is certain that, in order to preserve Life at a high level, severe internal disciplines must be retained in each polity. Anangke, on whose breast the Family itself reposes, and the omnipotential principle behind Life and Mind, will see to that. Youth, which should freely pass at adolescence out of the discipline of the home to that of the school, will have to acquire all the ancient successive indurations and disciplines imposed now amidst larger opportunities and choices of employment afforded by the expanding spheres of civilisation. Above all, direct personal service to the state of all young persons should be required. The whole youth of the country between fourteen and twenty years of age should be obliged to learn some technical pursuit during at least half his day. The rest of his time may go to leisure, play, and Anangke. One year should be given to pass each through some public service of a defensive discipline, or a dangerous or a repugnant kind, in order to brace and temper Life. Above twenty years of age every individual should be encouraged to choose an avocation with the utmost freedom, remembering only that that work is worth most to the state, into which only a man's whole weight of conviction, from the centres of his being, can be thrown.

XII

FINALLY, given the preservation of the Family, the formation of the greater areas of civilisation, which we have seen is proceeding, clearly enriches the world, through the influx and admixture of a larger number of stocks and races, with, therefore, better chances of cross-fertilisation. And all new inventions are thrown into a cauldron of more manifold opportunity. The growth of area insures the destiny of Man against adverse chances by spreading his bases of resource and action wider, and by drawing tributes of raw material from vaster orbits of climate.

355

And yet it remains that only in the person of great individuals of genius can these multitudinous elements fuse, by a detonating spark, into fresh inventions for humanity. After our debts to Chance and Anangke, we owe most to Genius. We owe to it, indeed, far more than invention. It is to Genius and to the Family that humanity owes such equipoise, love, and simplifying vision as it has attained. Genius is conscience and consciousness at its whitest heat, bearing the subtlest implications of the Family most clearly and steadily in mind. But the soul of a child of Genius requires to live long encysted and ensheathed. Encysted, first, in the warmth of love; and then in solitude, as were the shy souls of Shelley or Christ. The strength of Genius lies in its ignorances. For this child is Life itself, free and pure; older than its father, and abler to resort afresh to the primordial fountains. All that Polity, after the Family, can add to the instinctive endowment of the child is knowledge of the technical languages of the crafts, and of the various disciplines necessary to deal with his fellows and to meet Anangke. But these may all be learned in the Family. His children are the best teachers of any father. Therefore, the Polity and the World have not, in the main, much to teach. Rather they have to learn from the ultimate judgments of the Family and the Child. These are the lawgivers from whom all the values radiate.

THE TRADITION OF THE GREAT STATE

BY HUGH P. VOWLES

XIII

THE TRADITION OF THE GREAT STATE

TRADITION always has been and always will be a dominant factor in human association. Yet this is extraordinarily disregarded in contemporary discussion; at most, tradition is currently considered and discussed as exerting a diminishing influence in the onward sweep of civilisation. The purpose of this paper is to point out that tradition, great as its influence has been hitherto, is manifestly destined to exert a far greater influence in the future. And, the relation between tradition and formal education being very intimate, this function of Great State activities will receive especial consideration in this paper. To discuss tradition is in fact to discuss education.

No one will dispute that tradition dominates the Normal Social Life. Primitive men found in the beginnings of speech a means whereby to build up and transmit from generation to generation those superstitions, legends, prejudices, habits, and customs developed by conflict between man and his environment. Intensely localised, each group would have its particular ideas which would become the

substance of an education admirably fitted to meet
the needs of man under this form of association.
We see that such an education, though varying from
group to group, would have two leading characteristics. First it would be limited in amount, and
secondly it would be stereotyped. So long as the
relations between man and his environment are
limited and unchanging, not only must there soon be
a limit to the development and increase of tradition,
but there can be little further modification of its
character. That is, tradition is the outcome of relationship, and the Normal Social Life, as we writers
conceive it, is correlated with a general absence of
those disturbing forces, the tendency of which is to
produce new relationships and, therefore, new and
more elaborate tradition. Thus we find the Normal
Social Life still persisting over vast tracts of earth
to-day, primitive and fundamentally unchanged by
the passage of time and having an extraordinary
uniformity of tradition in regard to all the fundamental social relationships. Fallacious though the
clap-trap talked about "unchanging human nature"
often is, it approximates the truth when applied to
communities most nearly in the phrase of the
Normal Social Life.

But of course tradition has never been absolutely
inflexible or unprogressive. Always a number of
forces have been producing new ways of living, new
relationships, new modifications of tradition. And
if one believes, as we believe, that these extraneous

influences are becoming of rapidly increasing importance in relation to the Normal Social Life, it follows that tradition, instead of disappearing, will become more important than ever by reason of the resulting modifications in its character and range. Its potency, an interpretation and discipline of relationship, will need to be increased to a hitherto undreamed-of degree. Herein will be the essential value of tradition. The possibilities of a Great State must ultimately depend on the quality and harmony of its collective thought; and, that thought may be collective, it must rest on a broad basis of tradition, of interaction and understanding, common to all. Unless this amplified tradition is common to every citizen and to every child born into the community, the epithet "great" as defining that community will be misapplied. The development of such a community will be hampered on every side, and at last arrested by the appearance of a multitude of sects and castes, of specialised classes, suspicious and contemptuous of everything beyond their own peculiar circles of thought. Sectarianism is, as it were, an infantile disease of the Great State, and has slain hitherto every fresh attempt to exist of the Great State. Mutuality, co-operation, efficient criticism, and subtlety of thought are alike impossible; effort is fragmentary and wasteful, and the community has as little mastery over its destinies as an ailing child unless its tradition is adequate and universal.

Now, amplification of tradition in the past has always been accompanied by increasing range of intercourse. Those primitive men who wandered away from the tribe and survived, and perhaps returned or were fused into some alien group, would be certain to widen not only their own range of intercourse, but also that of those with whom they came in contact. No matter what influence brought man into touch with new relationships—it was more often than not slave-trading and war—this would be the probable result.

Not necessarily was the bringing into touch direct contact. With the invention of writing, tradition ceased to be purely oral: henceforth it could be recorded and multiplied and transmitted from a distance, from here to there, and from one age to another. Range of intercourse widened enormously, and more than ever it became possible to experience new relationships, as it were, vicariously—a thing already possible in a limited degree since the development of speech. Thus, step by step, tradition expanded and grew. . . .

From these considerations it is easy to pass on to the proposition that the school education of the Great State, so far as it enlarges and supplements the oral education of the Normal Social Life—so far, that is, as it is an adjustment of the new citizen to the larger society in which he finds himself—must be essentially a training in enlarged communications and the study of multitudinous relationships—must be essentially the imparting of the Great State tradition and its methods of enlargement.

Let us consider briefly the methods likely to be adopted to invigorate the general process of thought and to organise those forces which will be carrying on, modifying, and enlarging the collective body of tradition. There we reach what is probably the most vital consideration of all, the problem upon a solution of which the project of a Great State depends.

The study of communication in the education of the citizen of the Great State will probably be dealt with under various heads, such as language-training, drawing, painting, sculpture, and the like; mathematics, logic, and other symbolical methods. Whether there is likely to be one or several languages in current use is a question upon which it is impossible to form a judgment. It is another matter, however, to glance at general tendencies and from them form a plausible deduction. Here the accumulative growth of disturbing forces and influences points to certain probabilities. The immediate and most obvious outcome of these forces is the extraordinary extent to which man is being delocalised in both body and mind. One has only to think of such recent inventions as the electric telegraph, telephone, wireless telegraphy, steam and electric tractions, the motor-car and motor-vehicles of every description, the ocean liner and the æroplane, to see how quite common men to-day are enabled to sweep out ever - widening circles of mental and physical activity. Think of the stupendous growth of the penny-post alone! All these are things so recent that the effect upon human mentality can scarcely as yet be beginning. Bearing this in mind, it is difficult to believe that a multiplicity of languages, and all the barriers to the broadening of intellect that such a multiplicity implies, will prevail for long before the systematic enlargement of the means of communication which will be a distinctive characteristic of the Great State. While it is not within the scope of this essay to consider whether one language will overcome its rivals or whether there will be a world language resulting from the fusion of several existing tongues, it should be noted that the substitution of one general language for the babel of to-day would itself widen enormously the range of a general intercourse and tradition. In this connection we may remember that the Great State has been defined as a social system world-wide in its interests and outlook. Language-teaching would be greatly simplified. Having but one language to learn, there would be some prospect of the average citizen acquiring a really comprehensive knowledge of his tongue, which is far from being the case in any community to-day. How many contemporary English-speaking people know more than a tithe of their own language? Even the little knowledge they have is vague and misapprehensive to an astonishing degree. Much muddled thought in contemporary life springs from an imperfect apprehension of the

364

written and spoken language. No attempt is made to provide our youth with a liberally inclusive vocabulary. One's knowledge of English is often found on examination to be—no other word seems so apposite—*jerry built*. New words are acquired at random through reading and intercourse, a loose and distorted significance often being gathered from the context.

Language-training, then, must involve the acquisition of a vocabulary of the greatest possible content, each word in which must be thoroughly understood if such training is not to fail of its essential purpose, and through that work of definition and enlargement the amplification of tradition and thought to more and more spacious horizons, and the bringing of every citizen into understanding contact with that tradition. As to drawing and music, it is possible these will be taught chiefly as a means of expressing thoughts and emotions which cannot be communicated in words. Again, mathematics resolves on analysis into a system of symbol communication. Consideration will presently be given to the idea— glanced at in the opening essay—of a change in occupation being normal to the life of every citizen. Here it may be remarked that changes of occupation would be greatly facilitated by a wide-spread and thorough knowledge of mathematics, since the occupations involving such a knowledge form a considerable portion of present-day activities. No one can hope to be a competent astronomer without a knowledge of mathematics. Most of the physical sciences require its aid. Even music involves mathematics in its last analysis. Great armies of people calling themselves engineers would be unable to achieve their ends without this science, and everywhere we find a rapidly increasing number of men engaged in physical research and the application of scientific deductions to technical ends, the quality of the results being commensurate with the mathematical knowledge possessed by those carrying out the investigations. An endless diversity of intricate machinery grows and spreads about the earth, and a mathematician has taken a part in the evolution of every machine that is well proportioned and carefully designed. Even to-day people ignorant of mathematics show a disposition towards either an ignorant hatred or a superstitious awe of most of the beautiful apparatus that binds our civilisation together.

A superficial observer might argue that with the growth of knowledge standardisation of machinery and formulæ will ensue to such an extent that a general and advanced knowledge of mathematics will be unnecessary. No such hope is supported by the tendencies of contemporary engineering. The nearer the approach to perfection in any machine, the greater the subtlety and refinement of calculation required. Moreover, machines no sooner approach the measure of perfection possible to them than some new discovery is made which renders the whole design of that machine obsolescent. A good example of this is the present partial replacement of reciprocating steam-engines by the steam-turbine, which involves a whole host of new and intricate calculations. The increasing application of internal-combustion engines to ship-propulsion and the coming of the aeroplane place vast new fields of research at the disposal of the engineer with a knowledge of mathematics; and it may be that engineering problems will continue to increase in complexity and in universality of interest till at last our remote progeny will be within reach of the possibility of a system of controls of the earth's velocity, and will steer our planet nearer and nearer the sun as its heat and splendour wane. . . . But I have wandered away from my point, which is that mathematics, together with language-training and those activities of expression usually referred to collectively as "art," will form the necessary basis of education in the Great State—not the education, but the basis and means of education. To consider these fundamentals in greater detail would be to pass beyond the bounds of this essay. Let me, therefore, return now to a more general consideration of tradition in relation to the Great State.

It should, of course, be remembered that while the leading characteristic of tradition in the future will be its insistence on personal adaptability and its secular modification and development, there must always be a group of ideas that will persevere over long periods practically unchanged. Many of the needs of men are long-lived, and it is an open question whether most if not all of our present-day traditions will not go on to a fuller and completer influence in the lives of the citizens of the Great State. That large body of tradition we speak of as Christianity, for example, may conceivably serve as the basis of the moral tradition in the Great State. This matter is, I believe, to be discussed more fully in another paper in this book, but the present writer now ventures to offer a few remarks that seem to fall within his scope. In many ways he admits Christian tradition has been a beneficial factor in our evolution. Its teaching of love and concord is of the very essence of the Great State. Whatever broadens the basis of sympathy and mutual understanding is a force operating in the constructive direction, and so it would seem probable that Christianity will at least survive in its spirit and intermingle with the more elaborate traditions of the future. In no case can a tradition disappear without leaving behind it some effect or influence. But this is far from asserting that there need be or will be a definite survival of Christianity as such. Contemporary Christianity must purge itself from a multitude of defects before it can possibly be acceptable to the clear-headed men who will be the normal citizens of the Great State. A mere spirit of co-operation alone can never be all-sufficing for the religious basis of tradition. The Great State will be complex beyond all precedent;

and that he may cope successfully with these complexities, the average citizen must be trained to think clearly and exhaustively, and be given a wealth of tradition for his guidance multifarious beyond any the world has yet produced. Christianity as we know it at present makes no insistence upon understanding and mental alertness as duties, nor upon the supreme necessity of thoroughness in thought and work. It is not a critical religion; it is emotionally sound, perhaps, but critically careless, and the vital preservative of right in a complex situation is a critical faculty highly stimulated and fed.

It would be impertinent to discuss so detailed a thing as the probable tradition of the future in relation to moral ends. But it seems clear that we have to look rather to a living literature and drama, and it may be to a living pulpit for that perpetual stream of criticism which is the life-blood of a great community, which indeed must be deliberately fostered with a view to the continual reinvigoration of tradition and thought if the Great State is to remain in health. Quite possibly there will be no definite "moral" teaching by way of precept in the Great State in the sense in which "moral" is commonly understood to-day. The tendency of liberal thought to-day seems to be altogether away from definite moral controls towards a latitude which implies alternately that relationship should be judged upon its merits. We are slowly learning that no moral code can be framed of general appli-

369

cation without a vast amount of limitation and injustice in individual cases. The writer believes that if the Great State is to be possible at all, the traditional atmosphere surrounding each individual, from his youth up, must be such that a sense of social conduct will become intuitive. He will do right because his atmosphere is right, and not because his definite instructions are right. Meanwhile, on our way to the Great State, all moral laws and judgments, all arbitrary pronouncements regarding moral questions, must be submitted without bigotry and without prejudice to detailed scrutiny and criticism.

The age in which we live is characterised by the unprecedented intricacy of its relationships. Complex problems face us on every side. We are, as it were, entangled in a net, and in the measure that our schemes of extrication are dully conceived, carelessly and weakly planned, we shall be more and more hopelessly involved. Never was the need for penetrating analysis and criticism so pressing. Consider, for instance, the problem of the official and his relationship to the normal citizen—all the possibilities of demoralisation by office and the loss of sympathy of the citizen towards the official. How will criticism, aided by a fund of spacious tradition, be directed to the solution of such problems as these?

Whatever demoralisation takes place in an official is partly due to the fact that he is a specialist—that is, a human being who has narrowed the sphere of his activity at the expense of his social instincts, thereby becoming but a fraction of a man. He sees a field of activities as brightly lit, perhaps, but as limited as the field of a microscope; and not infrequently it is as though the microscope was a little out of focus. There is a blurring as of things too close to the eyes to be distinctly seen. Moreover, office usually implies a power over his fellows which inevitably breeds first pride and then corruption in little minds. Speaking generally, an official's pleasure in the direction and regulation of other people's lives is inversely proportional to his mental capacity and range. Amplification of tradition should therefore carry us at least half-way to a solution of this problem. Let it be granted that every child will acquire from his parents, his teachers, and his fellow-creatures a spacious and comprehensive outlook on life in all its manifold aspects and relationships, and it follows that the suspicions, prejudices, jealousies, the lack of sympathy and of generosity of dealing which are too often the concomitants of officialdom to-day, will be almost non-existent in the Great State. It is conceivable that constitutional methods such as change of office, short terms of office, would suffice to eliminate whatever remains of this, the supreme difficulty of all constructive projects.

And here perhaps I may venture to offer a few remarks upon specialists and specialisation in general.

It is a characteristic of specialisation that it encourages the fragmentation of human thought and effort. Essentially it belongs to the era of localised tradition and limited outlook and is everywhere reflected in the castes, cliques, cults, and classes which are so familiar a feature of the earlier social superstructures upon the Normal Social Life such as we find in India. It multiplies to infinity the possibilities of misunderstanding, jealousy, hatred, and dissension. We cannot here consider the historical aspect of specialisation in detail, but a general survey indicates that it originated in the segregation of the rulers, warriors, priests, traders, and slaves who until recent years formed the backbone of practically every human community. The caste system of India originated in this manner some three thousand years ago, developing in course of time into the most elaborate system of specialisation on record; and nowhere is the Normal Social Life more firmly rooted as the common way of living and its tradition as the universal tradition than in India. It must, however, be clearly understood that specialisation is not necessarily peculiar to the Normal Social Life. There can be few ideas more prevalent than those of domination, subordination, and specialisation; and since the ideas with which humanity is most familiar have a strong tendency to perpetuation it is conceivable that the persistence of these ideas into a period of change and comprehensive reconstruction may yet lead to a social order in which the bulk of humanity will be almost as specialised in function as the wheels and levers of a machine, and subordinated to and co-ordinated by a small class of wealthy, vigorous, and probably truculent overseers and "understanding persons"—in short, a Servile State. If, therefore, we are to escape both from the evils of the Normal Social Life and from those of the possible Servile State, we must systematically encourage forces adverse to specialisation of individuals. A tradition of liberalism and criticism must be consciously sustained. Granting that in the Great State each citizen will be brought into contact with the broadening influence of a catholic tradition, it is possible there will be no specialists at all in the ordinary sense of the word. That there may be a degree of specialisation in certain lives is quite probable. Not only has knowledge grown beyond the possibilities of individual intellectual grasp, but always there are men who at an early age show predilections for a certain class of work; and in so far as they excel in that work they will, no doubt, be specialists. But this need not involve, as it so often involves now, the atrophy of all those possibilities of development not brought to bear on the matter immediately in hand. A man will be able to specialise and yet remain a man. The tradition of his time and education, the new tradition of the Great State, will have fitted him to tackle widely differing classes of work; and even if he devotes his life to one field of narrowed limits determined by his special capacity, he will still have a sympathetic understanding of those activities which lie beyond his self-imposed range. With the normal run of humanity, however, it seems probable that change of work from time to time will give the best results for both the individual in happiness and for the community in product. It is extremely doubtful whether any man is a good and happy specialist all his life, any more than he can always be a good and happy lover. Even a lifetime wholly of work, albeit enlivened and enlarged by repeated changes of occupation, will probably be considered as regrettable in the Great State. To work, as to love, is but a phase in man's development. A balanced attitude towards life demands lengthy intervals of leisure, time for travel and recreation, periods devoted to thought and exercise, days of solitude and contemplation. Stevenson has pointed out that extreme *busyness* is a symptom of deficient vitality, and that a faculty for idleness—as opposed to the exercise of some conventional occupation—implies a catholic appetite and a strong sense of personal identity. This is profoundly true; and to concentrate the whole or even the greater part of a lifetime on any one aspect of life to the complete or partial neglect of all others is a waste of potentialities and by so much essentially a failure to live.

It seems to the present writer that there is a certain cycle of efficiency for the average human being. Every man's development as a worker appears to follow some law of accumulation and fatigue which involves first a period of interest combined with a certain lack of dexterity, then an interval of maximum interest and maximum efficiency, followed at length by a decline towards routine. Interest in most cases begins to flag before efficiency shows any serious signs of falling away, for after work has been well executed for a number of years mechanical aptitude may keep one going, though freshness and zeal have departed. An interesting side issue here would be to consider whether, generally speaking, our judges, bishops, admirals, and generals are not appointed at a period of life when fire and enthusiasm are declining and a certain staleness and secondary inefficiency are setting in. As a matter of fact, there comes to most specialists a time when they are glad to retire from the work to which they have devoted the greater portion of their lives. But this by no means necessarily indicates that their energies are exhausted. They are tired of their specialty, and at last comes a reaching-out to other things about which to centre their activities. Such names as Mr. Balfour, Lord Rosebery, and Sir Frederic Treves may be cited as British instances of this cessation of interests in a special occupation. The last is a particularly good example of a man who, having attained to an extreme eminence as a surgeon, retired deliberately while still in the prime of life to travel, to write, to become a more generalised man.

Now, bearing in mind the ample tradition and education of the Great State and the fact that mechanism and co-ordinated effort will have reduced the unavoidable work for each individual to a few hours a day, it is not difficult to imagine a man under these conditions spending a portion of his leisure in familiarising himself with the details of some occupation other than that primarily engaging his attention. As interest in his earlier occupation relatively or actually declines and proficiency in the new increases, the latter becomes the chief medium for the exercise of his faculties. Thus the normal citizen in the Great State may range over very wide fields of work indeed, broadening in outlook and understanding, growing in sympathy and toleration. And I think in all discussions as this there is too strong a disposition to that idea of a three or four hour working day. Why not a ten-year working life?—and do it jolly and hard while you are at it?

It may be argued that the result of such a reduction of specialisation as I am suggesting would be a community of incompetent amateurs. Such an argument ignores the fact that the very possibility of a Great State postulates a wealth of tradition and education available for each citizen, thus insuring knowledge and thoroughness being applied to whatever work is taken in hand. No doubt there may be differences in quality of output. Work may be crudely done here, elaborately and beautifully finished there. This does not invalidate our general proposition.

THE TRADITION OF THE GREAT STATE

At the present time there is far too general an acquiescence in the specialisation of individuals. Common people are dazzled by the brilliant light often focussed by the specialist on his specialty; they forget the worlds which, lying beyond the range of his imaginative grasp, the specialist cannot realise. And they fail to understand that a community of specialists must inevitably lack collective vision and understanding by reason of the inco-ordination of its units. The specialist may take you nearer the Great State in all sorts of ways, but it is very doubtful if he will ever get you or himself there. No attempt is being made to study the possible reactions of specialisation on the human mind. One thinks of specialists who are secretive and cunning, of specialised business men who prefer to work behind the scenes and who delight in letters that are "private and confidential." One thinks of the artful bureaucratic expert and the dull but crafty and intriguing diplomat. How far is all this "foxiness" mere coincidence, and how far is it a necessary characteristic of specialisation? This is but one of a countless number of such questions that must be answered on our way to the Great State. For his own part the writer cannot conceive any sort of Great State that will endure a year, where education, where tradition, does not first make its citizen a gentleman, and then, in a relation entirely secondary, a specialised worker.

But already this discussion of specialisation has

been carried beyond the limits of this paper. That so much contemporary writing expresses the conviction that any possible future state must be dominated by specialists and officials (using the words in their generally accepted sense of narrow concentration) will perhaps serve as an adequate excuse. The writer firmly believes in the possibility of a Great State which will include neither official as such nor specialist as such, a state in which this that he here throws out so sketchily will probably have been fully worked out; but he also believes that, without having at its base some such tradition and education as he has indicated, no Great State can possibly exist. Amplification of tradition, increasing enlargement of the means of communication, together with education developed to these ends, forming a foundation for vigorous, subtle, and all-embracing thought—these are our fundamental needs. Herein lie the seeds of unparalleled greatness, possibilities of development leading to ways of life more splendid than all our dreams.

Is it possible to have a world of men such that merely to live in it were a liberal education? The question is already answered. We of this book say: on certain conditions, yes. Dimly we perceive the road which, leading thither, winds darkly outwards across the centuries. There are ways leading elsewhere; humanity may take the wrong turning, and may yet be overwhelmed in a Red Sea of petty, trivial, immediate things. There are times, indeed,

378

when lack of faith gives the lie to one's hopes and the vision of a Great State wavers and fades. . . .

The permutations of life's possibilities are beyond our telling.   But this at least we steadfastly believe: there is no insuperable barrier between mankind and the goal of our desire.

THE END

5096